FLAWED SAINTS

To Jonathan & Margaret
with my love & prayers
B. Gladpi
(09/13)

FLAWED SAINTS

BIBLE FAMILY PROBLEMS AND THE
TRIUMPH OF GRACE

Emmanuel Oladipo

TATE PUBLISHING
AND ENTERPRISES, LLC

Published by Tate Publishing & Enterprises, LLC
127 E. Trade Center Terrace | Mustang, Oklahoma 73064 USA
1.888.361.9473 | www.tatepublishing.com

Tate Publishing is committed to excellence in the publishing industry. The company reflects the philosophy established by the founders, based on Psalm 68:11,
"The Lord gave the word and great was the company of those who published it."

Published in the United States of America
ISBN: 978-1-61862-861-9
1. Religion / Biblical Studies / History & Culture
2. Religion / Christian Life / Relationships
12.12.06

DEDICATION

TO JOHN DEAN

Thank you for training and trusting us.

ACKNOWLEDGEMENTS

This book has been a very long time in writing. Very many friends and a multitude of prayer partners who have supported us as a family have a hand in it. I will mention only a few by name—those in particular who were involved at the tail end of the process.

I cannot thank God enough for the privilege to count Margaret Dowson and her husband, Paul, among my friends. Margaret's advice was priceless, as usual, and I am similarly indebted to Robbie and Ruth Burns and Peter Kimber, erstwhile fellow-labourers in the Scripture Union sector of the Great Vineyard. There are David and Anna Boyce, Kristian and Toyin Lythe, my lifelong friend, Tunji Adebayo, and my son, Jesutosin, too, for their labour of love in reading through the manuscript, spotting many errors, and offering valuable comments and suggestions.

I express my hearty thanks for the many sources that I quoted in the book, especially Christianity Today, IVP, YWAM, and C D Maire, among those who freely and graciously gave their permission, and also to my editors at Tate Publishing.

Finally, with much praise to God, I gratefully acknowledge the woman who, for forty glorious years, has shared the joys and the pains of married love with me. Together we have worked through not a few family problems as joint recipients of extraordinary grace and favour from our incomparable God. Without Ruth's faithful companionship, most of what I accomplished in life would not have been possible—especially not this book. Four sons enrich our lives, the most wonderful any parent would wish to have, and I thank them for not featuring as negative examples in a book of family problems!

—Emmanuel Oladipo
Leicester, December 2011

TABLE OF CONTENTS

PREFACE

Satan does not like happy families. Everywhere in the world and in every area of family life there are pressures and troubles that lead to ever increasing breakdowns and unhappiness. We are tempted to think that the world has never had it so bad, but the fact is, as stated by the Preacher in Ecclesiastes, "There is nothing new under the sun."

To adapt the words of Job, "Families are born to trouble as surely as sparks fly upward." We have all had our share of it. Some wonder, like Jeremiah in the book of Lamentations, if there has ever been any sorrow like theirs. Others face problems so terrible that they totter on the edge of despair. All are inclined to pose the plaintive question to the God of love, "Why, dear Lord, why?"

This book is written for ordinary, Bible-believing, Christian families with the purpose of helping them appreciate how the worst that the devil throws at them is but a rehash of problems he had caused for men and women of God before them. Starting with the parents of the world's first murderer and his victim, it highlights all the significant family problems contained in the Bible, right up to those faced by the parents of our Lord Jesus Christ. It attempts to grapple with the complex issues involved and to provide encouragement in the struggles of family life, both for those directly involved in the problems and for those who stand alongside of them. It should also help to equip young couples just setting out on the adventure of marriage.

The saints of whom we read in the Bible were subject to the same human limitations and frailties we have today. They failed God just as often and as flagrantly as we sometimes do, but where they *did* succeed, the resources that enabled them to overcome their troubles there and then are equally and abundantly available to us here and now. Their God is our God, the same yesterday, today, and forever.

Written with an African mindset, the book brings a non-Western perspective to the issues addressed. These issues are universal, and the proffered lessons apply to all. Every passage cited is quoted in full as part of the text. This is to ensure that readers with only a limited knowledge of the Bible can derive full benefit from the book while also providing a ready reference for those who may be well versed in the Holy Scriptures.

A detailed background is provided to the situation in every chapter. The problems are analysed, using illustrations from different parts of the world and drawing out relevant lessons to foster hope and enhance faith in the God of grace. Each subsection ends with a question for personal reflection, and each chapter concludes with a set of questions for discussion suitable for use in small groups. The ultimate goal is that this may be a tool in the hands of the church to frustrate the purposes of the enemy and to help us build families that bring honour and glory to God.

—Emmanuel Oladipo
December 2011

ADAM AND EVE: FIRST MURDER IN FIRST FAMILY

Sin did not gradually evolve. It was not a steady degeneration from little lies to petty theft to bank robbery and on to murder. We read of rebellion in the Garden of Eden in Genesis 3, and the very next story in the very next chapter of the Bible is of one of the most despicable fratricides in human history.

It is customary to blame an unhealthy social environment, difficult political circumstances, or serious economic deprivation for crime on our streets. One extreme case of this thinking comes from England—Jason Cooper, the "Safari Boy." Jason began to make his mark quite early. He was expelled from one kindergarten at the age of four and then from two others. He became progressively unmanageable, but it was when he set fire to the family home at the age of twelve that his parents gave up on him and handed him over to Derbyshire Social Services.[1]

"Red House" was the special school they chose for him, and Red House sent him scuba diving in the Caribbean and cruising through the Everglades. He visited Disney World and Sea World, skied in Italy and Norway, toured Italy and Denmark, and went to Zimbabwe for the African safari, which gave him his nickname.

The idea was that his problems stemmed from the poor surroundings of his childhood and that exposure to the good life would cure him. It did him absolutely no good. Within a month of leaving care, he was imprisoned for robbery. He needed the money to feed a £350-a-week drug habit. In fact, he spent three of the next four years in prison. To add insult to injury, Jason Cooper obtained tax-funded Legal Aid to sue the government for giving him a taste for the expensive lifestyle he developed while in care without providing for him to maintain it afterward!

No such excuses may be adduced for the first murderer in history. No one had a better start in life than the world's first parents, and even though they were born outside of the Garden of Eden, the world's first siblings had everything going for them. Let us take a look at their family background.

Heaven on Earth

I suppose the first thing Eve ever saw were flowers. Conceived in the heart of God, she was born in the Garden of Eden, and what a garden it was! Stretching on and on as if forever, in full pride of their youthful bloom, were all the ancestors of the most beautiful plants and flowers that ever existed. Crickets crackled in the thickets, and frogs croaked in the ponds. Birds chirped in the trees, and fawns frolicked on the hillocks. Palms swayed in the breeze as alluring scents perfumed the air. This was a garden designed with infinite wisdom and was planted by the very hand of God. It was as close to heaven as this earth will ever get.

The first man had been made as the pinnacle of six days of extravagant creativity. It had started with the Spirit of the living God hovering over the still waters of a world waiting to be ordered into being. The Word of God pronounced light into the formless darkness of purposeful emptiness. That was the first day, and the heavenly Father noted with divine approval that it was good while angelic beings applauded in songs of joyous acclaim.

It was the opening act of the stunning drama of creation. Skies and lands and plants, seasons and years, sun and moon and stars, creepy-crawlies and beasts and birds, in the sea and on land and in the air, all followed in due order. Successively, the all-wise Father God declared that everything was good as a carefully ordained environment prepared the way for the special event of the sixth and final day. God fashioned a lump of clay, breathed into it the breath of life, and thus created man in His own image.

If there was ever a man in a state of "Hakuna matata," as the phrase goes in Swahili, it was Adam. He had no reason to worry about anything. Here was a man with no housing problems, no family crises, no health hazards, and no crime statistics to bother him. There were no economists to alarm him, no scientists to cajole him, no taxes to pay, and no journalists to bring bad news. Adam had more than enough of everything his heart could ever desire. Abundantly provided with food and drink and surrounded by all the animals in the world as pets, he was gainfully employed in a thoroughly fulfilling job, tending the most magnificent garden this world will ever know. Whatever else a man would want in life Adam had no idea.

But the triune God who created him is a God in community. He knew that it was not good for man to be alone. Joyful noises surrounded Adam day and night with birds and beasts twittering or bleating or roaring their carefree existence merrily around him, but he was still alone. "A man and his dog" is all well and good and has a role to play in promoting human happiness, but it does not supply companionship fit for purpose, and that is according to the Maker's opinion.

God decided to work out the solution to a problem Adam never knew he had. From his side He took out a rib which He used to create the Woman while this unsuspecting bridegroom was sleeping the sleep of the just. What Adam needed was a companion of the same kind as himself. The fact that God took his very rib to bring it about speaks eloquently of the status of this other being and the nature of the companionship He designed to exist between the two.

This was a creature possessing the same critical faculties as Adam. She had the same ability to laugh and to cry, to sing and to dance, to love and to hate, to think and to act, and she had exactly the same access to their common Lord and God.

And yet she was made to be different. Hers was a body designed for a complementary role in fulfilling the Creator's purpose of reproduction with an inbuilt capacity to attract the man, and she came fully equipped with astonishing mental strength and a baffling range of variable emotions.

Here comes the bride!

Gloriously attired in the unadorned beauty of her feminine innocence, Eve marched down the aisles for her nuptial coronation in the arms of her Father and God.

Adam awoke from his sleep to a sight that took his breath away. Talk about love at first sight! When at last he regained the use of his tongue, he waxed poetic, serenading his bride in the first love song ever composed:

> This at last is bone of my bones
> and flesh of my flesh;
> she shall be called Woman,
> because she was taken out of Man.

Genesis 2:23

Question for Reflection

Man and Woman are the same but also different. In what ways are we in danger of over-emphasizing or blurring the distinction between the two?

Enter Satan

Alas, it was too good to last! Satan saw to that. He tempted the woman and both she and her husband fell into his trap. This turned out to be the foundation of all the troubles every family has encountered and will encounter. He is the life-long, implacable enemy, not only of family life but of life itself.

It is this creature, "the dragon... that ancient serpent, who is the devil, and Satan" (Revelations 12:9), who came to the garden of Eden to spy out the idyllic happiness of our first parents, and what he saw presented him with an exciting challenge. His purpose is "to steal and kill and destroy" (John 10:10), and what better target than a couple at peace with each other, with all the world, and with their Maker? He employs the same tactics to lure us away from God's purposes today, and we must not be ignorant of his devices.

Adam and Eve had no reason to worry about the one fruit they were forbidden to eat from the tree of the knowledge of good and evil. They had any number of other delicious fruit ripening and falling off any number of trees all over the garden, but perhaps Samuel Clemens, aka Mark Twain, was rather unkind in his judgement:

"Adam was but human, that explains all. He did not want the apple for the apple's sake; he wanted it because it was forbidden. The mistake was in not forbidding the serpent; then he would have eaten it!"[2]

God makes no mistakes, but He did not forbid Adam and Eve from eating the snake, and the snake put the question delicately; "Did God actually say, 'You shall not eat of any tree in the garden?'" (Genesis 3:1).

This is not a request for information, madam! It is time to run! As the African proverb says, "For the eyes to see no evil, the feet provide the answer!" But Eve decided to engage in polite dialogue with the wily tempter.

"You will not surely die," he enthused, brandishing the luscious fruit in bald contradiction of the One who is the Way the Truth and the Life. It was not long before the Woman swallowed the bait—together with hook, line, and sinker.

Eve ate the fruit, and Satan nearly suffered a heart attack! He knew he had been lying and that God was telling the truth. Not being privy to all of God's counsel and wisdom, he must have expected the woman to fall down and die there and then, but she did not! We can imagine him doing a quick double-take.

"See? Didn't I say? You are still alive!"

Satan is not so foolish as to tell undiluted untruth. He was careful to ensure that the poison of his falsehood was well disguised.

The Wambuti are one of the Pygmy tribes of primitive hunter gatherers in the tropical jungle of Equatorial Congo. In the orgy of mindless warfare that has ravaged the country for decades, both the government and rebel forces terrorise forest tribes and devastate the wildlife with automatic firepower. But everyone is careful to avoid the territory of the Wambuti. This is because of their special weapon (bows and arrows) that put the fear of God into all and sundry. Their arrow consists of an ordinary reed with a jagged end dipped in poison. A simple scratch means instant death. Well, maybe not quite *instant*, since some brave stalwarts have been known to take as many as ten steps before succumbing. Of particular interest are the ingredients they use to make the poison. Five percent of it is concocted from various jungle herbs. The remaining ninety-five percent is pure honey from the honeycomb. In a similar way, Satan's deadly lies are often buried in a generous dose of attractive truth.

Knowledge was the bait behind which death was hiding its ugly head. Eve *did* gain a strange new knowledge of good and evil just as Satan had promised. This she offered along with the fruit to her husband, and he ate.

One of God's purposes in marriage, surely, is that the couple should help each other to stand. As the preacher was later to write, "Two are better than one, because they have a good reward for their toil. For if they fall, one will lift up his fellow. But woe to him who is alone when he falls and has not another to lift him up!" (Ecclesiastes 4:9-10).

Eve fell, and Adam did not help her up but was rather dragged down with her. It is a lesson that was lost on Ananias and Sapphira and one that must not be lost on us. That was the miserable couple who conspired to lie about the gift they brought to God.

> But a man named Ananias, with his wife Sapphira, sold a piece of property, and with his wife's knowledge he kept back for himself some of the proceeds and brought only a part of it and laid it at the apostles' feet. But Peter said, "Ananias, why has Satan filled your heart to lie to the Holy Spirit and to keep back for yourself part of the proceeds of the land?...You have not lied to men but to God."
>
> Acts 5:1- 4

Just like Adam and Eve before them, it was a rebellion that led to death. It is a warning to heed when the enemy brings a similar temptation to us.

Jonathan Aitken was a British politician who, along with his wife, trod the same unseemly path. As Chief Secretary to the Treasury in the British Cabinet, he was accused of unethical dealings with leading Saudis by an investigative journalist writing in *The Guardian* newspaper in April 1995. Aitken's protest was most robust, promising "to cut out the cancer of bent and twisted journalism in our country with the simple sword of truth and the trusty shield of British fair play."

The newspaper did not retract, and Jonathan Aitken carried out his threat to sue for libel. Like every good wife, Lolicia Aitken backed her husband's claim, testifying that she had paid for his hotel stay in France and not Prince Mohammed of Saudi Arabia as the journalist had alleged. But lawyers produced evidence to show that Lolicia was at the Ritz in Switzerland when she was supposed to be in France with her husband. Mr. Aitken's "simple sword of truth" turned out to be a dagger of falsehood. His case collapsed spectacularly, and he ended up in prison for perjury and for perverting the course of justice.[3]

In the garden, astounded that Adam and Eve did not fall down dead on the spot, the serpent slunk into the undergrowth in his puzzlement at the baffling ways of omnipotent God. With jangling nerves, he awaited what would happen next.

How did Adam handle the first crisis of his married life? Did he own up to his error of judgement and admit responsibility? Did he stand by his beloved spouse? Or did he penitently admit he had done wrong and say he was sorry? None of the above! When challenged to explain himself, he invented the blame game, passing on responsibility to his wife and to the Almighty who gave to him the wife. "The woman whom you gave to be with me," he replied, "she gave me fruit of the tree, and I ate" (Genesis 3:12).

By tasting of the fruit of the knowledge of good and evil, Adam and Eve did not immediately fall down and die physically, but they fell from their state of innocence and ushered in the regime of death, and in the process, they switched on the gene responsible for human sorrows and family woes. It is hard to improve on the way Dr. Chris Wright describes it:

> Human disobedience and rebellion against the Creator God brought disastrous results. Evil and sin weave their way into every aspect of God's creation and every dimension of human personhood and life on earth. *Physically*, we are subject to decay and death, living in a physical environment that is itself under the curse of God. *Intellectually*, we use our incredible power of rationality to explain, excuse, and "normalise" our own evil. *Socially*, every human relationship is fractured and disrupted—sexual, parental, familial, societal, ethnic, international—and the effect is consolidated horizontally through the permeation of all human cultures and vertically by accumulation through the generations of history. And *spiritually* we are alienated from God, rejecting his goodness and authority.[4]

To eat of the fruit of life would inscribe their guilt in indelible ink and seal them forever in a state of sin. For this reason they were expelled from the garden, and that fruit was temporarily withdrawn from the sin-polluted earth. It would later reappear in the New Jerusalem, and with enhanced capacity, but that is a story for another time and place.

In an intricate blending of judgment and mercy, God sentenced the pair to a life time of hard labour, pain and suffering, along with a pregnant promise and hopeful expectancy of the day when the seed of the woman would destroy the serpent, a promise which had its fulfilment in Jesus the Christ: "I will put enmity between you and the woman, and between your offspring and her offspring; he shall bruise your head, and you shall bruise his heel" (Genesis 3:15).

The first offspring of this couple was Cain, followed by his brother, Abel.

Question for Reflection

"Adam was not deceived, but the woman was deceived and became a transgressor" (1 Timothy 2:14). How do you understand this verse in light of the Genesis story? How should we answer those who seek to lay all the blame on Eve?

Fratricide

As they experienced the joy and the pride of parenthood, Adam and Eve took diligent care to introduce their sons to God. The two of them understood the value of worship, and both brought their sacrifices unbidden. The God who knows the secrets of the heart accepted the offering of the younger but not of the elder brother.

It would indeed be fair to suggest that Cain's heart was not right with God, as his rejection of a direct warning to desist from the path of evil was later to show: "The LORD said to Cain, 'Why are you angry, and why has your face fallen? If you do well, will you not be accepted? And if you do not do well, sin is crouching at the door. Its desire is for you, but you must rule over it'" (Genesis 4:6-7).

Abel's sacrifice was accepted by God while his brother's was not. How and why this constituted a reason for murder is hard to fathom. There are no two ways about it. Cain's act was one of premeditated murder in the first degree with no remorse or contrition after the event.

"Cain spoke to Abel his brother. And when they were in the field, Cain rose up against his brother Abel and killed him" (Genesis 4:8).

To kill a stranger is one thing. To kill a brother is another.

"Brother!" What a magical word to every African! And it does not have to be a sibling, either. I am not aware of any African language that uses a different word for "cousin." In some cases, the "brother" might even be a second cousin twice removed. A young man is sent from the village to seek his fortune in the city, and he stays with his elder "brother." Food, lodging, and travel, legal and health insurance, and every other aspect of personal welfare for as long as it takes are all rolled into that simple word—"Brother." Your elder brother is the one who looks after you come what may and defends you against all comers.

But Cain lured his brother to the field and killed him.

God pronounced a curse upon Cain and the murderer reacted with indignation:

> Cain said to the LORD, "My punishment is greater than I can bear. Behold, you have driven me today away from the ground, and from your face I shall be hidden. I shall be a fugitive and a wanderer on the earth, and whoever finds me will kill me."
>
> Genesis 4:8-14

Now we know: murderers do not want to be murdered!

Death is an erratic boulder on the route of God's intention, and we can look forward confidently to the day when death will die. Meanwhile, in the current order of human existence, death is the ultimate statistic. Until Jesus Christ returns, it continues to score 100 percent. Ten out of every ten people will die; hence, the pain of bereavement is a universal agony.

Thankfully, in spite of this, death is not the ultimate tragedy, in so far as we can look forward to a glorious resurrection. It is for this reason that St. Paul enjoins us to demonstrate our other-worldliness in the face of death. "But we do not want you to be uninformed, brothers, about those who are asleep, that you may not grieve as others do who have no hope" (1 Thessalonians 4:13).

This is not a call to pretend that the pain does not exist. How can we, especially when that pain intrudes into our everyday lives with violent finality? Rather, it is a call to acknowledge a special reality of the sure and certain hope that transcends all earthly pain.

Invariably, for parents to bury their son is a tragedy. Such was the very first experience of human death. How much worse when it results from murder?

Question for Reflection

In what ways does our Christian hope affect our reaction to the death of a loved one? How about if the deceased is not a believer?

Parents of the Victim

Poor Eve! Poor Adam! As if it was not tragic enough to have your son murdered, why must it be by his brother who should be looking out for him?

What can be worse than to have your son murdered? First, there is the numbing unreality at the news. "There must be a mistake somewhere. This cannot be true." But it is true. Your son is never coming back. His place in the family is forever void. All the labour of love invested in his bringing forth and bringing up. All the hope and expectations of what he would become and accomplish in life. All the succour that might be expected from him in your twilight years—all snuffed out by the mindless act of murder. How does one feel when their child is murdered? We can glean something from a modern tragedy that made sordid headlines around the world.

James Bulger was a two-year-old who was lured away from his mother at a shopping mall in Liverpool, led over two miles to a railway track to be brutally murdered, and then laid on the track for the next express train to run over. The murderers, Jon Venables and Robert Thompson, were only ten years old themselves that miserable day in February, 1993. The presiding judge in sentencing the pair declared theirs to be "a crime of unparalleled barbarity."

In an effort to rehabilitate them, the two were given the best psychiatric care available in Britain—and a good education to boot. Over time, their carers testified that their lives had changed. When they turned nineteen it was decided that they be released rather than be sent from juvenile detention to an adult institution.

Time, predictably, did not assuage the anger of the parents of James Bulger. The parole board was convinced that the pair posed no further danger to society, but for the parents, that was hardly the issue. Now divorced and both remarried to different spouses, such was the undiminished intensity of their anger that they were united in opposing the release of their son's killers.[5]

According to the bereaved mother, Denise, "If there is any such thing as a living hell, I and my family live it daily." This helps to underline how unnatural was the decision of the Reverend Walt Everett of United Methodist Church of Hartford, Connecticut, who not only forgave but helped with the release of his son's killer from prison. What he did was an act of human grace flowing from the grace of God.

It was on 26 July, 1987, when twenty-four-year-old Scott Everett was murdered by Mike Carlucci, a drug dealer who lived in Everett's apartment complex. The murderer apologised for his crime at his sentencing, but that brought no solace to the grieving father. To begin with, and for many months, according to a journalist's report,

> "Everett spent his days inflamed, stunned into livid silence. He withdrew from his wife of thirty years and went through the motions with his other children, a college-age son and daughter. During a sermon or a church supper, he would burst into tears, prompting parishioners to shift in their seats and grouse about 'getting over it.'"

Rev. Everett later described his state of mind:

> "I was just lost and saw no way out of the grief and powerlessness I felt ... I couldn't believe that one individual could do so much harm to my family, and though I didn't stoop to violent thoughts about him, I wanted him punished for a long, long time."[6]

On the first anniversary of his son's death, Walt Everett wrote a three-page letter and sent it to Carlucci in prison. Everett began the letter by describing the "extremely difficult" year since Scott was killed. Then he wrote, "I do accept your apology and, as hard as these words are to write, I add: I forgive you." He confessed that he did this for himself in order to overcome the anger and the hate that were consuming him. Such anger and hate add to the burden of all who are close to the victim. They are corrosive feelings for which they require some form of deliverance and healing. The sort of forgiveness which Reverend Everett was able to give, therefore, is a powerful therapeutic measure.

Carlucci replied from his prison cell and requested a visit from his victim's father. It was a visit that was to be repeated at least once a month over the next two years until Rev. Everett finally wrote to the parole board. "I told them I didn't think he was the same guy who had gone to prison, that he could be a productive member of society, and that God had made tremendous changes in Mike's life." The board agreed with him, and Carlucci was released after serving only three years behind bars.

It is the same Spirit of God in action in Rwanda that inspired a woman to demonstrate forgiveness to the man who wiped out her entire family. This is how it was reported in a YWAM news release in February 1997.

> "While visiting a jail holding many of those accused of killings during the bloodshed, when he preached about forgiveness, [the worker] was approached by a prisoner who had become a Christian during an earlier visit. He confessed that he had killed his neighbour and three children, but the wife had escaped," said Arne Petersen, YWAM's East Africa acting regional director. "Now he wanted to know how he could contact the widow to ask for her forgiveness for what he had done." The YWAM worker suggested he write a letter and promised to try to find the person concerned and hand deliver the note—which he was able to do later that same week. When the woman received the letter she began to weep, explaining that she had become a Christian after the murders and had been praying for the man who had killed her family. Later, the YWAM worker was able to arrange a prison meeting between the killer and the widow where they embraced as he asked for and received forgiveness. Since then the woman has returned to the prison to take more food to supplement the man's meagre diet.[7]

Question for Reflection

Why is forgiveness so important when we or our loved ones are victims of crime?

Parents of the Culprit

The question asked earlier, "What can be worse than to have your son murdered?" is not merely rhetorical. Here is one intriguing answer—*to be the parent of the murderer!*

The victim's parents receive support and sympathy from all and sundry, but the lonely journey for parents of a murderer begins with bland denial, hobbles through soul searching, and descends into guilt—"What did we do wrong?"

Jimmy Mizen's mother was extra-ordinarily perceptive as she grieved the loss of her gentle-giant of a son. The six-foot-four sixteen-year-old was stabbed with broken glass by a young man with whom he had refused to have a fight in a London baker's shop. His mother commented:

"We've got so much joy about Jimmy. Jimmy—we had him for sixteen years and one day, and he brought joy every day of his life."

She went on to say she had no anger toward his murderer but felt sorry for his killer's family.

"What are his parents' memories? I do feel sorry for them. I can't feel anger for them. They've got to live with this for the rest of their lives and this boy whatever he's done, his life will not ever be the same again."[8]

How can such parents ever forgive themselves for the wrong they are not sure if or how they had done? Then they run the gauntlet of their immediate community and of society at large as they are accused, tried, and condemned unheard in the court of public opinion. There is a saying in Spanish; "An ounce of parent is worth a pound of clergy." If a child turns out a murderer, who else is to blame but the parents? They are guilty as charged. There is no forum for them to declare their innocence or else to plead guilty, serve their sentence, and get on with their lives. Would it not be preferable if their child had died? They have lost him to an enemy more ruthless than death itself as they experience bereavement without closure where no inquest can determine the cause of death. Not surprisingly, the journey begins with denial.

Shaheed Hamad did not expect his son to live up to his name. He was shocked to the marrow when Jihad Hamad was arrested for attempting, together with a friend, to blow up a German train in a jihad against the infidels of his adopted country. It was he who insisted his son turn himself in to the authorities when he was declared a wanted man in Germany. He found it so incredulous that he said he would kill himself if his son turned out to be guilty as charged. "He cannot possibly be an extremist," his sobbing wife too told the magazine *Der Spiegel.*

A newspaper report filed by Hassan M. Fattah on 29 August, 2006, described how the Hamad family had struggled to shelter its children from a growing militancy taking hold near their home. The father had watched very carefully over his sons, preventing them from going out alone so as not to get mixed up with local gangs, and he enrolled them in Christian schools in order not only to provide them with the best education but also to keep them from trouble.[9]

Theirs was a desperate and sorry plight, but at least they did not get sued into the bargain, unlike Mr. and Mrs. Manzie.

Edward and Valerie Werner had no doubt it was poor parenting that let down Sam Manzie, who killed their son, and so they sued his parents. The fifteen-year-old killer had himself been the victim of sexual molestation by a predator he had met on the Internet. He became unmanageable in the home. When their best efforts proved unsuccessful, his parents had sought help for him in all the ways they knew how. Manzie Senior took his son to trained social workers, describing him as a time bomb on a short fuse. Far from helping, the learned professionals turned on the helpless father, accusing him of maligning his "innocent" son! He then appealed to a judge, but the judge reprimanded him for attempting to offload his parental responsibilities on others. Sadly, Sam Manzie confirmed his father's worst fears by killing

Eddie Werner, an eleven-year-old who was going door-to-door selling holiday items for the local PTA.

Sam Menzie was given a seventy-year prison term. The victim's parents, Edward and Valerie Werner, brought suit against Sam's parents, blaming them for failing to control their angry son. Thus, life can be a whole lot more unkind for the parent of the murderer than for the parent of the victim.

But what can be worse than either to be the parent of a murdered child or to be the parent of the murderer? Ask Adam and Eve. They were parents to both!

Who exactly was Adam going to sue for his son's murder? On whom was Eve going to foist her frustration and anger? With whom were the couple going to share a healing embrace? They inhabited the worst of all possible worlds!

Question for Reflection

In what ways is the tragedy that befell the first family an encouragement to us when we encounter family tragedies today?

The Wages of Sin

By persuading Eve to take the forbidden fruit, Satan succeeded in subverting God's creation beyond his wildest dream. Right from the moment our first parents left the garden, heart-rending tragedies became part of the lot of mankind. Every book of the Bible has something to say about one aspect or another of this consequence of human disobedience. It was an outcome that the tempter himself, not being omniscient, could obviously not foresee. Not only were the woman and her husband to die and to pass on death, there was also the death of innocence that has blighted all of human life from that day to this.

It takes all forms as Satan goes about his business, "to kill, to steal, and to destroy." It includes the exploit of fifty-three-year-old Duane Morrison, a drifter who took six girls hostage at Platte Canyon High School in Bailey, Colorado, and sexually assaulted some of them before fatally shooting one and killing himself as police stormed the classroom. Joe Morales, executive director of the Colorado Department of Public Safety, did not mince his words. "I think anybody who goes in—an armed individual—takes on innocent, unarmed children in the sanctuary of a school is the lowest of the most cowardly of the most yellow."[10]

It includes the fifteen-year-old student in western Wisconsin who shot and killed his Principal, John Klang.[11]

And it also includes, within the same fateful week in the United States, Charles Carl Roberts, who dropped his own three children at the school bus stop before going to shatter the peace of an Amish community in Pennsylvania with the shooting of their school children—killing five of them. Roberts had left a rambling suicide note and letter to his wife and children.[12] Referring to an event twenty years before, he was angry with life and angry at God. Spare a thought for his distraught wife, Marie Roberts, who could only sob and sob and ask for prayers for the families who lost their children—and for her own family, too.

People who are intimately involved with such tragedies, how do they find comfort in their grief? Where and what is the answer?

Thankfully, many of these poor parents sometimes find understanding, fellow-feeling, or empathy in victim support of one sort or another. We have seen several examples. We can also add the parents of Sam Manzie, whose desperate efforts to help their son had failed, and they had been sued into the bargain. Edward Werner eventually extended a hand to Nicholas Manzie by asking his pastor, the Rev. Thomas Geoffroy of the Christian Life Fellowship, to arrange a meeting. The fathers met in Geoffroy's presence. Manzie, the father of the killer, said, "We cried like babies. We just held each other and we couldn't hold each other tight enough."

The Amish went one further, taking a step that some found absolutely scandalous. Not only did they forgive the murderer, but they went out of their way to set up a fund for the family of the killer of their children, an act which they admitted weeks later they had not found easy or cheap.

Marie Roberts, his wife wrote to them, "Your love for our family has helped to provide the healing we so desperately need." But that was much too much for some. Although he was more than a tinge unfair in his assessment of the Amish, Jeff Jacoby of the Boston Globe spoke for many when he wrote:

> "Hatred is not always wrong, and forgiveness is not always deserved. I admire the Amish villagers' resolve to live up to their Christian ideals even amid heartbreak, but how many of us would really want to live in a society in which no one gets angry when children are slaughtered? In which even the most horrific acts of cruelty were always and instantly forgiven?"[13]

These examples do not in any way represent cases of "all is well that ends well." Rather, they are instances of redeeming grace at work in desperate situations. Even more importantly, they are instances of people not focusing on the wrong enemy but appreciating the fact that it is Satan who is the real enemy whose avowed purpose is to kill and to destroy.

Question for Reflection

What do you think of the action of the Amish community in relation to Marie Roberts in the light of the comment by Jeff Jacoby of the Boston Globe?

Where There Are No Answers!

There can be very few in this world whose heartache surpasses that of Adam and Eve. We are not given any insight as to how the first parents sought and found solace in their unprecedented grief. It is possible that they had other family members to share their grief on the assumption that at least some of their other children were already born at this time. Their situation was nonetheless unique. Nobody else in their world knew what it meant to lose an offspring—let alone by violent death. No one else knew what it meant to parent a murderer. There was nobody, absolutely no one, who could empathise with them in the tragic depth of their sorrow—except their God.

He was not indifferent to their pain. More than that, He was able to share it with them to the fullest extent. From before the foundation of the world, He had made adequate provision to cater for the darkest emotional needs that mortals would ever encounter.

Experientially, the great I Am knows from eternity what it means to be in the situation of Adam and Eve. His own Son was "the Lamb who was slain" (Revelation 13:8). And who did the killing? It was a people He claimed for Himself as His "son." This was what He made clear in His message through Moses requesting the King of Egypt to set His people free: "Then you shall say to Pharaoh, 'Thus says the LORD, Israel is my firstborn son" (Exodus 4:22).

But Israel was not exclusively guilty of that crime. His blood is on the head of all the other sons and daughters of God whose sins made it necessary for the Son of God to be murdered. As St. Peter put it,

> You were ransomed from the futile ways inherited from your forefathers, not with perishable things such as silver or gold, but with the precious blood of Christ, like that of a lamb without blemish or spot. He was foreknown before the foundation of the world but was made manifest in the last times for the sake of you who through him are believers in God, who raised him from the dead and gave him glory, so that your faith and hope are in God.
>
> 1 Peter 1:18-21

The God of Adam and Eve did not give them a burden too heavy for them to bear. Along with the curse on them for disobedience in the garden, He made adequate provision to alleviate their pain. Sin and death are not going to have the last word. There is going to be birth and renewal. There would one day come the Seed of the Woman, who would crush the head of the serpent. God's grace was already in evidence in the judgment He pronounced at the Fall. Adam and Eve did not understand it, nor indeed did the prophets of old. St. Peter describes it as a research topic for angels. But the grace of God makes it freely available to us in Christ:

> Concerning this salvation, the prophets who prophesied about the grace that was to be yours searched and inquired carefully, inquiring what person or time the Spirit of Christ in them was indicating when he predicted the sufferings of Christ and the subsequent glories ... things into which angels long to look.
>
> 1 Peter 1:10-12

The problems we face do not have the same universal implications as those of Adam and Eve. The same principles apply, however, in that they result from the curse which the Fall brought upon our world; also the same God who was there with them then is here with us now in the fullness of His loving grace.

Taking it Further

1. What can we learn from the interaction between Eve and the serpent to help us resist temptations?

2. Consider the four areas of human life affected by the Fall as described by Dr Chris Wright. How are these evident in your community and what is the Church doing about them?

3. Environmental factors on their own do not determine human behaviour and are not entirely responsible for wayward youth on our streets. In what ways do they contribute to these problems, and what can we do to help?

4. What help is available in your church or community for parents who struggle to manage children with criminal tendencies? How can such support be created if it does not exist or strengthened where it does?

5. "Satan is the real Enemy…" Is this a cop-out or a tenable argument? How can we be sure not to fight the wrong enemy, especially when we compare Psalms 35:1 and 35:6 with Ephesians 6:12?

ABRAHAM: CRISES OF FAITH FOR FATHER OF FAITH

Husbands, Love Your Wives

"Abram" means "exulted father," but there was nothing exalted or exulting about this man as a husband. He was one of the most gutless, self-serving specimens you would have ever encountered. Throughout this story, we shall call him Abraham, meaning "father of a multitude," the more fitting name with which the Lord later chose to honour him.

Those vaunted men of towering spiritual stature in those good old Bible times had feet of clay, and, at least in one respect, none to a more embarrassing degree than the illustrious "Father of Faith." May God deliver all faithful women from such a spineless husband as Abraham!

Here is a man who, together with his spouse, Sarah, provided an apt illustration of St. Paul's description of what married love requires.

In his seminal teaching on family relationship, St. Paul has many weighty instructions to impart. It comes at the conclusion of his teaching on Spirit-filled, Christian living in Ephesians 5. Contrary to the all too-human self-assertion that our culture promotes, he commands husband and wife to submit to one another[14]—not as an optional extra or a good idea to earn "brownie points," but as a matter of reverence for Christ.

St. Paul was operating at the confluence of Jewish, Greek, and Roman cultural norms. None of them had any lofty concept of the status or the role of the woman.

For millennia, every Jewish man made the standard prayer thanking God for not creating him "a slave, a Gentile, or a woman."[15]

The Greeks for their part, more often than not, "acquired" wives for material, territorial, social, or political gain rather than for companionship. This is how one of their famous philosophers explained the place of the wife in Greek family life: "Mistresses we keep for the sake of pleasure, concubines for the daily care of the body, but wives to bear us legitimate children."[16]

Roman law governed Palestine, and in Rome, married men as householders were "patres familias" a term for which there is no exact equivalent in English. The man was the husband, father, and master to whom Paul speaks in Ephesians 5:25-33. He was patron of his household where his word was law. More than that, the Roman tradition of *potria potestas* virtually put the power of life and death into his hands. He was responsible for whatever was done or not done in his household. Unlike Paul, therefore, social philosophers did not address their words to any other member of the household but only to patres familias.

Interestingly, the teaching of the Qur'an,[17] which came some six hundred years after Christ, was no different. Here, for example, is what it says, without note or comment, in its chapter on women.

> The men are made responsible for the women, and God has endowed them with certain qualities and made them the bread earners. The righteous women will cheerfully accept this arrangement, since it is God's commandment, and honour their husbands during their absence. If you experience rebellion from the women, you shall first talk to them, then (you may use negative incentives like) deserting them in bed, then you may (as a last alternative) beat them. If they obey you, you are not permitted to transgress against them. God is Most High, Supreme.[18]

Question for Reflection

The Bible's teaching on the place of the Woman ran counter to what obtained in the Greek, Roman and Jewish societies. In what ways is this also true of our own culture?

Exemplary Beginning

Abraham had commenced his life of faith ever so brilliantly. The son of a nomadic herdsman who had left Ur in Chaldea, literally for better pastures, he had travelled with his father, Terah, along the trade route of the fertile Tigris and Euphrates rivers. Terah had a mind to go to Canaan, taking with him his eldest son and daughter-in-law, and also his grandson Lot whose father had met an untimely death. The little band travelled as far as Haran where they pitched their tents. Shepherds were known to be tough and adventurous, constantly braving the dangers of the wild as they pastured their flocks. But that does not mean they were foolhardy. They preferred to limit their search for new pastures to tried and tested fields. Haran was as far as Terah and his little band could go without leaving the security of their country to enter into alien territories, and so he was careful to go no farther. Life took its natural course and, eventually, Terah went to join his ancestors, leaving Abraham in charge of the clan.

It was out of the question for Lot to return to Ur. He was a valued member of the household with his proper stake in the family business.

Thank God for places where children who do not know parental love receive good care. There was a dear missionary couple who set up such an orphanage at Oyi in central Nigeria. From near and far, little ones were deposited to their charge, each with a heartrending tale of woes, until they had several dozen in the home. After years of faithful love and labour, the couple had to retire but had no one to carry on the good work. They turned to the government to take over the orphanage as a last resort. In their wisdom, those in authority decided to close it down. What happened next? Every single child went back home, and not one of them had any difficulty finding a next of kin to assume full responsibility. When the orphanage existed, its offer to look after the children was gratefully accepted, but before it came into being and after it ceased to exist, traditional options were available for looking after the orphans.

Fatherless Lot was Abraham's responsibility fair and square, and Abraham did not renege. Lot simply remained with the clan, now under new leadership. Then Abraham heard the voice of God, telling him to step out into the unknown.

Exactly how God spoke to Abraham, we shall never know. Was it by a dream or a vision of the night? Was it by some thought He put into his heart and continued to reinforce day in day out until it took hold of him? Was it by an audible voice that made him feel at first as if he was "losing it?" This God is the God of infinite variety, and the ways He calls His servants are many and varied.

Moses had to step aside to marvel at the burning bush, but He chose not to speak to Elijah in the earthquake, wind, or fire—only in the quietness of a whisper. For the young King Solomon, it was in his dream. For Balaam, God resorted to the mouth of a donkey, while Isaiah saw a vision of angels adoring the thrice holy God seated on His glorious throne as His splendour filled the temple. There was the arrogant scamp who told the preacher that if God needed him, he would send a blinding flash of light as He did to Saul of Tarsus. The answer he got was that "God does not swat mosquitoes with sledge hammers." He knows exactly how to get the attention of each one of us, and He has the habit of making His call clear enough to those who have a listening ear. Significantly, in Islamic countries closed to normal avenues of hearing the gospel proclaimed, an incredible number of people experience visions and dreams of Jesus revealing Himself as the One in whom alone is life eternal. It even happened when some were circling the Ka'aba during their pilgrimage to Mecca!

How He chose to speak to Abraham is immaterial. What matters is that the Creator of heaven and earth does speak to men and women, and Abraham heard the call of God as all will hear who desire to be guided by Him.

To hear God's call, however, is only the first half of the deal. Moses asked Him to think again, and Gideon politely requested Him to repeat Himself. Jeremiah explained very carefully to Him that he was only a child. Jonah took a boat and headed in the opposite direction. But "Abraham believed God and it was counted to him as righteousness" (Romans 4:3).

His obedience was unquestioning and instantaneous. He stepped out at the head of his family and flock into the land of Canaan. This mysterious God had promised him blessings beyond what he could ever imagine, and he trusted His word without reserve.

Then his troubles began! There was nothing to lead Abraham to expect that there would be famine in the land, and this famine was severe. Very much an infant in the school of faith, he had not realised that going where the Lord directed did not obviate the hazards of travel. How did it work in the life of the Son of God?

> And when Jesus was baptized, immediately he went up from the water, and behold, the heavens were opened to him, and he saw the Spirit of God descending like a dove and coming to rest on him; and behold, a voice from heaven said, "This is my beloved Son, with whom I am well pleased."
>
> Matthew 3:16-17

You know the next verse that followed? "Then Jesus was led up by the Spirit into the wilderness to be tempted by the devil" (Matthew 4:1).

In the circumstance, it did not make sense to Abraham to stay put. If Terah did not go far enough to enter the land of Canaan, his son's problem was that he went beyond the place the Lord appointed. That was how he arrived at the country where he saw the need to make special arrangements for his personal safety at the expense of his wife:

> Now there was a famine in the land. So Abram went down to Egypt to sojourn there, for the famine was severe in the land. When he was about to enter Egypt, he said to Sarai his wife, "I know that you are a woman beautiful in appearance, and when the Egyptians see you, they will say, 'This is his wife.' Then they will kill me, but they will let you live. Say you are my sister, that it may go well with me because of you, and that my life may be spared for your sake."
>
> Genesis 12:10-13

"The hyena," as the saying goes, "does not smell its own stench." Here is Abraham concerned about the godlessness of Pharaoh and his people that would put his life in danger. He did not see his own godlessness that would endanger his wife. Oh no, no one caught Abraham telling an outright lie, as indeed Sarah was his half-sister. And when in a tight corner, how many of us have not opted for the path of expediency?

True, instances do occur in life when it is manifestly unwise to go out of our way to tell the truth, the whole truth, and nothing but the truth, and Abraham could perhaps be forgiven for deciding that this was one of them. As one of his illustrious descendants was later to caution, "Be not overly righteous, and do not make yourself too wise. Why should you destroy yourself?" (Ecclesiastes 7:16).

The problem was not so much the fact that Abraham did not tell the truth. It was his underlying motive that was singularly unbefitting. He did what he did in order to save his skin at the expense of someone he was duty bound to protect.

One significant change in the position of women under the Taliban regime in Afghanistan was noted by keen observers. This was the uncompromising Islamic sect that came to power after the Soviet Army had been driven out in disgrace. With their strict interpretation of the Qur'an, they made the lives of women miserable. Many atrocious laws were passed, including one which forbade girls from going to school.

From time immemorial and for reasons lost in antiquity, a woman would normally walk behind her husband when going about in the countryside. The new development was that women were made to walk in front, and the husbands took care not to follow too closely behind. This change had nothing to do with extreme Taliban religious zeal or to any strict interpretation of their holy book. It had everything to do with landmines!

Abraham's behaviour was of that order. It raises the question of how much, and with what kind of love, he loved his wife.

Question for Reflection

The risk to Abraham's life was very real. What would we have done in his position?

"Wives, Submit to Your Husbands ..."

Strangely enough, when God instructs wives to submit to their husbands in all things, He evidently included the likes of Abraham. In laying on women this injunction, St. Paul did not try to be diplomatic or to be politically correct. He did not use language that required trained legal practitioners or doctoral dissertations in theology to unravel.

> Wives, submit to your own husbands, as to the Lord. For the husband is the head of the wife even as Christ is the head of the church, his body, and is himself its Savior. Now as the church submits to Christ, so also wives should submit in everything to their husbands.
>
> Ephesians 5:22-24

41

Downtrodden daughters of their culture, none of Paul's earliest female audience would have seen anything earthshaking in this injunction. Society at large, the church, and their parents all expected them to be submissive to their husbands. The apostle did not remodel life for them by maintaining they should not only submit to their spouses but do so "in everything."

Unmarried though he was, it is likely that Paul had come across some wives in his day who had IQs somewhere in the stratosphere. Some of them must have been married to pretty clueless husbands, to put it politely. He made no exceptions. Such women, too, should submit to such husbands *in everything.*

That was what was expected in his day and age, but he did not give us room to suggest that it should be any different with any changes that might occur in societal norms at any other time in history. Two things he said make that plain as plain can be.

First, wives are to submit to their husbands "as to the Lord." There is no getting around that on any cultural bypass. Wherever and whenever a Christian woman lives, her submission to the Lord remains the same, and so should her submission to her husband.

Then there is his invocation of the relationship between Christ and the church. If the wife is to submit to her husband as the church submits to Christ, then we are talking about a situation that does not change with time or place.

The universality of this injunction is reaffirmed in St. Paul's first letter to Timothy:

> Let a woman learn quietly with all submissiveness. I do not permit a woman to teach or to exercise authority over a man; rather, she is to remain quiet. For Adam was formed first, then Eve; and Adam was not deceived, but the woman was deceived and became a transgressor.
>
> 1 Timothy 2:11-14

Notice how he qualifies the type of submission—not partial, not intermittent, but *full* submission. And notice the link reference to what transpired in the garden of Eden. Dr. John Stott addresses the point:

> Since it is mainly on the facts of creation that Paul bases his case for the husband's headship (Ephesians 5:22f.), his argument has permanent and universal validity, and is not to be dismissed as culturally limited ... the man's (and especially the husband's) "headship" is not a cultural application of a principle; it is the foundation principle itself. This is not chauvinism, but creationism. The new creation in Christ frees us from the distortion of relations between the sexes caused by the fall (e.g. Genesis 3:16), but it establishes the original intention of the creation. It was to this "beginning" that Jesus himself went back (e.g. Matthew 19:4-6). He confirmed the teaching of Genesis 1 and 2. So must we. What creation established, no culture is able to destroy.[19]

Some have sought to reduce this to Paul's ill-disposition toward women in general. After all, he chose not to be too closely yoked together with any of them, a good reason for remaining single all his life. Dr. Stott, again:

> All attempts to get rid of Paul's teaching on [male] headship (on the grounds that it is mistaken, confusing, culture-bound or culture-specific) must be pronounced unsuccessful. It remains stubbornly there. It is rooted in divine revelation, not human opinion, and in divine creation, not human culture. In essence, therefore, it must be preserved as having permanent and universal authority.[20]

But even if we could dismiss St. Paul on whatever grounds, we have the same message from yet another apostle. It would seem that the Holy Spirit does not want us to lose sight of this lesson; "Wives, submit to your husbands as to the Lord."

The apostle Peter had this to say:

> Likewise, wives, be subject to your own husbands, so that even if some do not obey the word, they may be won without a word by the conduct of their wives, when they see your respectful and pure conduct...as Sarah obeyed Abraham, calling him lord.
>
> 1 Peter 3:1, 6

Sarah was very different from Queen Vashti, who stood up to her husband in a manner that would gladden the heart of the modern day feminist. Her husband, the Persian Emperor Ahasuerus, was celebrating, and Queen Vashti was content to give a parallel feast for women at the palace. When, his heart merry with wine, the King ordered that the Queen be paraded in royal robes simply to show off her beauty, Queen Vashti asserted her independence by simply refusing to obey. It is doubtful whether she had reckoned on the likely cost, since she *did* lose her crown and station as a result, and for good reason too, according to one of the King's counsellors.

> "Not only against the king has Queen Vashti done wrong, but also against all the officials and all the peoples who are in all the provinces of King Ahasuerus. For the queen's behaviour will be made known to all women, causing them to look at their husbands with contempt, since they will say, 'King Ahasuerus commanded Queen Vashti to be brought before him, and she did not come.'"
>
> Esther 1:16-21

The man Sarah is commended for obeying was not just being vainglorious. His was a calculated plan to betray her honour in order to save his skin. But it was a pardonable weakness on the spur of the moment—was it not? Or was it perhaps the deliberate, studied, self-serving action of an inconsiderate spouse?

Question for Reflection

What are the pros and cons of a woman submitting to her husband as it operates in your cultural context?

"...As to the Lord"

No thanks to her reprehensible husband, God preserved the honour of Sarah, inflicting punishment on the household of insatiable Pharaoh who, for his part, considered any beautiful woman as another trophy to add to his harem. Abraham's wrongdoing was made clear to him in no uncertain terms. Through the sheer act of God's special favour, he was allowed to depart in peace with his wife and suffered no adverse consequences for his misdeeds. This God is a God of grace, but St. Paul warns us, "What shall we say then? Are we to continue in sin that grace may abound? By no means! How can we who died to sin still live in it?" (Romans 6:1-2).

But Abraham did not yet get it, and so he did it again with Abimelech, King of Gerar.

It is hard to find any defence for Father Abraham. Whatever may or may not be his other laudable qualities, on this same matter of his personal safety and security, he again demonstrated a pathetic failing in his duty of care. What he did in Egypt was not due to a momentary lapse in judgement but rather demonstrates the shameful characteristics of a shameless husband.

Astoundingly, once again, the Lord intervened, preserving the hapless woman untainted and, incredibly, enriching her contemptible husband into the bargain.

> Then Abimelech took sheep and oxen, and male servants and female servants, and gave them to Abraham, and returned Sarah his wife to him. And Abimelech said, 'Behold, my land is before you; dwell where it pleases you.' To Sarah he said, 'Behold, I have given your brother a thousand pieces of silver. It is a sign of your innocence in

the eyes of all who are with you, and before everyone you are vindicated.' Then Abraham prayed to God, and God healed Abimelech, and also healed his wife and female slaves so that they bore children. For the LORD had closed all the wombs of the house of Abimelech because of Sarah, Abraham's wife.

Genesis 20:14-18

Here is a lesson on grace unmerited in all its overwhelming abundance! Here is proof if ever it was needed that Abraham had no claim on God's blessing on the basis of his good works. Rather, it was his faith that the God of grace decided to honour: "The scripture was fulfilled that says, 'Abraham believed God, and it was counted to him as righteousness'—and he was called a friend of God" (James 2:23).

God, it would seem, has a soft spot for new and weak believers. "Beginner's luck," we might say, but the fact is that luck has absolutely nothing to do with it. It simply is the result of divine favour undiluted. C.S. Lewis sounds the warning that when marvellous acts of grace are evident in our lives, it behoves us not to attribute them to any merits of our own.

> "Little people like you and me, if our prayers are sometimes granted, had better not draw hasty conclusions to our own advantage. If we were stronger, we might be less tenderly treated. If we were braver, we might be sent, with far less help, to defend more desperate posts in the great battle."[21]

There is a very important caveat in Paul's teaching that must not be ignored; "Wives, submit to your own husbands as to the Lord."

To bring the husband's headship under the authority of Christ introduces a new dimension to the concept of submission. How are we to understand this?

Let us consider one popular way of looking at it. It is an argument that goes something like this: the Lord loves unreservedly and has the wife's best interests at heart. The text goes on to say that husbands should love their wives as Christ loves the church. In so far as the husband demonstrates these characteristics of God, therefore, the wife would be in a position to submit to him as to the Lord. If he fails to do his part, she is relieved of the burden of submission and is thereby spared his tyranny. It is a matter of give and take; husband and wife have to contribute fifty-fifty to the relationship and meet each other halfway.

With this understanding, wives can exercise godly discernment as to the type of husband who deserves their submission and on what occasions to withhold that submission. Some husbands are simply not deserving of respect—let alone submission. See what Abigail says of her husband, Nabal, in saving him and his entire household from destruction by David and his troop: "Let not my lord regard this worthless fellow, Nabal, for as his name is, so is he. Nabal is his name, and folly is with him." (1 Samuel 25:21-25).

Obviously, it is not to this kind of wicked fool of a husband that a godly wife is expected to be submissive! The one problem with such an understanding, however, is that it does violence to the text of Scripture. It is simply different from what St. Paul says. Let us take another look at the text in its context.

> Wives, submit to your own husbands, as to the Lord. For the husband is the head of the wife even as Christ is the head of the church, his body, and is himself its Savior. Now as the church submits to Christ, so also wives should submit in everything to their husbands.
>
> Ephesians 5: 22-24

First, a word of caution is in order before we continue. We have already referred to 1 Peter 3:1. The phrase used there is identical to what we have here, urging wives to submit *"to your own husbands."* This underlines the fact that the teaching has to do with the ordering of relationships within the family. It must never be misconstrued, therefore, as indicating a general subservience of women to men!

It is important to pay particular attention to the different points of comparison in this passage. The church is the body of Christ, and the wife is the body of the husband since the two are one flesh. There is full correlation here.

But the church is the body of Christ of which He is Saviour, while the wife is the body of the husband, of which he is *not* the Saviour!

As the church submits to Christ the Saviour, the wife is to submit to the husband, who is nothing of the sort.

The text, then, is asking the wife to submit to a husband who does not and cannot have the attributes of Saviour. It does not say to submit only on such occasions as he attains to certain attributes of the Saviour, either. It says to submit, *"in everything."*

It goes on:

> Husbands, love your wives, as Christ loved the church and gave himself up for her, that he might sanctify her, having cleansed her by the washing of water with the word, so that he might present the church to himself in splendor, without spot or wrinkle or any such thing, that she might be holy and without blemish. In the same way husbands should love their wives as their own bodies. He who loves his wife loves himself.
>
> Ephesians 5:25-28

Unlike Taliban men, the husband should love the wife enough to give his life for her. That is what Jesus Christ did for the church, and He is the model St. Paul sets before every husband. But he does not make it a condition of the wife's submission.

And again comes the divergence. The consequence of Christ's sacrifice is beyond the capacity of any husband. He should encourage his wife in the way of faith and may indeed give up his life for her, but nothing he can ever do will result in making her "without stain or wrinkle or any other blemish, but holy and blameless."

Also, we should take note that Scripture does not refer only to Christian spouses. The unbelieving husband, too, is head of his wife to whom she should submit as unto Christ in everything. This is the point Peter makes in his treatment of the subject. "Likewise, wives, be subject to your own husbands, so that even if some do not obey the word, they may be won without a word by the conduct of their wives" (1 Peter 3:1).

When he says, "likewise," Peter is harking back to what he said in the previous chapter where he addressed the need of citizens to submit to rulers and servants and slaves to submit to their masters with all respect "not only to the good and gentle but also to the unjust" (1 Peter 2:18). He then goes on to commend to them the example of Christ's unmerited suffering.

Thus, St. Peter leaves us in no doubt that he does not enjoin wives to be submissive to unbelieving husbands only when they are good and gracious and saintly! The only qualification of submission for the Christian wife, then, is "as to the Lord."

Before considering this point, we must not lose sight of where we started. The first point St Paul made is to do with mutual submission. A wise husband will not simply see his word as law. On many issues great and small, he will learn to submit to his wife's counsel after diligent consideration. Failure to do so would be to neglect the special help the good Lord has sent to him in His wisdom!

But what does it mean for the wife to submit to her husband "as to the Lord"? It means that the wife submits to her husband only in so far as such submission is consistent with submission to Christ. Sarah, for example, did not need to submit to Abraham's cowardly scheming. To make herself available to satisfy the lust of men who knew no better would hardly be in keeping with her submission to God! Or for the wife of an unbelieving husband, when he requires her to carry out any act of worship that violates her Christian conscience, she must obey God rather than man.

This is the limit of the wife's submission; when it would require her to dishonour the Lord or go contrary to His teaching in any way, she must draw the line.

Let us for a moment consider the practical outworking of the alternative—that the wife submits to the husband only as and when he proves himself deserving of her submission. Her submission would be conditional upon his good behaviour, and she would be the sole judge of that. Is this not the same as saying that it all depends on the husband's compliance with the wife's definition of deserving behaviour? Would that not in fact be standing "submission" on its head?

How about the other side—the husband who loves the wife only when he finds her submissive and otherwise withholds his love. This "love" would be her reward for good behaviour. How can any wife endure the ensuing tyranny?

A concept of meeting halfway in a fifty-fifty contribution to a successful marriage is perhaps the most brilliant recipe for disaster ever concocted. Human nature makes us more generous in estimating our own contribution of fifty percent. "The camel does not see its own hump," and we rarely see ourselves the way we really are. It is normal for us to feel that we are doing all the giving and the partner is doing all the taking!

God's way is that the husband should carry out his assigned responsibility to the wife one hundred percent, regardless of what the wife does or fails to do. In fact, it is not his role to *demand* submission. We shall see an example of this when we consider Hosea. And the wife should carry out her own assigned responsibility one hundred percent regardless of what the husband does or fails to do.

God judges each of His children according to how much exposure they have to the light of His truth, and so He did not place on Sarah the mature responsibility of New Testament revelation. She was not censured for failing to contradict and stand up to her husband's sinful scheming. In a similar way to Rahab the prostitute many centuries later, she was true to that which she knew and understood, and for this she received due accolade and praise.

The quotation is usually attributed to Samuel Clemens, alias Mark Twain, "It is not what I do not understand in the Bible that troubles me. It is what I do understand!" And even St. Peter acknowledges in one of his letters that there are some things in Scripture that are hard to understand.

> And count the patience of our Lord as salvation, just as our beloved brother Paul also wrote to you according to the wisdom given him, as he does in all his letters when he speaks in them of these matters. There are some things in them that are hard to understand, which the ignorant and unstable twist to their own destruction, as they do the other Scriptures.
>
> 2 Peter 3:15-16

Since there are indeed many things hard to understand in the Word of God, we should be careful not to join ignorant and unstable people in distorting them but leave them to our learned brothers and sisters who are given the theological muscle to wrestle with tough texts. Most of the time, however, what God tells us to do or not to do is not hard to understand. If only we could be true to what we do understand, we would earn the commendation due to those who are humble in spirit.

This hardly seems like one of those teachings that are hard to understand, but it is certainly not among the easiest to obey!

Question for Reflection

Do you agree with the explanation of the limits of submission, "as unto the Lord" or do you understand it differently? What are your reasons?

Stuttering Faith

It was Abraham's faith that sets him apart. He stepped out into the unknown because of this faith in the self-revealing God who had called him out of home and country.

Any divinity could promise a child to a childless couple of child-bearing age, but they would hardly target a woman who was biologically dead as far as concerns the natural mechanism for pregnancies. That was what Abraham's God did. It could not have been too hard to believe at first. He was a mere seventy-five years old, not an impossible age to be a father, even in these times of diminished human capabilities. Indeed, the famous still-film actor Charlie Chaplin was seventy-three when his last son was born to his thirty-seven-year-old wife Oona in 1962. More recently still, Jamie Rai was born to seventy-nine-year-old Raymond Calvert in a Lancashire Hospital in England in April, 2010.[22] The mother, Charlotte, was only twenty-five. Sarah, however, was much, much older than either mother, even though we have to concede she was rather unusual by all accounts. At sixty-five, this woman still turned heads!

Months turned to years, and years turned to decades, but the promised child did not show up. First Abraham, then Sarah started to analyse the original promise. What exactly did God say, and is there another way to understand it?

> I will make of you a great nation, and I will bless you and make your name great, so that you will be a blessing. I will bless those who bless you, and him who dishonors you I will curse, and in you all the families of the earth shall be blessed.
>
> Genesis 12:2-3

Lot was already his own man. There was a servant, more likely a slave, Eliezer of Damascus, who could legally inherit all that Abraham possessed if he died childless. He could then go on to become a great nation. But Abraham did not find that to be a satisfactory fulfilment of what God had said, and neither did God, who reiterated and clarified the promise.

> And behold, the word of the LORD came to him: "This man shall not be your heir; your very own son shall be your heir." And he brought him outside and said, "Look toward heaven, and number the stars, if you are able to number them." Then he said to him, "So shall your offspring be." And he believed the LORD, and he counted it to him as righteousness.
>
> Genesis 15:4-6

No problem here. Except that the baby still did not arrive, and Sarah was not growing younger. Then she had a brainwave. An idea came to mind which originated from one of the earliest pioneers of family jurisprudence. Hammurabi was the ruler who gave her native Chaldea, and indeed the world, its first set of Codified Law.

Neither God's initial promise nor the subsequent clarification indicated that Sarah would of necessity be biologically involved. Under the Code of Hammurabi that governed her native country, she could give her slave girl to her husband. There would be two main advantages if she bore him children. First, the husband could no longer treat the wife as if she was childless and take on another wife on that score. Second, he would have offspring who could legally inherit from him so long as he acknowledged them as his. This is what Hammurabi's Code 170 says,

> If his wife bear sons to a man, or his maid-servant have borne sons, and the father while still living says to the children whom his maid-servant has borne: "My sons," and he count them with the sons of his wife; if then the father die, then the sons of the wife and of the maid-servant shall divide the paternal property in common.[23]

Obviously, if the wife has no sons of her own, the sons of the maidservant would simply inherit the man. This was what Abraham, Sarah, and Hagar all thought would happen.

Question for Reflection

What do you think you could have done differently if you were in Abraham's position?

Domestic Violence

Abraham did not need much persuading before he took the young lady to bed. In no time at all a baby was on the way, and, just as quickly, like goat's milk in their desert climate, the triangular relationship began to sour. Hagar's pregnancy placed her in a position of power over her mistress, or so she thought. Then Sarah showed her who was boss, making her flee into the trackless wilderness on the way to her home country of Egypt.

There is enough blame to go round. Should Sarah not have counted the cost of vacating her marital bed for her slave girl? It was her idea, but the way she blamed it all on her compliant husband smacks of the sort of logic that keeps men for ever perplexed.

> And Sarai said to Abram, "May the wrong done to me be on you! I gave my servant to your embrace, and when she saw that she had conceived, she looked on me with contempt. May the LORD judge between you and me!"
>
> Genesis 16:5

But surely she does have a point, Father Abraham, does she not? Where was your manly resolve to wait on the God who had promised? Are you not responsible, indeed, for making the final decisions that govern your family? Are you so naïve in your appreciation of human nature that you could not foresee the denouement of your eager compliance with your wife's fraught proposition? How about your pastoral responsibility to encourage her to stand firm in the grace you have both received?

Hagar, oh Hagar! How readily you forgot your station! Did you learn nothing from the godly comportment of your master and mistress? And if you can have a child but another woman cannot, what credit, exactly, do you have in the matter?

This incident happens to be the one case of domestic violence we have recorded for us in Scripture. Even though it was perpetrated by one woman against another, the husband was far from blameless. His exact words to Sarah sounded like instigation to brutality. "Behold, your servant is in your power; do to her as you please" (Genesis 16:6).

The older woman did not need any further prompting. "Then Sarai dealt harshly with her, and she fled from her." More usually, it is the man who indulges in direct physical violence against his wife, contrary to the clear direction God gives to us through the teaching of St. Peter: "Likewise, husbands, live with your wives in an understanding way, showing honor to the woman as the weaker vessel, since they are heirs with you of the grace of life, so that your prayers may not be hindered" (1 Peter 3:7).

In the United Kingdom, one incident of domestic violence is reported to the police every minute.[24] It is estimated that one in four women will be a victim of domestic violence in their lifetime.

Even "weaker vessels" than wives and no less "heirs of the grace of life" are children, but they too are often victims of domestic violence from the hands of one parent or both!

Nor are men exempt. They too are sometimes victims of domestic violence. US Department of Justice researchers say that while there were approximately 4.5 million intimate partner physical assaults perpetrated against women in the twelve months preceding their survey, approximately 2.9 million men were similarly assaulted.[25] I once happened on a BBC radio programme where a caller described how he lived in terror of his wife and was condemned to suffering in silence. She regularly hit him with whatever came to hand, and he feared he could end up in prison if he ever touched her, even in self-defence, for no one would ever believe he was indeed the victim. He was six-foot-plus, and she was five-foot-nothing!

Battered victims often feel responsible for their plight and silently carry with them unwarranted burdens of guilt along with their sufferings. The protection traditionally offered by close-knit families with several generations living together or in close proximity no longer avails, as people move out and into the anonymity of large towns and cities to establish nuclear families. Thank God for societies that have established means of dealing with domestic violence, but far too often it goes unreported until irreparable damage results—up to the point of murder. In the UK, on average, two women a week are killed by a current or former male partner.[26]

Writing to the Philippian Christians, St. Paul enjoined them to live a life above reproach "that you may be blameless and innocent, children of God without blemish in the midst of a crooked and twisted generation, among whom you shine as lights in the world" (Philippians 2:15).

It is not enough that we should be blameless of actual involvement in violence. The local church as a community of God's people has a responsibility to protect the weak and be a voice for the voiceless. As individuals and as communities of light, under no circumstance should we turn away our faces or walk the other way whenever we come across this gross crime.

"To enter into disgrace may take but a moment, to get out can take forever." May God rescue us from the small beginnings of irreversible tragedies. How many men and women of God have taken the first seemingly innocent step away from the path of moral rectitude only to live a life of regrets as a result! Still, it is safe to say that nothing any of us is capable of doing can result in anything remotely approaching the dramatic, long lasting and earth-shaking consequences of Abraham's compromise.

Ishmael was born, and the course of world history was changed forever. That was the sordid beginning of the problem we still have today in the Middle East.

The Jews and their Arab neighbours indulge in a dialogue of the deaf and the nations of the world prescribe largely self-centred non-solutions while the Holy Land continues to bleed. Thankfully, there is one Jerusalem on high, way above the fray, where descendants of Isaac and Ishmael can have an equal claim to the hard-won victory of the Prince of Peace. But here below, true justice and lasting peace are tantalizingly beyond our reach as eminently demonstrated by the unfulfilled promise of Israeli/ Palestinian conflict resolution efforts.

"Whether the knife falls on the melon or the melon falls on the knife, it is the melon that suffers the bruise." It was Hagar the slave woman who had to leave the house together with her son.

Question for Reflection

In what ways did Abraham fail his wife Sarah, his slave girl Hagar, and his son Ishmael?

Wait on the Lord!

Whoever says God's clock is never slow is not reckoning time on a human calendar. Ishmael was now a teenager. Abraham was knocking on his centennial and his beloved wife, a mere ten years behind, remained as barren as ever. Of His own initiative, God reassured Abraham He had neither forgotten His promise nor changed His mind. He decided to renew His covenant with him—with circumcision as the sign. It was at this point that he received a new name—Abraham. His wife, too, had a name change from Sarai to Sarah, that is, from "my" princess to "Princess" as in a generic title.

That was when Abraham chose to do a very noble thing; the sort of thing you and I would do for a friend. The friend makes a promise which he had not thought through carefully and now finds it harder to keep than he had envisaged. Abraham offered to let God off the hook:

> Then Abraham fell on his face and laughed and said to himself, "Shall a child be born to a man who is a hundred years old? Shall Sarah, who is ninety years old, bear a child?" And Abraham said to God, "Oh that Ishmael might live before you!"
>
> Genesis 17:17-18

This God, however, is more than able, and in His own good time, the child of promise was born, from the sperm of Abraham, and from an ovum of the wife of his youth.

Two observations conclude this section. First is God's surprising evaluation of Abraham as recorded for us through St. Paul:

> He did not weaken in faith when he considered his own body, which was as good as dead (since he was about a hundred years old), or when he considered the barrenness of Sarah's womb. No distrust made him waver concerning the promise of God, but he grew strong in his faith as he gave glory to God, fully convinced that God was able to do what he had promised. That is why his faith was "counted to him as righteousness."
>
> Romans 4:19-22

What are we to make of this when we take note of how he did weaken in his faith and waver concerning the promise of God? There are some things which, in His incredible generosity of spirit, the Creator of memories chooses to forget. "Forgive and forget" rarely, if ever, happens with us human beings, but God is not like us. This is what He said to the sin-prone people of

Isaiah's time. "I, I am he who blots out your transgressions for my own sake, and I will not remember your sins" (Isaiah 43:25).

As someone has pointed out, sometimes we repeat a sin which we had confessed to God and had been forgiven. And so, we exclaim, "Sorry, Lord, I've done it again!" His response is, "Done what?"

Abraham's faith in God was imputed as righteousness, but he was every bit as human as you and me. That faith was far from perfect, but God credited to him the perfect righteousness that belongs to Him alone. This is grace at work, and it is what He does for us, too.

I think of how Sue once brought a little earthenware pot to show at our Home Group. It was a pot like only a child can make a pot. It is of no value for any household use, but Sue explained how she treasured it more than any of her expensive porcelain. It was a present her son brought home to her from his first camp. To her it is an object of incomparable beauty, even now that the son is grown up and is a father. Is this not the way our heavenly Father receives and treasures whatever we offer to Him in faith, ignoring all its flaws? In our familial relationships as in all other departments of our lives, we are far from perfect. Knowing all there is to know about our human limitations, however, God takes that which we have to offer and transforms it into something beautiful and wholesome in His reckoning. As husbands and wives, we must learn to do the same.

Second, Israel as a nation did not make Abraham's mistake. They never wavered in their expectation of God's promise of the Child who would be born in the house of David. It is true that they had a wrong conception of what the Messiah was coming to do, but the passing of centuries did not diminish their hope or dampen their expectation.

It is this example of Israel, rather than that of Abraham, which we must follow in all our dealings with God. We must hold on to whatever He says to us, once we hear Him clearly, and hold on to it without letting go, regardless of circumstances. Here is what He says through the prophet Habakkuk:

> "Write the vision; make it plain on tablets, so he may run who reads it. For still the vision awaits its appointed time; it hastens to the end—it will not lie. If it seems slow, wait for it; it will surely come; it will not delay."
>
> Habakkuk 2:2-3

And it is Peter's word for us in his general letter to the saints:

> The Lord is not slow to fulfill his promise as some count slowness, but is patient toward you, not wishing that any should perish, but that all should reach repentance. But the day of the Lord will come like a thief, and then the heavens will pass away with a roar, and the heavenly bodies will be burned up and dissolved, and the earth and the works that are done on it will be exposed.
>
> 2 Peter 3:9-10

And the psalmist:
"I believe that I shall look upon the goodness of the LORD in the land of the living! Wait for the LORD; be strong, and let your heart take courage; wait for the LORD!" (Psalms 27:13-14)

Question for Reflection

In what way is Paul's assessment of Abraham's unwavering faith in Romans 4 an encouragement to you?

Isaac on the Altar

The God of Abraham is the God of the unexpected. Those who decide to follow Him must be constantly ready for anything. But not in a million years would Abraham have expected God to ask for this child in sacrifice, this unique child on whom His promise rests!

The sacrifice of children was nothing new. It was practiced in Abraham's home and culture along with many, many others all over the world. For Abraham's God to demand that Abraham's son be given to Him in sacrifice would only bring Him in line with other local deities. By obeying, Abraham was only doing what other devotees of other gods did all the time. But presumably for such devotees, it would not be their only child; they would most likely be in their prime of life and be well able to have other children, and they would not be confined to a wife now in her nineties!

As far as we can tell, Abraham did not seek the opinion of his beloved Sarah before setting out for Mount Moriah in grim obedience. We are free to speculate all we want as to the thoughts churning the numb misery of his weary mind as he hiked his way toward the fateful rendezvous. That the core remained intact is demonstrated by the involuntary truth in the answer he gave to his son's only-too-reasonable question:

> And Isaac said to his father Abraham, "My father!" And he said, "Here am I, my son." He said, "Behold, the fire and the wood, but where is the lamb for a burnt offering?" Abraham said, "God will provide for himself the lamb for a burnt offering, my son." So they went both of them together.
>
> Genesis 22: 7-8

In his user-friendly overview of the Bible, Whitney Kuniholm, president of Scripture Union in the United States, points out the significance of the seemingly bizarre incident as a symbol of our salvation. "As the tension mounts in front of the makeshift altar, Abraham unwittingly prophesies God's plan of salvation: "God himself will provide the lamb for the burnt offering."[27]

God obviously knew in advance that Abraham would pass the test. Until he actually did, however, Abraham had no way of knowing! At the last moment, God *did* provide a ram for sacrifice in place of Abraham's son, and He later made it an article of the

Law that the children of Israel were not to follow the practice of the nations in sacrificing their children.

> When you come into the land that the LORD your God is giving you, you shall not learn to follow the abominable practices of those nations. There shall not be found among you anyone who burns his son or his daughter as an offering...
>
> Deuteronomy 18:9-10

Sadly, this lesson was lost on at least one of the Judges of Israel. Jephthah thought he was doing God a favour when he sacrificed his daughter, a willing but unnecessary victim, in payment of a rash and ignorant vow as recorded for us in Judges 11.

> Then the Spirit of the LORD was upon Jephthah, and he passed through Gilead and Manasseh and passed on to Mizpah of Gilead, and from Mizpah of Gilead he passed on to the Ammonites. And Jephthah made a vow to the LORD and said, "If you will give the Ammonites into my hand, then whatever comes out from the doors of my house to meet me when I return in peace from the Ammonites shall be the LORD's, and I will offer it up for a burnt offering."
>
> Judges 11:29-31

The endowment of the Spirit does not render any man infallible! The Spirit of God was on this man of war to enable him prosecute a military campaign, but that did not prevent him from the blunder of a rash oath to sacrifice whoever came out of his house to meet him. Did he simply decide to ignore the Law, or was he ignorant of what it teaches? Neither one nor the other is acceptable. It so happened that it was his daughter who came out to meet him with tambourines and dances!

When a man is filled with the Spirit of God, he ought to be even more conscious of his human frailty. This story should be a salutary lesson to us all as we are involved in spiritual conflict.

It is true that an oath should be kept and at great cost if necessary. Among the attributes of the upright man in Psalm 15, for instance, is that he is a man, "who swears to his own hurt and does not change" (Psalm 15:4). Jephthah's, however, was one oath that should not have been kept, because it was against the Law of the God that he was seeking to honour. He thereby failed to learn a lesson which was to prove the undoing of a future king of Israel when the Prophet Samuel explained to Saul. "Has the LORD as great delight in burnt offerings and sacrifices, as in obeying the voice of the LORD? Behold, to obey is better than sacrifice..." (1 Samuel 15:22)

We too must be careful not to fall down at this hurdle. No sacrifice, however costly, is a substitute for obedience.

Question for Reflection

Is it sometimes easier for us to offer sacrifices to God rather than to obey Him? What sort of sacrifices do we usually like to make?

Why the Test, Lord?

The question remains; why would God, loving, caring, and omniscient as He is, put His avowed devotee such as Abraham through such a cruel test? It brings to mind what St. Teresa of Avila said to God in a moment of exasperation: "If this is the way You treat Your friends, it's no wonder You have so few!"[28]

Charles Tindley wrote a song about it in 1905. It is entitled "When the Morning Comes."

Trials dark on every hand, and we cannot understand
All the ways that God could lead us to that blessèd promised land;
But He guides us with His eye, and we'll follow till we die,
For we'll understand it better by and by.

By and by, when the morning comes,
When the saints of God are gathered home,
We'll tell the story how we've overcome,
For we'll understand it better by and by.

Temptations, hidden snares often take us unawares,
And our hearts are made to bleed for a thoughtless word or deed;
And we wonder why the test when we try to do our best,
But we'll understand it better by and by...[29]

It is no use trying to defend God since we can never fully understand His motives, and His reasoning is of a totally different order from ours. This much we can say, however. He never invites us to go to a place where He Himself would not go. When the time came to sacrifice His only Son, He did not answer His prayer and remove from Him the sentence of death.

As C.S. Lewis puts it, "Sometimes it is hard not to say, 'God forgive God.'

He didn't. He sacrificed Him!"[30]

Abraham passed the test, and God reaffirmed His blessing on him and through him and his offspring to all the nations of the earth.

But how about us? Does God call us sometimes to make such costly sacrifices today? We can think back a few generations before ours, to the time before the discovery of Quinine. Parents released their bright young sons and daughters for missionary service in malaria-infested climates. At one stage, the average lifespan of newly arriving missionaries in West Africa was six weeks, but that did not stop them from going!

The story of Elisabeth Elliot is much more recent. She was barely three years into her marriage when her husband, Jim, was murdered in 1956, along with fellow pioneer missionaries, by Huaorani Indians they were trying to reach. What did she do as a

FLAWED SAINTS

result? She took great pains to learn their language and then went to live among them together with her infant children in order to bring to them the glorious good news of the saving grace of Jesus.

In short, in ways not too dissimilar to what He asked of Abraham, God *does* require us to make costly sacrifices. When He does, are we ready and willing to comply? What is it that we have and is so precious to us that we begrudge Him who gives us our life and livelihood and His one and only Son to boot? Evidently, the pathway of God's grace sometimes passes through strange alleyways!

Taking It Further

1. Abraham was an outstanding example as a man of faith, but he fell far short in his relationship with his wife. How can we identify our own areas of weakness so we can seek the necessary help?

2. In what ways do we stand by families undergoing any type of serious trauma in our Christian community?

3. *Patres familias* had great authority over their households. Do you believe that some of our government regulations have a tendency to erode the authority of parents today? If so, what can the church do concerning this?

4. Have you experienced or witnessed domestic violence first-hand? Does it sometimes happen in Christian homes? What can we do about the issue as a church and as a service to our community?

5. Why do you think God invited Abraham to sacrifice his son? Do you know individuals or families who are having to make costly sacrifices today? How can you or your church support them?

LOT'S UNENVIABLE LOT

Gay Pride?

With Abraham and Sarah having no child of their own, his nephew Lot was, naturally, his heir in Canaan—except he had other ideas. He grew up to be his own man, determined to make a name for himself. He had herds of his own, and they were growing, so much so that there was not enough room for his herdsmen and his uncle's. Thus clashes ensued. Abraham offered to Lot the freedom he craved. The younger man did not even accord to him the courtesy of first choice of territory that cultural norms demanded. An archetypical, enterprising go-getter, Lot knew exactly what he wanted, and he went for it.

Was it perhaps this rupture that led Abraham to pass over Lot as heir of all his inheritance? We have no way of knowing for sure.

Lot's choice of a well-watered valley to tend his flock was a decision that took him all the way to Sodom, a city that turned out to be antipathetic to his godly upbringing and training—a city that the apostle Peter was later to write, "tormented him in his righteous soul" (2 Peter 2:7-8). It was a choice that left his uncle with the more arid territories of Canaan, but that did not reduce God's blessings on him and on his flock—a worthwhile lesson for all who expect to prosper by adhering to conventional wisdom and logical economic strategies to the exclusion of God's leading. Rather, it is much wiser to heed the injunction, "You shall remember the LORD your God, for it is he who gives you power to get wealth" (Deuteronomy 8:18).

Even in his adopted home, Lot retained enough of his upbringing under Abraham to practice the brand of hospitality which led him to entertain angels unawares.

Thank God for those who have the gift of hospitality. For them, it is simply the normal thing to do. In my travels that took me to over a hundred countries, I have been blessed by not a few of them. Additional mouths at the table with little or no notice is not a problem for those endowed with this capacity to bless visitors of all hues. They never have to apologise for whatever they set before their guests, be it meagre or sumptuous, because it is the very best they have. Nor do they share with Martha her sense of irritation when she appealed to Jesus Christ to send her sister Mary back to join her in the kitchen, because they know how not to go beyond what is required.

Two Latin words provide the root for our English word "hospitality." The first is "*hostis*," which is also the root for "hostility" and has the connotation of "stranger." The second is "*potentia*." Hospitality, therefore, is dealing kindly with a stranger who could harbour hostile intentions and who, potentially, has the power to harm us.

As it turned out, Lot was not at risk from these unknown wayfarers in Sodom. He brought them into his home, alas, only to have gangsters descend on the household.

To compare the men of Sodom to animals would be an insult to beasts of every description, and this is before touching on the question of homosexuality. Animals may hunt in packs, but they most certainly do not descend to the level of gang rape.

"When you live next to the cemetery, you do not weep at every funeral." Righteous Lot lived in Sodom, and sin gradually lost its horror for him—until the time came when he evidently considered it a mark of honourable hospitality to offer his daughters to rapists in lieu of his guests. This really was an indication of how much he had strayed from the strait and narrow path and imbibed the culture of Sodom. We must all heed the warning from Paul in 1 Corinthians 15:33, "Bad company ruins good character."

The men of Sodom were the first on record to have sexual relationship with fellow men. In this, it is important to take time to understand them, and especially others who share their sexual orientation, and to react to them in love. The particular family problem their story introduces is one that is tearing the church of God apart in our generation, and so it is right to go into it in considerable detail and to seek the light of God's grace through it.

The awe-inspiring vista of nature does not only present us with profuse diversity. There are also numerous egregious aberrations. Not every child is born with perfect limbs. Some come into the world with webbed toes, twelve fingers, stumps where their hands should be, or an extra hand or two. And there is the extreme case of Nick Vujicic who, for no medical reason, was born without arms or legs and has to make do with what he calls a "chicken drumstick." None of these makes them less human than the rest of us. They are equally the handiwork of the same Creator God. Of that, Vujicic leaves no one in any doubt as he goes around the world proclaiming, "No arms, no legs, no worries!"[31]

There are many examples we could cite in the world of top rank sports, and the International Amateur Athletics Federation (IAAF) has a lot of experience of trying to determine whether an athlete is more male than female! Examples include the Polish American sprinter, Stella Walsh who competed as a female but was found to be actually male after she died.[32] More current is the young South African long distance runner, Caster Semenya who was suspended and investigated because of the unusual make-up of her gender before being reinstated as a female athlete.

As in the physical realm, so it is with the ways our minds are ordered. Just as most of us are either male or female, there are some who are in-between. Most human beings are sexually attracted only to people of the opposite sex. It is a biological fact, however, that some are born with a natural desire for sexual relation with people of the same gender as themselves. That is not wrong in itself. If they are born that way, why should anyone blame them for the way they are made? Let us compare this with a universally repugnant example. To the consternation and revulsion of all right thinking people, some have a natural predisposition to paedophilia—their innate desire is to have sex with children. In so far as we can concede that they did not make themselves that way, we can hardly blame them for it! It is not that predisposition in and of itself that is the problem. It is what they do with it. The fact that they have such a desire does not automatically mean that they have to act on it.

The Bible makes it clear that homosexual practice is not acceptable in God's ordering of human relationships.

In the Books of the Law, it is written, "You shall not lie with a male as with a woman; it is an abomination" (Leviticus 18:22). And again, "If a man lies with a male as with a woman, both of them have committed an abomination; they shall surely be put to death; their blood is upon them" (Leviticus 20:13).

Does this perhaps merely reflect unenlightened cultural attitudes of the Old Testament? In the New Testament, the Epistles are no less direct. In his letter to the Romans, St. Paul applies his formidable intellect to reason it out with consummate logic. He wrote about people who wilfully pervert God's purposes for human life:

> For although they knew God, they did not honor him as God or give thanks to him, but they became futile in their thinking, and their foolish hearts were darkened. Claiming to be wise, they became fools, and exchanged the glory of the immortal God for images resembling mortal man and birds and animals and creeping things.
>
> Therefore God gave them up in the lusts of their hearts to impurity, to the dishonoring of their bodies among themselves, because they exchanged the truth about God for a lie and worshiped and served the creature rather than the Creator, who is blessed forever! Amen. For this

reason God gave them up to dishonourable passions. For their women exchanged natural relations for those that are contrary to nature; and the men likewise gave up natural relations with women and were consumed with passion for one another, men committing shameless acts with men and receiving in themselves the due penalty for their error.

Romans 1:21-27

And he presents us with God's final verdict on the matter in his first letter to the Corinthians. "Or do you not know that the unrighteous will not inherit the kingdom of God? Do not be deceived: neither the sexually immoral, nor idolaters, nor adulterers, nor men who practice homosexuality" (1 Corinthians 6:9).

In the world of professing and confessing Christians, opinion is sharply divided about what to make of this and other similar passages even though the plain meaning, which is the traditional understanding of the church, would seem clear enough.

Question for Reflection

Lot got into trouble as a result of living in Sodom and also when living in the hills with his daughters. How do you see this in light of the injunction that we are "to be in the world but not of the world"?

A Church Divided

Some people accept what it says as what it means but are of the opinion that the message is based on the mores of bygone times and needs updating to conform with the spirit of our times. For example, the Bible does not condemn slavery or polygamy but is opposed to female leadership in the church and long male hair. On all of these matters, however, Christians generally consider it a mark of progress under the guidance of the Holy Spirit to take a contrary view. Homosexual practice, they argue, falls into this category, and to jettison biblical teachings that disapprove of it would be more in conformity with the concept of a God of love than the disgraceful treatment the church has accorded homosexuals through its history.

Such views, geared as they are at updating the Bible itself, are obviously not open to discussion on the basis of the final authority of Scripture. As Rev. Canon David Anderson, President of the American Anglican Council, pointed out,

> On the topic of Holy Scripture, the Bishop of Pennsylvania, the Rt. Rev. Charles Bennison has remarked, "We wrote the Bible and we can rewrite it."[33]

"We wrote the Bible, and we can re-write it," and the push is to re-write it to conform with enlightened modern secular philosophy.

The 1998 Lambeth Conference disagreed and appealed to Scripture in its resolution. This is the conference where Bishops of the world-wide Anglican Church come together every ten years for fellowship and to share together their vision of ministry in the world at large. "This Conference...in view of the teaching of Scripture, upholds faithfulness in marriage between a man and a woman in lifelong union, and believes that abstinence is right for those who are not called to marriage."

The seventy-sixth General Council of the Episcopal Church of the USA that took place the following year was of a different opinion. Rather than Scripture, it puts prior emphasis on "changing circumstances" in the United States and other countries resulting from legislation authorizing marriage, civil unions, or domestic partnerships for gays and lesbians. On these bases, Resolutions were passed with a clear majority in favour of accepting practising homosexuals as ministers of the church at every level.[34]

Thus, for the Episcopal Church, the Bible is not considered to be a relevant arbiter in these matters, let alone the Supreme

Court of appeal. Instead, human experience and the collective wisdom of the surrounding culture have the final say.

This, surely, is not a safe attitude to adopt with regard to the Word of God. Wisely has it been said that if you are married to the spirit of the age you will be a widow tomorrow!

Interestingly enough, the erudite Archbishop of Canterbury, Rowan Williams, usually cautious to the point of being overly nuanced, was uncharacteristically lucid in his rebuttal of Resolutions of the seventy-sixth General Convention of the Episcopal Church. His official, twenty-six-point response includes the following:

> In the light of the way in which the church has consistently read the Bible for the last two thousand years, it is clear that a positive answer to this question would have to be based on the most painstaking biblical exegesis and on a wide acceptance of the results within the Communion, with due account taken of the teachings of ecumenical partners also. A major change naturally needs a strong level of consensus and solid theological grounding.
>
> This is not our situation in the Communion. Thus a blessing for a same-sex union cannot have the authority of the church Catholic, or even of the Communion as a whole. And if this is the case, a person living in such a union is in the same case as a heterosexual person living in a sexual relationship outside the marriage bond; whatever the human respect and pastoral sensitivity such persons must be given, their chosen lifestyle is not one that the church's teaching sanctions, and thus it is hard to see how they can act in the necessarily representative role that the ordained ministry, especially the episcopate, requires.
>
> In other words, the question is not a simple one of human rights or human dignity. It is that a certain choice of lifestyle has certain consequences. So long as the church Catholic, or even the Communion as a whole does not bless same-sex unions, a person living in such a union cannot without serious incongruity have a representative

function in a Church whose public teaching is at odds with their lifestyle.[35]

When the Anglican Diocese of New Westminster in Canada decided to bless same-sex marriages in 2002, the eminent theologian, Dr. J.I. Parker was one of those who walked out of the synod. What he subsequently wrote to explain the decision is best quoted at length:

> To bless same-sex unions liturgically is to ask God to bless them and to enrich those who join in them, as is done in marriage ceremonies. This assumes that the relationship, of which the physical bond is an integral part, is intrinsically good and thus, if I may coin a word, *blessable*, as procreative sexual intercourse within heterosexual marriage is. About this assumption there are three things to say. First, it entails *deviation* from the biblical gospel and the historic Christian creed. It distorts the doctrines of creation and sin, claiming that homosexual orientation is good since gay people are made that way, and rejecting the idea that homosexual inclinations are a spiritual disorder, one more sign and fruit of original sin in some people's moral system. It distorts the doctrines of regeneration and sanctification, calling same-sex union a Christian relationship and so affirming what the Bible would call salvation in sin rather than from it. Second, it threatens *destruction* to my neighbour. The official proposal said that ministers who, like me, are unwilling to give this blessing should refer gay couples to a minister willing to give it. Would that be pastoral care? Should I not try to help gay people change their behaviour, rather than to anchor them in it? Should I not try to help them to the practice of chastity, just as I try to help restless singles and divorcees to the practice of chastity? Do I not want to see them all in the kingdom of God? Third, it involves the *delusion* of looking to God— actually asking him—to sanctify sin by blessing what he

condemns. This is irresponsible, irreverent, indeed blasphemous, and utterly unacceptable as church policy.[36]

Rev. Dr. John Stott, as usual, is unambiguous as to what he considers the Biblical position:

> Acceptance or tolerance of a same-sex partnership rests on the assumption that sexual intercourse is "psychologically necessary." That is certainly what our sex-obsessed contemporary culture says. But is it true? Christians must surely reply that it is a lie. There is such a thing as the call to singleness, in which authentic human fulfilment is possible without sexual experience. Our Christian witness is that Jesus himself, though unmarried, was perfect in his humanness. Same-sex friendship should of course be encouraged, which may be close, deep and affectionate. But sexual union, the 'one flesh' mystery, belongs to heterosexual marriage alone.[37]

But that is not his final word on the matter: "However strongly we may disapprove of homosexual practices, we have no liberty to dehumanize those who engage in them."[38]

Question for Reflection

What do you think of the comments of Archbishop Rowan Williams and Dr Parker on same-sex union?

Personal Battles

The approach of the US Episcopal Church that is shared by the Canadian Diocese of Westminster, of course, is not the only one taken by those with a dissenting opinion. There are those who accept the Bible's teaching as the standard for all matters of faith and life but believe, nonetheless, that the traditional belief and practice of the church based on the texts cited above are in error because they are based on misinterpretation and consequent mis-understanding of their true meaning.

There is no doubting the sincerity of many who have to fight a personal battle to ascertain God's mind for them and to please Him in their choices regarding homosexuality.

Justin Lee, for example, founder of the Gay Christian Network, deserves high marks for his effort in seeking a biblical basis for active homosexuality, especially in light of his claim that he is single and does not sleep with any man.[39] He makes a heartfelt pitch as he delves into Scripture in his determined contribution to "The Great Debate" on the Gay Christian Network website.[40]

Lee begins by taking the four traditional arguments against homosexual practice head on. First, he concedes that our bodies are designed for heterosexuality but points out that none of us would consider sign language sinful simply because hands are primarily designed for anything but talking! Second is the idea that gay sex must be wrong because it cannot fulfil God's purpose of procreation, but infertile couples have sex legitimately know-ing full well that a child will not result. Next is the argument from silence; there is no example of same-sex marriage in the Bible, and "if extramarital sex is wrong, then sex would only be permis-sible in a gay marriage." Agreeing with part of this argument, he roundly condemns promiscuity and all forms of casual sex, citing Cameron Diaz's character in *Vanilla Sky,* "Don't you know that when you sleep with someone, your body makes a promise even if you do not?" His main rebuttal here is that the Bible merely records the cultural norms of its time. Finally, he comes down hard on the argument that gay sex must be wrong because the Bible says it is …because he does not agree that the Bible does.

For all his impressive effort, Justin is in the end unconvincing in his response to what he described as "homosexuality proof-texts" against gays and lesbians who engage in homosexual prac-tice. It would seem he took his cue from Dr. Tony Campolo, the respected Baptist minister and evangelist and professor emeritus of sociology at Eastern College in suburban Philadelphia, whose audio contribution is featured on the same website alongside of his wife, an advocate for the acceptance of openly gay relationship among the clergy.[41] Dr. Campolo is amazingly lackadaisical in his approach to Biblical exegesis and interpretation, and Justin Lee echoes his words. Classifying homosexual practice with the ritual rather than moral aspects of the Law, he dismisses Old Testament teaching on it along with "abominations" such as feeding on carrion-eating birds. And with conjecture rather than proof, he deflects New Testament disapproval away from active homosexuality by concluding that St. Paul was probably referring to a practice that was fairly common in the Greek culture of his day whereby married men had sex with male youths on the side.

The response by Justin Lee's gay colleague and fellow member of the Gay Christian Network, Ron Beglau, leaves nothing to be desired.[42] He seems to me like a man who fulfils Jeremiah's prophecy, "You will seek me and find me, when you seek me with all your heart" (Jeremiah 29:13).

Evidently seeking the Lord with all his heart, Ron studied Greek so that he could make an in-depth, first-hand research of the texts involved, and it paid off handsomely. These texts he analyses skilfully, and in particular the word *arsenokoitai*, which those who favour homosexual practice often attempt to explain away.

He begins with people who argue that Jesus Christ had nothing to say against homosexual marriage by pointing out that, in His teaching on divorce, He invoked and endorsed the original, divine ethic of marriage:

> Have you not read that he who made them from the beginning made them male and female (cf. Genesis 1:27), and said, 'For this reason a man shall leave his father and mother and be joined to his wife, and the two shall become one flesh' (cf. Genesis 2:24)? So they are no longer two but

one flesh. What therefore God has joined together, let not man put asunder.[43]

On 1 Corinthians 6:9-11 he writes:

> The key debate over this passage concerns the meaning of the term *arsenokoitai*. There is a lot of debate over this word, but having studied Greek, it seems to me fairly self-evident that *arsenokoitai* is a compound word referring to those offenders condemned in Leviticus 18:22. In the Septuagint, we find "You shall not lie *[koiten]* with a male *[arsenos]* as with a woman; it is an abomination" (Leviticus 18:22).… It is true enough that there are some Greek scholars who reject this interpretation just as there are some Biblical Scholars who argue that God is not the Creator or that Christ was not born of a virgin or that He wasn't the Son of God or that He did not rise from the dead. But if Christians had to give up their beliefs every time a scholar professed disbelief, Christianity would not have survived a week.… There is a tiny amount of room for scepticism about the meaning of *arsenokoitai*, but in order to make a compelling case against the obvious meaning, one would need to propose an alternative meaning, find documentation of that alternative meaning, and show that the alternative meaning would make at least as much sense out of Paul's argument as does the grammatically obvious meaning.[44]

As a man who wished it were not so, Beglau confronted the facts of the Bible's teaching honestly and came out in favour of what mainline Christianity has always believed. He made an in-depth, common sense study of the words in contention in the Greek original, in a manner very different from Tony Campolo's rather sloppy approach which was adopted by Justin Lee. But he is not done. He went on to analyse 1 Timothy 1:8-11:

> Paul argues that homosexual acts can 1) keep us from the Kingdom of Heaven; 2) defile the temple of the Holy

Spirit within us; and 3) place us back under the judgment
of the law. Given the stakes involved, it is not a risk I am
willing to take. Even more so, I would never risk inflicting
consequences that serious on another man whom I loved.[45]

It is truly heart-warming to read Ron Beglau's testimony. For
those of us who do not know gay feeling experientially in our
bodies and our minds, it could sound merely theoretical when
we say these same things. There are those who, in an attempt
to be charitable, especially in light of the hateful response from
the church in the past, seek to tone down the Bible's teaching on
the subject. Beglau, however, speaks from the background of personal experience and an earnest desire to seek the Lord's face and
do only what is pleasing to Him. What he demonstrates most
decisively to us is that the grace of God does not compromise the
Word of God.

Clearly, God's plan for sexual relations is exclusively between
a man and a woman. The homosexual option is one He definitely rejected. With Adam's rib as the raw material He chose
to employ, surely, the Almighty could not have found it hard to
make a clone of the man in order to produce "Adam and Steve,"
as Justin Lee puts it, instead of Adam and Eve!

Few countries make a law against adultery so long as the other
party is willing and of age.[46] Although the law of the land may
allow adultery or even homosexuality, however, the law of God
does not. He looks with favour on the sexual act only and exclusively between two persons of the opposite sex who are properly married to each other. His law is that heterosexual men and
women must not satisfy their natural desire for fornication and
adultery. His law is that the one who feels pre-disposed to paedophilia must rein in those desires. His law is that the one who feels
attracted to members of the same sex must not indulge in sexual
acts with them. And His law is non-negotiable.

The fact that most people, at least in the Western world,
would prefer it not to be so does not alter God's position. He

does not govern the world by majority opinion. He is not asking for anybody's endorsement. He is not canvassing for popular vote at the next election. That is what it means to be God.

Nobody should pretend that it is easy; and it is obviously more difficult for some than for others. It behoves none of us to look with disdain on those who have a different or harder struggle than ourselves. "What do you have that you did not receive? If then you received it, why do you boast as if you did not receive it?" (1 Corinthians 4:7).

Which of us has not struggled with a so-called "besetting sin" against which we seem powerless and paralysed in spite of our best efforts to use all the physical, human, and spiritual resources at our disposal? We need to learn from a stalwart in the faith of the calibre of St. Paul who confesses in Romans 7,

> For we know that the law is spiritual, but I am of the flesh, sold under sin. For I do not understand my own actions.... I have the desire to do what is right, but not the ability to carry it out. For I do not do the good I want, but the evil I do not want is what I keep on doing.
>
> Romans 7:14-15; 18-19

Happy is the man or woman who receives adequate help and support when battling with sin at this level of intensity! Others in the Christian community often pretend as if they never face such battles themselves, and so we feel all alone and too ashamed to own up to our needs and seek for help. Far from being helpful, those to whom we appeal sometimes add to our pains as a result of their own inadequacy.

Here is a question for those of us who are smug in our assurance that homosexual practice deserves the sternest condemnation. How would we react if our teenage son or daughter were to confide in us that they were a practising homosexual? Leaders do not always take to heart the injunction of St. Paul in his letter to the Galatians.

Brothers, if anyone is caught in any transgression, you who are spiritual should restore him in a spirit of gentleness. Keep watch on yourself, lest you too be tempted. Bear one another's burdens, and so fulfill the law of Christ.

Galatians 6:1-2

Take the case of Shawn O'Donnell who grew up in lively Pentecostal churches as a kid. He was told that being gay was a sin, and so he sought to subdue his feelings. At age eighteen, he began counselling to overcome homosexuality. He attended faithfully once or twice a week as required, for two years. It didn't work, and at age twenty-one he slashed his own wrist in a suicide attempt. His desperate cry for help was heard and further assistance provided, for the next three years, at New Hope Ministries. Altogether, ten years of active therapy failed to turn him around. Who of us can condemn him for lack of effort? Sadly, he finally gave up trying and joined a church that welcomes him and his gay sexuality.[47]

This, however, does not negate the testimonies of others who have received the sort of help that Shawn O'Donnell sought in vain. One fortunate such person is Mario Bergner, who has written a very helpful book to describe his experience.[48]

"Exodus International" (to which O'Donnell refers), "Pastoral Care Ministries" headed by Leanne Payne, "New Hope," and other similar ministries have helped many people to put homosexual lifestyles behind them. Thankfully, there is a growing number of such ministries to which people can turn for help, but many more are needed, and needed in every country.

The most successful of these ministries insist that ceasing to be a homosexual never comes quick and easy for anyone. It is like the battle with addiction. Alcoholics Anonymous trains those they help not to describe themselves as "cured" but as "recovering" lest they become complacent and put themselves at risk.

The words of Frank Worthen of New Hope ministries are pertinent:

To begin to understand the meaning of "ex-gay," we can correlate it with the sanctification process described in 2 Corinthians 1:10, "Who delivered us from so great a death, and doth deliver: in whom we trust that he will yet deliver us." The ex-gay knows that something has definitely happened in his life. Change has come. Perhaps the most important change is that he has come into agreement with God that homosexuality "misses the mark," which is the definition of sin. Attitudes have also changed so that what was once called "love" is now seen as possessiveness. The ex-gay can agree with Paul that he has been delivered. So there is now a new position in Christ where the ex-gay is freed from sin by the atoning blood of Jesus on the cross. God now views that person through the sacrifice of Jesus Christ. At the same time, the change that we are experiencing is also a process of growth that goes along day by day, even minute by minute… Becoming ex-gay does not guarantee that there will be no stumbles. Daily, each Christian needs to be delivered from tempting thoughts and sexual availability. He knows that Jesus will deliver him from these things because Christ has already begun the change process in his life. When one has already seen the hand of God at work in one's life, it is easier to trust God and to rely on Him in times of trouble.[49]

These sentiments come from the head of a ministry that has enough success to blow its own trumpet if it were so inclined as the study by two eminent scholars clearly indicates.[50] No matter how rigorous their methodology in demonstrating religiously mediated change in sexual orientation, however, it would be overly optimistic to expect that researchers such as Stanton Jones and Mark Yarhouse will ever gain popular acclaim in the current social and scientific climate. Authoritative voices from the psychological, psychiatric, and other relevant health professions deride all talk of possible changes in a person's sexual orientation on a scale ranging from pitiable delusion to homophobic wickedness.

No amount of learned opinion, however, can cancel out God's work of grace. Far too often, unfortunately, the problem is with God's people who fail to mediate His truth in love. An article entitled "The Road to Healing: Battling Homosexual Attraction One Day at a Time," was posted anonymously in *Christianity Today* online, April 13, 2007.

> Over the years, I have taken huge risks to share my experiences with some Christian friends whom I thought I could trust. Needless to say, several of those friends wounded me deeply when they conveniently found ways to exit from my life. What if the church were full of people who were loving and safe, willing to walk alongside people who struggle? What if there were people in the church who kept confidences and who took the time to be Jesus to those who struggle with homosexuality? What if the church were what God intended it to be? What if broken people could safely do what James said, "Confess your sins to one another and pray for each other that you may be healed"?
>
> When I told another pastor my story, he loved me, prayed for me, encouraged me, and helped me in my journey toward wholeness.

Whenever people seek to honour God in their choice of lifestyle regardless of their human flaws, the grace of God is demonstrated in a glorious manner. The former Archbishop of York, Dr. David Hope, is one such example. Peter Tatchell, the Gay Rights campaigner wrote him a letter urging him "to be true to his nature" by proclaiming his gay sexuality to the world in order to help change the church's attitude by coming out in favour of open homosexual liaisons. What Bishop Hope did was to call a press conference where he did concede that his sexuality was "a grey area" but added that he had made a deliberate choice to be celibate. Peter Tatchell subsequently lamented:

> Like most Anglican leaders, Dr. Hope opposes an equal
> age of consent for gay men, supports the ban on gay foster
> parents by the Children's Society, endorses the sacking of
> clergy in loving gay relationships, and colludes with reli-
> gious cults that attempt to 'cure' gay people.[51]

In light of this, gay activists would most readily have brought
out any skeletons the esteemed bishop might have been hiding
in his ecclesiastical cupboard. David Hope was wise enough to
forestall insinuations. According to his biographer, he made sure
that nobody, male or female, gay or straight, ever stayed over-
night in his bachelor apartment.[52] Jesus Christ says that "there
are eunuchs who have made themselves eunuchs for the sake
of the kingdom of heaven" (Matthew 19: 12). The general verdict, even of a scandal-mongering tabloid press was that Bishop
Hope lived a life above reproach. "This is a positive way of life
for me," added the godly prelate. "I am happy and content with
and within myself."

For all his failings and imperfection, Lot was counted among the
righteous. Evidently, he was able to live above the level of the
general sinful populace to the extent that his life brought the sins
of his community into sharp relief. The rampant homosexuality which was a feature of their immorality provoked a backlash
against homosexuals for millennia, until only a few short years
ago when the practice suddenly became fashionable in Western
countries. Now, it is not merely that gay unions are legal but
those who disapprove of it for whatever reason are being demon-
ised. As for us, we have a responsibility to know and to obey what
our Lord requires. That is why the testimonies of Ron Beglau
and Bishop Hope and the principled stand of Rowan Williams
and Dr Parker are so heart-warming. To all that we must add
another fact. What homosexuals need is not condemnation but
help. Unfortunately we rarely know or care enough to be able to

provide the needed help, and yet it is through us that God wants to minister His grace to the gay men and women among us.

Sadly, Lot did not win many converts in Sodom—not even the young men who were planning to marry his daughters. Whatever God counted for him as righteousness was sufficient only to save him and his family, but even that was reduced by the vacillation of his wife who could not take her eyes away from the doubtful delights of Sodom. If only there were a handful of others like him, the twin cities of Sodom and Gomorrah would have been saved in answer to Abraham's prayers. Such was the ambition of one dear sister I got to know in Nairobi.

"I do not know how many righteous people for whose sake God will save my country," she confided. "Perhaps ten. Maybe a hundred. Or a thousand. But my one desire in life is to be one of them."

From that day to this, I have made that my own desire, too, for my country.

Question for Reflection

How would you respond if one of the youth in your church came to you for help because they are gay? What if it was your son or daughter or little sister? What would be the likely reaction if one of the young people comes out as gay in your church?

The Problem of Singleness?

"The child that is burned by fire is afraid of ashes." Learning the hard lessons of his precipitous exit from Sodom, Lot was too scared to live in Zoar. From the ultra-modern civilization of his former abode, he became a cave dweller together with his daughters. One aspect of it did not sit well with the young ladies, and they felt they had to find a remedy. There were no men in their lives.

> Now Lot went up out of Zoar and lived in the hills with his two daughters, for he was afraid to live in Zoar. So he lived in a cave with his two daughters. And the firstborn said to the younger, "Our father is old, and there is not a man on earth to come in to us after the manner of all the earth. Come, let us make our father drink wine, and we will lie with him, that we may preserve offspring from our father."
>
> Genesis 19:30-32

Far too often we make the same mistake as the daughters of Lot. We look at the unmarried state as a "problem," and we set out trying to solve it by marriage, being the one and only answer we know. "The one whose only tool is a hammer sees every question in the shape of a nail."

That is not the way the Almighty God sees it. He is not limited to one method of ordering human existence. It is not his purpose for each and every person in the world to marry. The one perfect Man that ever lived did not! St. Paul actually recommends singleness over the married state for anyone who would like to serve the Lord with minimum encumbrance. He begins his teaching to the church in Corinth on the subject of marriage with the astonishing declaration. "It is good for a man not to marry" (1 Corinthians 7:1 NIV).

This was an audacious statement to make in any context, but more so when writing to people in a city which was a byword for immorality. Even among the Greeks whose worship routinely included sexual orgies, "to Corinthianize" was a term of particular depravity.

The Christian God demands absolute sexual purity. Marriage, the apostle went on to explain, was a concession to prevent immorality as members of the community of faith could not always dissociate themselves from the practices of the godless society among whom they lived. Not surprising, therefore, this is one of three reasons given for marriage in the Anglican form of solemnising a wedding as contained in the Book of Common Prayer:

First, It was ordained for the procreation of children, to be brought up in the fear and nurture of the Lord, and to the praise of his holy Name. Secondly, It was ordained for a remedy against sin, and to avoid fornication; that such persons as have not the gift of continency might marry, and keep themselves undefiled members of Christ's body. Thirdly, It was ordained for the mutual society, help, and comfort, that the one ought to have of the other, both in prosperity and adversity.[53]

I have had the privilege of working with single ladies in an itinerant ministry. Those of us who are married, of necessity, can be away from home only for very limited periods on God's wider ministry, turning our attention from the mission field to the other ministry that we have to our families in our homes. These ladies, however, pack their suitcases, hop on the plane, and are away for months on end, fully focused on putting their heart and soul into the service of the Master! This has helped me to appreciate in some measure what a gift God has given to His church in such devoted single people.

As Jesus Christ once explained to His disciples,

Not everyone can receive this saying, but only those to whom it is given. For there are eunuchs who have been so from birth, and there are eunuchs who have been made eunuchs by men, and there are eunuchs who have made themselves eunuchs for the sake of the kingdom of heaven. Let the one who is able to receive this receive it.

Matthew 19:11-12

Each one, therefore, needs to determine the mind of God for their particular life. I learned as much from my mentors as a teenager. There was a time I seriously considered whether I might be one of the special group the Lord calls to serve Him without marrying. Was it perhaps because of the high view I had of some of my single missionary teachers? In my African society, I did not know one adult who was not married, but among the missionaries, there were many. Humans marry—angels do not. Some missionaries married, some did not, and so I esteemed missionaries as something akin to the missing link between humans and angels! Aspiring to be rated among the seraphim, I sought the counsel of one of them, a middle-aged saint as attractive in her life as in her figure. She helped me to understand that singleness is a calling that some receive, and then they can choose to embrace or to reject it. I will never forget her words. "The gift to remain single," she told me, "is one which very few people can receive with both hands from God and say, 'Thank you.'"

It became clear soon enough that I did not qualify!

The very possibility of the single life did not occur to the daughters of Lot. Perhaps, like the situation in many traditional cultures, it was not even considered an option in theirs. What they really wanted was to have children, and, until our generation came along, that invariably required the service of a man in a sexual encounter.

> ## Question for Reflection
>
> Why do you think that singleness is considered a "problem." What should the church be doing to change this perception?

"Wine is a Mocker"

One unfortunate fact about Lot is shared by many fathers. He did not really know his children, although they knew him only too well!

He no doubt had his own plans to fulfil his paternal responsibility to get them decent husbands in due course. It would seem that he failed to share such happy thoughts with them, and they could not wait forever.

Tasteless, odourless, and colourless, Rohypnol, Gamma Hydroxy Butyrate (GBH) and Ketamine Hydrochloride are popular "date rape" drugs. Slipped into the drink of some unsuspecting female, they are quick acting and difficult to detect in toxicological tests. They render their victims unconscious but responsive, and without a memory of whatever happened to them in the interim.

In light of such diabolical risks, how important it is to be careful in choosing where one goes to drink what and in whose company!

A few thousand years before these clever modern chemical compounds came on the market, poor Lot was the victim of a much more common drug, and he did not have to leave his home and family.

Among the habits he had picked up in Sodom was a love for drink, and his daughters knew it. On the basis of wisdom distilled perhaps from bitter experience, King Solomon was later to write with mature reflection: "Wine is a mocker, strong drink a brawler, and whoever is led astray by it is not wise" (Proverbs 20:1).

Now reduced to living the life of hermits, Lot's daughters were deprived of the gaiety and frivolity they had enjoyed in Sodom. Only one man existed in their world, and he was far from eligible. What is more, in his right senses, there was zero chance in a billion that he would lie with either one of them. Three and a half thousand years ahead of their time, the two ultra-modern young ladies were interested in having babies without the "irrelevant" intermediary of husbands. What to do?

They were sufficiently streetwise to know how to exploit the weakness of their father. All they needed to do was get him to drink himself into a stupor, and in the surrounding fields they managed to find the necessary ingredients. Their plot succeeded, and instead of the blessing of a father, what they earned for themselves was the curse of the prophet: "Woe to him who makes his neighbours drink—you pour out your wrath and make them drunk, in order to gaze at their nakedness!" (Habakkuk 2:15).

It is not surprising that some in their zeal to avoid such trouble make it a law that a Christian should abstain from all alcoholic beverages. It has to be made clear, however, that nowhere does the Bible forbid drinking. The only exception was the Nazirite vow, such as applied to Samson and even to his mother when she was pregnant with him, and that encompassed not only alcoholic beverages but anything that came from the vine:

> He shall separate himself from wine and strong drink. He shall drink no vinegar made from wine or strong drink and shall not drink any juice of grapes or eat grapes, fresh or dried...he shall eat nothing that is produced by the grapevine, not even the seeds or the skins.
>
> Numbers 6:3-4

Apart from this, not even the Pharisees, who distilled 613 laws from the books of Moses, could include a prohibition of wine as one of them. The best wines at weddings in all cultures and in all history have always been alcoholic wine. Evidently, Jesus did not turn water to lemonade. The Master of Ceremonies at the wedding in Cana was no teetotaller; it is safe to assume he knew what he was talking about when he pronounced the wine produced by His first miracle as the genuine article. "Everyone serves the good wine first, and when people have drunk freely, then the poor wine. But you have kept the good wine until now" (John 2:10).

And when Paul prescribed a little wine for Timothy's ailing stomach, it was not to use wine as an ointment to rub on it! "No longer drink only water," he counselled, "but use a little wine for the sake of your stomach and your frequent ailments" (1 Timothy 5:23).

What exists in plenty throughout the Bible, Old Testament and New, are injunctions to self-restraint. King Solomon did not mince his words:

> Who has woe? Who has sorrow? Who has strife? Who has complaining? Who has wounds without cause? Who has redness of eyes? Those who tarry long over wine; those who go to try mixed wine. Do not look at wine when it is red, when it sparkles in the cup and goes down smoothly. In the end it bites like a serpent and stings like an adder. Your eyes will see strange things, and your heart utter perverse things.
>
> Proverbs 23: 29-33

Paul gives clear guidance to deacons and to older women. "Deacons likewise must be dignified, not double-tongued, not addicted to much wine, not greedy for dishonest gain" (1 Timothy 3:8). "Older women likewise are to be reverent in behaviour, not slanderers or slaves to much wine" (Titus 2:3).

In light of such strong words, anyone who feels they are in danger of failing or of leading others to fall would be very wise to choose to abstain completely. This, after all, would be a very minor sacrifice compared to those, for example, who make themselves eunuchs for the sake of the kingdom of God! St. Paul gives the encouragement in one of his letters:

> Do not, for the sake of food, destroy the work of God. Everything is indeed clean, but it is wrong for anyone to make another stumble by what he eats. It is good not to eat meat or drink wine or do anything that causes your brother to stumble.
>
> Romans 14:20-21

Question for Reflection

Increasingly, heavy drinking is a problem in many countries especially among the youth. What should the church be doing about it?

Sin Ruins Reputations

Lot would very much wish he had never tasted his first mug of wine, but by the time he discovered his indiscretion he was an expectant father and grandfather twice over. Surely, this must be one of the saddest verses in the Bible: "Both the daughters of Lot became pregnant by their father" (Genesis 19:36).

Some sins are particularly disgusting right across cultures the world over, and incest is one of them. What is a man or a woman to do when the enemy succeeds in luring them into an act which most people would find nauseating? It is clear in this and many other narratives through the Scriptures, such things can sometimes happen to prominent and effective men and women of God. And if they happened in Bible times, they happen today.

Some of us are not too keen on television evangelists, especially those whose emphases seem to be as much on money as on souls. We are saddened but are not too surprised when they get caught in sex scandals and fall spectacularly from grace. Some Protestants succumb to self-righteous indignation at the news of Catholic priests involved in sex scandals—priests who are happy for everybody to call them "Father" except their actual children! "If only they do not espouse the unhelpful theology of celibacy," we piously reckon, "they would not be in such a mess." But it does happen also to seasoned, married Protestant leaders. We have to acknowledge and lament the frailty of our human condition.

Gordon MacDonald was pastor of Grace Chapel in Lexington, Massachusetts, for twelve years. He left in 1984 to join World Vision International and then became President of InterVarsity Christian Fellowship. He also taught at Bethel Theological Seminary in St. Paul, Minnesota, and Gordon Conwell Theological Seminary in New England. Any one of these positions signifies top-shelf evangelical credentials, but Gordon MacDonald had them all under his belt. And then his world imploded. He came crashing down from these lofty heights when he got caught with his pants down.

There are others like him.

Even though he had been married for twenty-eight years with one of his five children in pastoral ministry, Ted Haggard was another prominent Church leader who had to learn the hard way. He was the pastor of New Life Community Church in Colorado Springs with a congregation of fourteen thousand, and president of the thirty-million-strong American National Association of Evangelicals. This is not the profile of a man one would expect to admit to buying sex and drugs from a male prostitute, but that is exactly what happened to him.[54]

There is one thing we can say for sure. God forgives sin when the sinner repents. Both Ted Haggard and Gordon MacDonald experienced tough love from their churches, which put them under both discipline and counselling, and these led to restoration as St. Paul taught in his letter to the Corinthians.

> Now if anyone has caused pain, he has caused it not to me, but in some measure—not to put it too severely—to all of you. For such a one, this punishment by the majority is enough, so you should rather turn to forgive and comfort him, or he may be overwhelmed by excessive sorrow. So I beg you to reaffirm your love for him.
>
> 2 Corinthians 2:5-8

In fact, Gordon MacDonald was not only restored but became better able to help other leaders enmeshed in the web of Satan, especially through sexual sin. *Rebuilding Your Broken World*, a book which came out of his unhappy experience, has been a help to thousands.[55] This famously included Bill Clinton, president of the United States of America, when Gordon Macdonald joined Tony Campolo and Philip Wogaman in providing him and his wife Hilary with six months of intensive counselling.[56]

The tenor of Bible witness is that Lot received forgiveness for this wine-induced culpable incest with his two daughters. Significantly, St. Peter was able to refer to him as "a righteous man" in spite of this blot on his record.

Of particular interest is the way God dealt with the children born as a result of this sin. Just as with any other children, He treats them as normal heirs of their father. The manner of their conception and birth did not stop Him from giving special instruction concerning their descendants to Moses for the Israelites on their way to the Promised Land:

> Do not harass Moab or contend with them in battle, for I will not give you any of their land for a possession, because I have given Ar to the people of Lot for a possession.
>
> Deuteronomy 2:9

This is wonderful news and encouragement for all children born out of wedlock or as a result of liaisons that are not in line with God's commands. God recognises their claim on His love and His Fatherhood just like any other child of saints born in the most virtuous way imaginable.

Taking It Further

1. The law in most countries of the Western world grants the same rights to gay couples as obtain in traditional marriage while rampart discrimination exists in most countries of the developing world. In either case, what should be our stand as individual Christians and what should be the stand of the church?

2. Check out "The Great Debate" on the Internet and read the opinions of Justin Lee and Ron Beglau in full. (www.gaychristian.net/greatdebate) How would you relate to someone having the same opinion as either one of them?

3. Homosexual people have been very badly maltreated in many cultures and even churches. What should we be doing today to redress this?

4. What effects do you think that drinking has on family life in your culture and what role does the church play?

5. What do we need to do in order to value and support "singles" appropriately in our Christian communities?

JACOB: REAPING, SOWING, AND GRACE AT WORK

Daylight Robbery

In his popular overview of the Bible, *Essential 100*, Whitney Kuniholm introduces the story of Jacob and Esau in the following way:

> A psychiatrist could have a field day analyzing this dysfunctional family: a permissive father, a controlling mother, an errant older son, and a deceptive younger son. Get them all fighting for the family inheritance and, hey, presto! You've got a great pilot line for any TV soap. But this is one of the most important families in the Bible because God used them to build the nation of Israel.[57]

Isaac was old, frail, and blind, and he wanted to give to his older son, Esau the hunter, his final blessing before he died. He requested that Esau go into the field to hunt game for him, and then receive the blessing. His wife overheard this and decided to help the younger twin brother, Jacob, receive the blessing instead. "Go to the flock and bring me two good young goats," she instructed him, "so that I may prepare from them delicious food for your father, such as he loves. And you shall bring it to your father to eat, so that he may bless you before he dies" (Genesis 27:9-10).

In her book on parenting, Grace Onamusi describes a mother as the only one capable of dividing her love between several children so that each one of them has one hundred percent.[58]

Not a few mothers fall short of this ideal, and Rebekah is the great-grandmother of them all. For whatever reason, many parents do have favourites among their children. Problems come when they allow that to lead to preferential treatment. There is nothing here to suggest that Isaac did anything untoward because of his preference for Esau, the gallant hunter, who brought him that venison to which he was particularly partial. Not so Rebekah. She was prepared to bend the full force of her not inconsiderable feminine wiles to aid and abet Mother's favourite son. Together, they pulled off a high risk, high stakes, cloak-and-dagger operation of the first order. Before Esau could return from a hunting trip at the behest of his father, they had substituted a goat for game, and the younger brother for the elder who should receive the father's blessing.

The result left a venerable father befuddled, a dutiful son swindled of his inheritance and a trickster unjustly rewarded. Seeing that fratricide was a clear possibility, the deceitful twin brother fled the scene with all the haste his guilty conscience could summon.

But what was God's role in it all? He could have stopped it at any stage, but He did not. Why does He allow such gross injustice to triumph?

In one of his most memorable turns of phrase, the great British politician and orator, Winston Churchill, once referred in a wartime radio broadcast to the action of Russia as "a riddle wrapped in a mystery inside an enigma." It is the same here with the action of God.

At first, it would appear to be a simple matter of cause and effect—of reaping and sowing. Esau did lose his birthright to his younger twin brother with the despicable connivance of their scheming mother. But this is only because Esau had already sold it...for a bowl of pottage.

Once when Jacob was cooking stew, Esau came in from the field, and he was exhausted. And Esau said to Jacob, "Let me eat some of that red stew, for I am exhausted!" … Jacob said, "Sell me your birthright now." Esau said, "I am about to die; of what use is a birthright to me?" Jacob said, "Swear to me now." So he swore to him and sold his birthright to Jacob. Then Jacob gave Esau bread and lentil stew, and he ate and drank and rose and went his way. Thus Esau despised his birthright.

Genesis 25:29-34

Esau, therefore, had only himself to blame. He merely reaped what he sowed. If he had not taken this action in the first place no ruse in the world would have been clever enough to dispossess him of what God assigned to him as his.

But it is more complicated than that. Did God indeed assign it to him as his? There is significant evidence that He did not!

When Rebekah had conceived children by one man, our forefather Isaac, though they were not yet born and had done nothing either good or bad—in order that God's purpose of election might continue, not because of works but because of him who calls— she was told, "The older will serve the younger." As it is written, "Jacob I loved, but Esau I hated."

What shall we say then? Is there injustice on God's part? By no means! For he says to Moses, "I will have mercy on whom I have mercy, and I will have compassion on whom I have compassion." So then it depends not on human will or exertion, but on God, who has mercy.

Romans 9:10-16

This is the "riddle wrapped in a mystery inside an enigma." It is hardly anybody's definition of fairness! For Isaac or Rebekah, with their all-too-human failings, to have favourites, or for Rebekah to jeopardise her older son's welfare as a result is disagreeable enough. For the all-wise, all-knowing God to choose to hate Esau even before he was born is utterly beyond comprehension! But is this not the key to our enigma? The fact that He is all-knowing and all-wise? That Esau did not have to act before God knew what action he would take? And in His wisdom, therefore, to decide Esau was not fit to obtain the birthright he despised?

The words of the old poet provide valuable insight to resolving our dilemma when he sought to explain the complete responsibility of our first parents at the Fall, having been created as free agents to choose between right and wrong.

> They themselves decreed their own revolt, not I;
> if I foreknew, foreknowledge had no influence on their fault,
> which had no less proved certain unforeknown.
> So without least impulse or shadow of fate, or aught by me immutably foreseen ...
> for so I form'd them free: and free they must remain...[59]

Hence, it is pertinent to heed the warning in the book of Hebrews:

> [See to it] that no one is sexually immoral or unholy like Esau, who sold his birthright for a single meal. For you know that afterward, when he desired to inherit the blessing, he was rejected, for he found no chance to repent, though he sought it with tears.
>
> Hebrews 12:16-17

Rebekah had it all planned to the last detail. She was counting on time to heal Esau's bleeding heart, and so it was going to be. She would then send for Jacob to come back, but that was not to be. That hasty good-bye was to be the last she saw of her favourite son.

Question for Reflection

How would you explain the fact that God used a dysfunctional family like Isaac's to fulfil His purposes?

An Unusual Marriage Proposal

As he fled in the way his mother pointed, Jacob was in unfamiliar territory in more ways than one. Miles out of his comfort zone, he lay down to sleep exhausted, vulnerable, and all alone in the wilds, at the end of a long, hard day.

The God who helps those who cannot help themselves chose this time to reveal Himself and lay His claim on the fugitive reprobate and confirm to him the promise made to his illustrious ancestors. Thus a patch of igneous outcrop was turned into hallowed ground, a surreal foretaste of the time when true worship would not depend on time and place but be enacted only "in spirit and in truth," and when all miscreants at the end of their tether would find full acceptance in the Son of God.

God conducted Jacob safely to his uncle's homestead where he learnt to earn his keep and work to obtain what his heart desired.

Foolish young man blinded by passion! Already in his early forties, he was no longer a stripling. But he was obviously deficient in his understanding of social conventions and pitiable in his negotiating skills. His uncle offered to pay him fair wages for his labour and requested him to name his price. He offered to work seven years to earn the hand of his strikingly beautiful younger cousin. Seven whole years! Did nobody tell him that it took his mother all of seven seconds to decide to marry his father without having set eyes on him? Or of how she actually set out seven hours later on the long and perilous journey to join him in distant Canaan? And it isn't as if there was much by way of competition, either. No other suitors were in evidence, and the older sister was still at home.

But we have to admit that, unlike his father, he had not exactly sent ahead a caravan of camels laden with gold and goodies!

Uncle Laban must have marvelled at his good fortune as he pondered the proposal of his nephew so naïve. He put into gear a scheme to double the price, turning seven years of free labour into fourteen by the simple expediency of substituting the dreamy-eyed older sister for her alluring younger sibling on the wedding night. Was this groom the same man who had deceived his father and older brother? It seems that God sometimes gives us a taste of our own medicine!

Seven years hard labour to get a bride—was Laban selling his daughters? What if someone else had offered ten years instead of seven? Would he be open to bargaining? What is the sense in the whole dowry system, anyway?

The payment of dowries is a very important aspect of the marriage process for more than half of the world's population today. It is evidently a custom that predated Hammurabi, the Babylonian king who gave the world its first codified set of laws, for he included it in his famous Code, describing how it was to be handled in various circumstances.[60]

Also, in ancient Rome, the bride-to-be received financial gifts including a ring to wear on her middle finger, which, as was then believed, contained a nerve that ran straight to the heart. With the advent of Christianity and religious orders, women also brought their dowries with them when they became nuns.

Dowry payment was widely practiced in Europe and continued to Victorian times in England. It was seen as an early payment of a daughter's inheritance, such that only daughters who had not received their dowry were entitled to part of the estate when their parents died, and if the couple died without children, the dowry reverted to the bride's family.

The dowry system does have high moral justification as originally conceived, whether we think of the old Europe, Hindu

India or Confucian China, in that it served as a way for the family to secure some of its wealth for its daughters since women could not inherit property while sons inherited from their fathers and carried on the family name. When a daughter got married, it was only fair that she took with her a portion of the family wealth into her new home.

The underlying philosophy is different in traditional Africa, where it is the man and not the girl who pays the dowry. In southern Africa it is called the "*lobola*" and is usually in the form of cows. One positive aspect of the system is that it involves close relatives investing in the marriage. Uncles and aunties join the immediate parents by contributing one or two cows from their own herds to make up the required number. Subsequently, they see themselves as parents-in-loco for the bride in her new home, putting her right when she takes the wrong turning and putting her husband in his place if he attempts to subject her to any form of ill-treatment. This goes to underline the fact that in traditional societies a marriage is not a private affair between a young man and his bride but a social bond between families and even communities.

Cows are all important to the Maasai in East Africa. Indeed, they believe that when God made the cow, He gave it to the Maasai to look after. Traditionally, Maasai youth did not marry until they had killed a lion to demonstrate they were able to protect their cowherd. There was the case of a young Maasai from Kenya who went to study abroad and, to the consternation of his people, came back with a bride. Even though times were changing and the government had seen to it that the killing of lions was no longer mandatory, this marriage, to a rank outsider, had not been properly sealed with the payment of a dowry with the relevant number of cows. It was considered an anomaly of such enormity that the tribal elders had to summon their collective wisdom to come up with a ruling. They concluded that they had only themselves to blame for allowing the young man to go to foreign lands where he took it upon himself to get married without due process. They, therefore, decided to regularise the marriage by adopting his bride as a member of the tribe. The couple went back to the city to live and work until the thoughtless young man came back to drop another bombshell on the tribe. He had decided to divorce his wife! Fortunately, as everybody knows, "Young heads do not rot where hoary heads abound." This time, the elders were on hand to straighten out the confused young man. They explained to him that a decision of such magnitude was not for him to make on his own. The entire tribe was involved in his marriage, and he could carry through his foolish decision only if he first decided to divorce himself from the tribe! As this was more than he bargained for, he found it possible to return to his wife, and the two resolved their differences.[61]

Unfortunately, the dowry system has been subverted in various ways in different cultures. It is reckoned that as many as 7,000 brides a year are killed in India for the "capital crime" of insufficient dowries. It was in this context that Nisha Shama of Noida became a *cause célèbre* when she got her groom and in-laws sent to jail for their excessive greed on her wedding day![62]

On the question of dowries, as in everything else, Christian believers in every society have to come to a correct appreciation of what is expected of them by their tradition and culture and then work out from the Scriptures what exactly should be their response. Abraham's servant did not go empty handed in his quest for a wife for Isaac. A retinue of ten camels laden with costly gifts was considered a reasonable investment for the enterprise, and his calling card of twenty-four-carat gold bracelets very quickly got the attention of the bride's brother Laban with his shrewd eye for pecuniary rewards. It is not difficult to see how these would have played a role in the prompt decisions!

In a similar vein, the Upper and Lower springs that Caleb gave to his daughter Acsah in Judges 1:13-15 would qualify as the dowry she took with her to the gallant husband he found for her.

Indian Christians, therefore, arrange marriages for their children in good conscience before the Lord, paying and receiving dowries for their sons and daughters. African Christians pay and receive *lobolas* while eschewing the excesses sometimes evident in the rest of society. It is one way of being in the world but not of the world. Hopefully they do not get exploited by avaricious in-laws like Laban!

Duplicitous from head to toe, Jacob at last has met his match, but this was only the beginning of his family troubles.

> ## Question for Reflection
>
> Why do you think that Jacob offered to work seven years for his bride?

Fertility Problems

Several scientific studies have highlighted problems that arise from inbreeding in mammals, including reduced fertility and sperm viability, increased genetic disorders, lower birth rate and higher infant mortality.[63]

At one stage in European history, the ruling houses were on the verge of extinction. Infertility was rife, and infant mortality was higher than the average for the general populace, which was high enough in the period before the discovery of penicillin. One of the main factors responsible was severe inbreeding among the royal houses, with the marriage of cousin to cousin producing fragile offspring when any babies were born at all. King Henry the Eighth, for example, resorted to desperate measures, casting off one wife after another until the sixth could produce the male heir he craved. If only they had learned from the story of the Patriarchs in the Bible!

We do not know the relationship between Abraham's father and mother, but he married his half-sister, who had trouble conceiving a child. Their son married his cousin Rebekah, and we are told that they too had fertility problems. "Isaac prayed to the LORD on behalf of his wife, because she was barren" (Genesis 25:21).

Now, here is one of their twin sons returning to their ancestral home and marrying his cousins. Thankfully, one of the two had no problem having children, but it was not the favoured, beautiful Rachel.

> When Rachel saw that she bore Jacob no children, she envied her sister. She said to Jacob, "Give me children, or I shall die!" Jacob's anger was kindled against Rachel, and he said, "Am I in the place of God, who has withheld from you the fruit of the womb?"
>
> Genesis 30:1-2

It is a sentiment common to all generations until ours. Since the Lord commanded His creatures to be fruitful and multiply, many children have always been considered a blessing, and none at all a curse. It was mostly a rural world, and in all rural societies, the number of children is linked to the family's economic well-being. There are more mouths to feed, but for every mouth that joins the family, there are also two hands to till the soil, and so the more the merrier.

The world started to move away from land-dominated economies at the period of the Industrial and Agrarian Revolutions. One man and a machine could now perform the task that previously required large families. Henceforth, one important reason for producing numerous children became irrelevant.

But there is another good reason for having large families that these revolutions left intact. Far too many children died in childhood. The more that are born, the more likely that some would at least survive to carry on the family name. It was not infrequent for a woman to be survived by only one or two children at the time of her demise, even though she had experienced a dozen confinements or more, as was the case with my mother in rural Africa.

Another revolution was soon on the way. Wonder drugs cured a whole variety of frightful diseases. With radical improvements in maternal health care, infant mortality lost its authority to control attitudes to human reproduction. Even taking into account the periodic Malthusian checks of epidemics and wars, most of the children survived into adulthood.

That is good news for parents in their old age. They can be sure that their offspring will take good care of their twilight years. But pension arrangements and state welfare programmes soon eliminated that need, too. Children, lo and behold, were beginning to lose their value. To increase and multiply no longer sounded like such a good idea in a world at risk of overpopulation. Having ceased to be a factor in their parents' future well-being, babies came to be regarded increasingly as a liability in affluent societies.

But they kept coming anyway, in unrelenting numbers, as a normal, inexorable by-product of sexual enjoyment. What to do to stem the tide?

Onan's is the first and only instance of human contraception recorded for us in Scripture. He wanted the pleasures of sex with Tamar, the widow of his deceased brother as the Law allowed, but he did not want the responsibility that comes with an offspring resulting from the liaison as the Law required.

"But Onan knew that the offspring would not be his. So whenever he went in to his brother's wife he would waste the semen on the ground, so as not to give offspring to his brother" (Genesis 38:9). His method was the crude and cruel expediency of premature withdrawal, which left the woman high and dry. The good Lord who judges the motives of the heart did not think much of it and punished him severely. And that led to serious problems for his father, too. Not wanting a similar end for Onan's little brother, Judah prevented him from marrying the widow according to the tenets of the Law. The woman resorted to an unorthodox stratagem by posing as a prostitute to Judah, obtaining personal tokens in lieu of payment. Her plan was to provoke a rather original scandal, and she succeeded more than she ever intended when she had twin sons fathered by her father-in-law! Here is one more reason not to consort with prostitutes—you never really know what you are getting, and it could turn out to be a whole lot more than you had in mind!

> As she was being brought out, she sent word to her father-in-law, "By the man to whom these belong, I am pregnant." And she said, "Please identify whose these are, the signet and the cord and the staff." Then Judah identified them and said, "She is more righteous than I, since I did not give her to my son Shelah."
>
> Genesis 38:25-26

For motives good and bad, the human race has sought means to restrict reproduction through the ages. It was not until our generation that the almighty Pill came to usher in an era when it became possible to choose not to have babies while enjoying the pleasures of sex to the full. And there is RU-486, the "morning-after" pill for those who omit to take the usual contraceptive precaution. If all else fails, there is the ready option of clinical abortion, now legal on demand, particularly in the most affluent countries of our world. Department of Health statistics in England reveal that scores of girls have had their third abortion before they are eighteen years old, and thousands of women have had four or more terminations of pregnancy by age thirty.[64]

Thus, for those who do not want to have a child, the problem is well and truly solved. But some *do* want to have a child but cannot. The odd world we inhabit was brought home to me by a doctor friend. One moment, his professional expertise would be called upon to terminate a healthy pregnancy of twenty-four weeks, and his next assignment would be to save the life of a premature baby born at twenty-four weeks!

The anguish of infertility has not diminished with the passing of millennia. It used to be the case that a couple's childlessness was blamed solely on the woman. As it has often been said, "It's a man's world!" Traditional societies exercise a greater stricture on a woman's sexual purity outside of marriage and fidelity within it than they do for a man's. They would usually have well developed modalities by which, if a husband could not make his wife pregnant, another man, perhaps some close relation, would perform the office. This is the case among the Yorubas in Nigeria, for example. Thus, the man's deficiency in this area can be hidden from public view. For a woman who cannot bear a child, however, there is no place to hide. It is not for nothing that Rachel majored on her expunged "disgrace" as the aspect most to be celebrated when her dolorous years of barrenness came to an end.

"Then God remembered Rachel, and God listened to her and opened her womb. She conceived and bore a son and said, 'God has taken away my reproach'" (Genesis 30:22-23). Over a thousand years later, on becoming pregnant with John the Baptist, Elizabeth expressed exactly the same sentiment. "After these days his wife Elizabeth conceived, and for five months she kept herself hidden, saying, 'Thus the Lord has done for me in the days when he looked on me, to take away my reproach among people' (Luke 1:24-25).

The question for us is whether it is any different today, two thousand years further on. In reality, roughly a third of infertility may be traced to the man, a third to the woman, and the remaining third either have contributory factors from both of them or else have causes yet to be understood at the current level of our medical science. Some natural physical anomaly in the reproductive system of man or wife is the most usual reason. Sometimes, unfortunately, infertility results from self-generated and preventable factors. These could be as simple as waiting too long to have a child, only to discover that the woman has passed the most favourable period for child-bearing in her life, the peak of which comes in her early twenties. Or it could be the consequence of some sexually transmitted disease.

Adoption has always been a way by which infertile parents can have children that are legally their own, but many do not find this satisfactory. They want a child who, biologically, is a piece of themselves.

A lot of sympathetic counselling help is required to stand alongside of faithful, believing men and women who find it difficult to accept their childlessness. They might not necessarily see it as a curse or a mark of God's disfavour, but the fact remains that it constitutes a major incidence of unanswered prayer for them and for their circle of family and friends.

Thankfully, modern medical advances now provide a range of options not available to earlier generations. Among them is In-Vitro Fertilisation, IVF, by which the mother's egg is fertilised outside the womb and then re-implanted in her; and surrogate motherhood, by which her fertilised egg is re-implanted in some other woman. This is what makes it possible for a South African woman to give birth to her three grandchildren. Mrs. Pat Anthony had been implanted with the ova of her twenty-five-year-old daughter, Karen Ferreira-Jorge, who had been inseminated artificially with her son-in-law's sperm. It was a story strange enough to be reported by the press in distant New York.[65]

All these came about four thousand years too late for Rachel and Isaac. What she did was to offer her slave girl to her husband. "Then she said, 'Here is my servant Bilhah; go in to her, so that she may give birth on my behalf, that even I may have children through her'" (Genesis 30:3).

He must have had a poor sense of history, for this was a formula that ill-served his grandfather Abraham. The result this time, fortunately, was not particularly dramatic. Bilhah's two sons, Dan and Naphtali, duly took their place among the offspring that turned out to be the patriarchs of the twelve tribes of Israel.

Thus, Laban got his two daughters, both the attractive one and the not-so-attractive one, happily married. He had fourteen years of free labour from a highly motivated farm manager. And he was surrounded by a happy crowd of grandchildren. Life was on the up and up, and it was going to get better still. Jacob made yet another propitious proposal—another six years service in order to build up a flock of his own. Uncle Laban seized the opportunity with both hands.

Question for Reflection

What are the similarities and what are the differences in the problems of infertility in Bible times and now?

Irate Fugitive

In his transactions with this double-dealing uncle and father-in-law, Jacob the inveterate deceiver was on the receiving end for the first time in his life. He had good grounds to be angry, and he did not mince his words:

> These twenty years I have been with you. Your ewes and your female goats have not miscarried, and I have not eaten the rams of your flocks. What was torn by wild beasts I did not bring to you. I bore the loss of it myself. From my hand you required it, whether stolen by day or stolen by night. There I was: by day the heat consumed me, and the cold by night, and my sleep fled from my eyes. These twenty years I have been in your house. I served you fourteen years for your two daughters, and six years for your flock, and you have changed my wages ten times. If the God of my father, the God of Abraham and the God of Isaac, had not been on my side, surely now you would have sent me away empty-handed.
>
> Genesis 31: 38-42

In-laws have a bad press, and a lot of it may be well deserved. Most happily for me, I am not in a position to say from personal experience. Thank God for those of us with mothers-in-law as loving and caring as our very own mothers, but we must be a rare breed if even ten percent of the stories we hear are true!

Jacob's problem, rather unusually, was from his father-in-law, and matters got into such a state that his final recourse was flight, reversing the journey he had made twenty years before.

This time he was pursued, overtaken, and, but for the direct intervention of the God of his ancestors, could have been dispossessed of his family and goods by his more powerful antagonist. Justly accused though he was, he was boiling over with indignation. He no doubt would have toned down his self-righteous rhetoric a little if he had been aware that his favourite wife was at that very moment sitting on idols stolen from his despised adversary. But the fact is that both Jacob and Laban have finally found the measure of each other. "A fox can hide from a dog, but it cannot hide from another fox!"

All is well that ends well. Jacob got the blessing of his father-in-law. But what goes round must come round. He now had to face the brother from whom he had fled those many years before, the older brother whose inheritance he had obtained by deceiving their father. Having sown the wind, he feared he was about to reap the whirlwind.

> And the messengers returned to Jacob, saying, "We came to your brother Esau, and he is coming to meet you, and there are four hundred men with him." Then Jacob was greatly afraid and distressed. He divided the people who were with him, and the flocks and herds and camels, into two camps, thinking, "If Esau comes to the one camp and attacks it, then the camp that is left will escape."
>
> Genesis 32:6-8

Panic stations! Thankfully, this fear proved unjustified and his despicable efforts to buy Esau's favour turned out to be totally unnecessary. As Peanuts' Charlie Brown said to Lucy in the popular cartoon, "Who says worrying doesn't help? Most of the things I worry about never happen!"[66]

God's favour, totally unmerited, rested on Jacob. This is the meaning of grace, and it came through the wronged brother. For God's grace was also at work in the life of Esau, who turned out to be the unlikely channel of fraternal love and mercy. Far from seething with anger and seeking revenge, he demonstrated a settled contentment with what he had, astonishing his frightened brother with a loving embrace and accepting his presents only as a gesture of brotherly kindness and not as the inducement which Jacob had in mind. It is not customary to give Esau due credit for this gracious acceptance of God's verdict on his life. It is important that we do not look on anyone as being damned beyond redemption!

Question for Reflection

How can you explain the difference between Jacob's attitude to Laban and Esau's attitude to Jacob?

"Honour Killing"

Immigrants enrich nations by bringing a kaleidoscope of cultural diversity. Sadly, some also bring atrocious traditions to their adopted home. The dishonourable rite of "honour killing" is one that the British judiciary occasionally has to handle.

On 20 July 2007, journalists Adam Fresco and Steve Bird filed a report for *The Times* in London—"Honour killing father jailed for life." The article begins,

> Banaz Mahmod was killed by her father and uncle for shaming the family. A strict Muslim father who murdered his daughter in an "honour killing" because she brought "shame" on his family by falling in love with the wrong man was jailed for life today. Mahmod Mahmod was told that he would serve a minimum of twenty years for the murder of Banaz Mahmod. Her uncle, Ari Mahmod, was also jailed for life and told he would serve a minimum of twenty-three years at the Old Bailey today. Ms Banaz,

twenty, had already displeased her family by walking out of an arranged marriage. After she was caught kissing Rahmat Sulemani, an Iranian Kurd, it was decided at a family meeting that they both had to die. Two months later, Miss Mahmod vanished. None of her family reported her missing. Only Mr. Sulemani went to the police to say that his girlfriend's worst fears had come true. Three months later, her naked body was found crammed into a suitcase and dumped in a six-foot, makeshift grave below a pile of bin bags, a rusting fridge and a discarded television in a back garden in Birmingham. The bootlace that was used to strangle her was still tied around her neck. A third killer, Mohamad Hama, thirty, was told that he would spend at least seventeen years behind bars.[67]

It is probably not particularly objective of the journalists to bring religion into it. Such honour killing is more a cultural than an Islamic issue.

Back in the land of his younger days, Jacob was now a man of means, with flourishing herds tended by his dutiful sons. Predating the Mahmods by four thousand years, his boys had an identical concept of family honour and how to defend it. Dinah was the lone girl in the family, with twelve brothers to cherish, spoil, protect, and defend her. Their sister was raped, and their family was thereby dishonoured, and they would not rest until she was avenged.

It is without question that Shechem loved Dinah.

Ordinarily, an unmarried woman is devalued in the face of a man who has had sexual intercourse with her. One Danish teenager once came to ask me for counselling on the pros and cons of premarital sex. At fifteen years old, he was still a virgin, which his friends found retro and bizarre. And yet he did not find the stories those friends told him about their sex lives to be particularly attractive. One of them, for example, had said that the most precious thing a girlfriend could give to him was sex, and once she has given it, the relationship was doomed as there was nothing else worth aspiring to attain. I could confidently assure him that his friend was right, and that is another good reason for waiting until marriage—after which the couple could look forward to life-long intimacy and friendship until death!

But unusually, Schechem continued to love Dinah after violating her. Even though he allowed his passions to run away with him, he was evidently not a wholly dishonourable man out for a one-night stand. He wanted to marry Dinah but had not learned the lesson that "true love waits." He was ready and willing to give very much for his love and convinced his father of the same. Jacob's sons insisted that the whole town first had to be circumcised. It was purely mercenary considerations, however, which persuaded them to agree when Hamor put the matter to them:

> "These men are at peace with us; let them dwell in the land and trade in it, for behold, the land is large enough for them. Let us take their daughters as wives, and let us give them our daughters. Only on this condition will the men agree to dwell with us to become one people—when every male among us is circumcised as they are circumcised. Will not their livestock, their property and all their beasts be ours? Only let us agree with them, and they will dwell with us."
>
> Genesis 34:21-23

Three days after being circumcised, the men of the city were sore and defenceless. That was when Jacob's children pounced on them. An eye for an eye is bad enough, but how about a head for an eye, or rather a multitude of heads? Even for that brutal age, this was as heinous and cowardly a massacre as can be found anywhere in the annals of ancient literature. Spearheaded by Simeon and Levi but aided and abetted by all their brothers, it made the clan of Jacob odious in the sight of all surrounding tribes.

Two wrongs, as the saying goes, do not make a right, but the demonic spirit that spurred the sons of Jacob to murder is alive and well today, and it is spawning low, mean, dastardly offspring.

Turkey aspires to join the European community and is therefore required to bring its laws in line with what obtains in the rest of Europe. This is one of the reasons it has cracked down on this monstrous crime of honour killing, and perpetrators are being brought to justice. Does this succeed in stemming the tide? If only! Now there is a new phenomenon of honour suicides!

Diana Nammi, an Iranian refugee in England, is the founder of the "International Campaign against Honour Killings." One of her colleagues describes how "honour suicide" operates. The family would bring pressure to bear on the young lady to the effect that having dishonoured the family, the only way to redeem herself is by committing suicide! They would then isolate the poor girl in a room equipped with the means to kill herself, tablets with which to overdose, or a noose into which to insert her head! In one extreme case, a young bride reported unacceptable advances from her husband's cousin and was encouraged to commit suicide in order to avert the dishonour the wayward man was going to bring on the family through her.[68]

It all goes to show that once the devil is allowed a place in the mores of any society, he goes about expanding his role. Our duty is to resist him with every ounce of energy we possess. His ways are the very antithesis of the grace of God.

Hoodwinked into connivance in this atrocity, distraught Father Jacob felt betrayed.

> Then Jacob said to Simeon and Levi, "You have brought trouble on me by making me stink to the inhabitants of the land, the Canaanites and the Perizzites. My numbers are few, and if they gather themselves against me and attack me, I shall be destroyed, both I and my household." But they said, "Should he treat our sister like a prostitute?"
>
> Genesis 34:30-31

This must be the lamest defence any lawyer would ever have to present in a murder trial! The consequent risk to the clan was real; they could easily have been wiped out in a spiral of vengeance. In yet another act of His saving grace, however, the good Lord spared them from the consequences of this gruesome crime against humanity.

> God said to Jacob, "Arise, go up to Bethel and dwell there. Make an altar there to the God who appeared to you when you fled from your brother Esau." ... And as they journeyed, a terror from God fell upon the cities that were around them, so that they did not pursue the sons of Jacob.
>
> Genesis 35:1, 5

But it would not be the last act of betrayal that Jacob would experience from his sons. A common and double-edged prayer among the Yoruba people says, "May your children do even more for you!" Whatever you do for your parents, be it good or bad, you can safely expect your children to repay you with interest. Also, the elders insist that a snake will give birth to something long. Was it poetic justice or something in the genes that makes this man's children to betray him even more cruelly than he betrayed his father?

Question for reflection

Compare the way the grace of God operates in Jacob's family with how it operates in yours. What items can you derive for prayer and for praise as a result?

Father's Favourite Son

"The wise man is not the one who learns from his own mistakes but from the mistakes of others." Some people, like Jacob, seem allergic to learning. His parents chose favourites among their children, and it led both the parents and the children to untold grief. Now Jacob decided to choose a favourite among his children, settling on Joseph, the first son of his favourite wife, thereby setting the scene for fresh heart-aches all round.

"Now Israel loved Joseph more than any other of his sons, because he was the son of his old age. And he made him a robe of many colours" (Genesis 37:2-3).

What role do dreams play in human affairs? Ancient cultures took dreams very seriously and their interpretation features as part of the role of priestcraft in traditional religions.

But dreams are not only of interest to ancient cultures and credulous religionists. It is an established field of study not merely in parapsychology but in psychology and psychiatry. One of the main claims to fame of Sigmund Freud was his scientific study of dreams and the methodology he developed for interpreting them in his influential work *The Interpretation of Dreams*.[69] There are some Christians who believe that we should pay much more attention to our dreams and that they form part of the means of grace by which God communicates with His people today. Without doubt, dreams play a more important role in the lives of some people than the rest of us, and Joseph is a particular case in point. It has to be admitted that, while the significance of dreams cannot be denied, assigning meaning to them boils down to a matter of opinion. Joseph's dreams, however, were not too difficult to decipher. Hopelessly naïve, and with more than a little dose of arrogance, Joseph shared them with all their disconcerting implications with his uncouth and jealous older brothers.

> Now Joseph had a dream, and when he told it to his brothers they hated him even more. He said to them, "Hear this dream that I have dreamed: Behold, we were binding sheaves in the field, and behold, my sheaf arose and stood upright. And behold, your sheaves gathered around it and bowed down to my sheaf." His brothers said to him, "Are you indeed to reign over us? Or are you indeed to rule over us?" So they hated him even more for his dreams and for his words. Then he dreamed another dream and told it to

his brothers and said, "Behold, I have dreamed another dream. Behold, the sun, the moon, and eleven stars were bowing down to me." But when he told it to his father and to his brothers, his father rebuked him and said to him, "What is this dream that you have dreamed? Shall I and your mother and your brothers indeed come to bow ourselves to the ground before you?"

Genesis 37:5-10

Three times in this chapter it is reiterated that his brothers hated him (verses 4, 5, and 8). Away from the protection of his doting father in the wilderness of Dothan, they contemplated killing him but settled for selling him into slavery while pretending to their distraught parent that he had met with a tragic accident.

Then they took Joseph's robe and slaughtered a goat and dipped the robe in the blood. And they sent the robe of many colours and brought it to their father and said, "This we have found; please identify whether it is your son's robe or not." And he identified it and said, "It is my son's robe. A fierce animal has devoured him. Joseph is without doubt torn to pieces." Then Jacob tore his garments and put sackcloth on his loins and mourned for his son many days. All his sons and all his daughters rose up to comfort him, but he refused to be comforted.

Genesis 37:31-35

When he latched on to God, good old Father Abraham had been assured that all would be well with his descendants. Faithfulness being one of the immutable attributes of this incomparable Deity, the apostle Paul was later to write in his second letter to Timothy, "If we are faithless, he remains faithful— for he cannot deny himself" (2 Timothy 2:13).

The poor young man just happened to be sold to Ishmaelites who just happened to be on their way to Egypt where they just happened to sell him to Potiphar, who just happened to be

Pharaoh's chief bodyguard—a whole series events leading the slave boy all the way to become the Prime Minister of Egypt. It would seem that when God chooses to intervene directly in human affairs, such chance coincidences just happen to multiply!

Question for Reflection

Are dreams a significant feature in your life of faith or of anyone known to you? Should we make more effort to understand the meaning of our dreams?

The Boss's Lustful Wife

The Lord was with Joseph, as the remarkable story in Genesis 39 reminds us not once or twice but *three* times, and Joseph for his own part was faithful to God, refusing to take advantage of the wayward wife of his trusty master.

> Now Joseph was handsome in form and appearance. And after a time his master's wife cast her eyes on Joseph and said, "Lie with me." But he refused and said to his master's wife, "Behold, because of me my master has no concern about anything in the house, and he has put everything that he has in my charge. He is not greater in this house than I am, nor has he kept back anything from me except yourself, because you are his wife. How then can I do this great wickedness and sin against God?" And as she spoke to Joseph day after day, he would not listen to her, to lie beside her or to be with her.
>
> Genesis 39:6-10

We live in an age in which human sexual appetite has no brakes. The only type of philosophy acceptable in the civilized West is to teach our youth to practice "safe sex" by using condoms in order not to contract HIV/AIDS. Even if health issues are the only ones, how about all the other members of the distinguished club of Sexually Transmitted Diseases for which condoms can at best reduce but never completely eliminate the risk of infection? How about Syphilis, Gonorrhoea, Herpes, Pubic Lice, Jock Itch, Kangus, or "the silent disease" Chlamydia[70]? It is true that there are other possible causes for some of them, but invariably, sexual abstinence cuts out the most obvious route of infection. But sexual abstinence outside of marriage, it would seem, is an alien concept to our health professionals!

Rightly concerned about teenage pregnancy in the country being the highest in Europe, the British government spent £6 million on a special project designed to persuade teenage girls not to get pregnant by handing out condoms and teaching them more about sex. But the pregnancy rate actually doubled! In London, *The Daily Mail* reported,

> A multi-million pound initiative to reduce teenage pregnancies more than doubled the number of girls conceiving... Research funded by the Department of Health showed that young women who attended the programme, at a cost of £2,500 each, were 'significantly' more likely to become pregnant than those on other youth programmes who were not given contraception and sex advice.[71]

This is not surprising, considering the sort of advice sometimes given.

Sheffield NHS Trust, for example, produced a leaflet which carries the slogan, "an orgasm a day keeps the doctor away." Guidelines were sent out with self-confident effrontery to challenge the youth:

> Health promotion experts advocate five portions of fruit and vegetables a day and thirty minutes' physical activity three times a week. What about sex or masturbation twice a week?[72]

Steve Slack, the director of the Centre for HIV and Sexual Health at NHS Sheffield is one of the leaflet's authors. By some logic entirely his own, he comments that instead of promoting teenage sex, this approach could encourage young people to delay losing their virginity until they are certain they will enjoy the experience.

"Flee youthful lusts" is the old rendering of 2 Timothy 2:22 in the King James Version of the Bible. It is a message this generation believes it is too civilised to consider. With all the advances in our medical science and technology, we are only slowly discovering the sheer, egregious stupidity of our supposed wisdom. There is every reason to pay attention to what we are told in the Good Book. "For the foolishness of God is wiser than men, and the weakness of God is stronger than men" (1 Corinthians 1:25).

Joseph took to heart the word of God and successfully resisted attempted rape by his master's wife. This is how John Ortbeg sees it:

> Joseph could have thought, *Where is God? I'm far from home, hated by my brothers, isolated from my father. I wore the Robe, but now I am a slave, and a slave is all I'll ever be. I'll never have what my father has, what I dreamed of having, what I deserve to have – my own life, wife, family, property, and name. Why shouldn't I reach for what little happiness I can get? It's not like I have anything to lose.* But Joseph says no. He speaks of the trust that Potiphar has placed in him and about the significance of honouring trust. His life and world are given meaning by loyalty and honouring relational commitment. To follow another way would be to enter a world of darkness that would destroy life as he knows it... Potiphar's wife persists, "And although she spoke to Joseph day after day, he would not consent to lie with her or to be with her." The implication of that last phrase is that she may have moderated her demand in hope of getting Joseph to take the first step—just a small step over the line. "Let's just be together for a while. Just be with me." She wants Joseph to be with her, revel in her attentiveness and flattery, make

fun of her husband as she does, exchange glances and notes and touches that are full of promise until, eventually, they would cross the final line. Still, Joseph refuses...[73]

Here are integrity and moral rectitude of the loftiest brand, and what did Joseph get for it? A very long term of imprisonment! Potiphar trusted Joseph, but the evidence was incontrovertible, as his wife produced the garment she grabbed from Joseph who was running away to escape her lustful embrace, and twisted the evidence to make him the aggressor.

It would be wonderful if virtue were always rewarded in this world, but that is very often not the case. On the contrary, many have to suffer precisely because they do the right thing—enough to turn a man cynical or worse! "Some people," we are told, "are like sugar cane—they are devoured for being sweet!"

But Joseph continued to be true to himself and to the God of his fathers. Was he expecting it all to work out positively in the end? Even in prison, we learn that the Lord was with Joseph. Is this or is this not reward enough for anyone who is faithful to God? Is this not God's promise to Abraham, at a time when he expected to see tangible reward for his faith in the shape of a son, that He, God Himself, was his reward?

"Do not be afraid, Abram. I am your shield, your very great reward" (Genesis 15:1, NIV).

But it also happened that two high ranking officials of Pharaoh joined Joseph in prison, and they both happened to dream dreams that Joseph happened to succeed in interpreting, resulting in the liberation of one and the beheading of the other.

Then, finally, it happened that the high and mighty lord of Egypt also had a dream, or rather a pair of dreams. His cleverest enchanters could not bluff their way into an interpretation sufficiently plausible to set his troubled breast at peace, and his troubled state of mind meant the whole state was troubled. Then the forgetful nobleman remembered the remarkable young Hebrew who had interpreted his dream in prison.

Joseph was summoned to interpret the dreams of the King, which he said was a forewarning of seven years of plenty to be followed by seven years of famine. An astute manager was needed to save the kingdom, and the lot fell on Joseph.

> And Pharaoh said to Joseph, "See, I have set you over all the land of Egypt." Then Pharaoh took his signet ring from his hand and put it on Joseph's hand, and clothed him in garments of fine linen and put a gold chain about his neck. And he made him ride in his second chariot. And they called out before him, "Bow the knee!" Thus he set him over all the land of Egypt. Moreover, Pharaoh said to Joseph, "I am Pharaoh, and without your consent no one shall lift up hand or foot in all the land of Egypt."
>
> Genesis 41:41-4

"The mills of the Lord grind slowly, but they grind exceeding small." Joseph was rewarded beyond the wildest dream of the most inveterate dreamer in Scripture. God does not always deal thus with those who are faithful to him, but how refreshingly reassuring when He does, when we see the just gloriously rewarded in the here and now!

Question for Reflection

What factors do you think helped Joseph resist temptation from his master's wife? How can they be harnessed by Christian youth today?

A Brother's Grace

The deadened consciences of Joseph's older brothers were not in danger of forgetting the Dreamer, but this is only because their father's obstinate, raw grief kept his memory alive. Thirteen long years elapsed, and then the day arrived when they came to bow before their little brother as his dreams foretold they would, and they had time enough for remorse. Unknown to them, the man in charge of the grains they came to buy in the time of famine was none other than the brother they had sold into slavery, and the grilling he gave them was most disconcerting:

> If you are honest men, let one of your brothers remain confined where you are in custody, and let the rest go and carry grain for the famine of your households, and bring your youngest brother to me. So your words will be verified, and you shall not die." And they did so. Then they said to one another, "In truth we are guilty concerning our brother, in that we saw the distress of his soul, when he begged us and we did not listen. That is why this distress has come upon us.
>
> Genesis 42:19-21

According to Yoruba wisdom, "When a man conceals treachery within, secret woes gnaw at his insides." The woes surfaced in the presence of the Viceroy of Egypt and accompanied the guilty brothers on their forlorn journey home to their distraught father and back again in the company of Joseph's little brother, Benjamin. It brought about a remarkable transformation. Each and every one of the heartless miscreants was now ready to guard the little one with his very life.

Joseph soon tired of playing cat and mouse with the culprits and revealed himself as their long-lost brother. What stupefaction! Here was the fulfilment of the most unlikely dream in history, as Joseph's aged father also came under his authority and care. When father died, Joseph's bewildered and cringing brothers fabricated a plausible scheme to assure their safety. They were not counting on his generosity of spirit or his knowledge and fear of God.

> When Joseph's brothers saw that their father was dead, they said, "It may be that Joseph will hate us and pay us back for all the evil that we did to him." So they sent a message to Joseph, saying, "Your father gave this com-

mand before he died, 'Say to Joseph, Please forgive the transgression of your brothers and their sin, because they did evil to you.' And now, please forgive the transgression of the servants of the God of your father." Joseph wept when they spoke to him. His brothers also came and fell down before him and said, "Behold, we are your servants." But Joseph said to them, "Do not fear, for am I in the place of God? As for you, you meant evil against me, but God meant it for good, to bring it about that many people should be kept alive, as they are today. So do not fear; I will provide for you and your little ones." Thus he comforted them and spoke kindly to them.

Genesis 50: 18-21

Now that was something! Consider all that Joseph suffered as a direct result of the hatred of these brothers. They took from him the protection and comfort of home and hearth under the watchful eyes of his loving father, leading to thirteen desperate years in slavery in an alien land and a good spell in prison unjustly convicted as a sex offender. And it was all during that momentous period when he transitioned from boyhood into manhood. Indeed, their original, more sinister intention was nothing short of cold-blooded murder, but selling him into slavery had two advantages. It gave them some pocket money, and they could placate their uneasy consciences with the thought that they did not have his blood on their hands.

The time came when they had no illusion about the gravity of their crime and the punishment they justly deserved. Joseph had the power and authority to inflict that punishment on them when they came crawling to him for mercy. He did not give them their just deserts. He forgave instead of punishing them, and he did more. He spoke a message of peace to their guilty souls. And he blessed them copiously out of the abundant resources at his disposal. Whitney Kuniholm makes the interesting observation:

The main reason Joseph didn't blow his brothers away is that he still loved them. Often we find that underneath our angriest feelings is a deep love. That's why lashing out is the worst thing you can do when you're angry. Joseph wisely finds a private place to weep, (43:30). Honest grieving about the hurts of the past is another essential step in the healing process…[74]

This is brotherly love at its most exemplary. But it is only a shadow of what Jesus Christ would do for us.

If Joseph was guilty of recounting his honest dreams the guilt of Jesus Christ consisted in proclaiming the goodness of God to wayward humanity. Those to whom He came disowned and sold Him for thirty pieces of silver, still the price a slave, but most likely worth considerably less than in the days of Joseph. For Him, it did not result only in thirteen years of hopelessness and despair in foreign servitude. It cost Him His life. He could have called ten thousand angels to destroy the culprits, but instead, He asked His Father to forgive them. He did not merely provide sustenance for the years of scarcity but provided the gift of Life, opening to us the boundless resources that are His by right, both in this world and in the world to come.

Philip Yancey quoted an incident in the life of C.S. Lewis.

During a British conference on comparative religions, experts from around the world debated what, if any, belief was unique to the Christian faith. They began eliminating possibilities. Incarnation? Other religions had different versions of gods appearing in human form. Resurrection? Again, other religions had accounts of return from death. The debate went on for some time until C.S. Lewis wandered into the room. 'What's the rumpus about?' he asked and heard in reply that his colleagues were discussing Christianity's unique contribution among world religions. Lewis responded, "Oh, that's easy. It's grace."[75]

There was nothing Joseph's brothers could do to right the wrong they did to him. The only way their relationship could be restored was through his act of forgiveness. Religions in general major on what we ought to do in order to be in right standing with our Maker. Christianity majors on what He did to make us right with Him, and it was not cheap. Elsewhere, this same C.S. Lewis made the shrewd observation, "It costs God nothing, so far as we know, to create nice things, but to convert rebellious wills cost him the crucifixion."[76] His sacrifice led to our forgiveness. This is why He was able to instruct us to forgive our brothers not seven times but "seventy times seven times" (Matthew 18:21-22).

Taking It Further

1. Why would parents want to favour one child against another? What can help them maintain a healthy balance?

2. What do you consider to be the appropriate attitude of the church in cultures where dowries are paid before marriage?

3. How can our churches help its young people to understand and to live out the concept that "true love waits"?

4. Government policy is normally directed by secular ideology which is often godless in practice. Do you know examples of this with regard to policies affecting the family in your country? What should individual Christians do about it? What of the Church?

5. God worked through unlikely incidents in the life of Joseph. Can you testify to the truth of Romans 8:28 in your personal and family life?

GENTLE MOSES: MEEK AND MURDEROUS!

"Ajunilo!" and Child Protection

In Yoruba, *Ajunilo* is a nightmare of a bully who uses your own hand to slap your face. Pharaoh, the king of Egypt, was worse, much worse, because slapping was not all that he had in mind. His ultimate goal was genocide, as he aimed at nothing short of the extermination of the Hebrew race by killing off all their male children, and he was going to use Hebrew hands to do the killing.

The second book of the Bible begins with the fascinating story of the birth of Moses. It was long after the time of Joseph. The children of Israel had grown quite considerably in numbers and were well and truly settled in the land of Egypt. Then a new king arose who saw them as a national threat and decided to suppress them at all costs. The records paint a grim picture of their ordeal:

> They ruthlessly made the people of Israel work as slaves and made their lives bitter with hard service, in mortar and brick, and in all kinds of work in the field. In all their work they ruthlessly made them work as slaves. Then the king of Egypt said to the Hebrew midwives, one of whom was named Shiphrah and the other Puah, "When you serve as midwife to the Hebrew women and see them on the birthstool, if it is a son, you shall kill him, but if it is a daughter, she shall live." But the midwives feared God and did not do as the king of Egypt commanded them, but let the male children live.
>
> Exodus 1:14-17

How can we begin to appreciate the torment of motherhood when at the mercy of an all-powerful sadist? The parents of fair-haired, blue-eyed Aryan babies favoured by Adolf Hitler and therefore taken away to be brought up to become the elites of the "Master Race" had this in common with Jewish parents of twin children who were confiscated for vivisection in scientific experiments. We do not have to go so far back into history. Arab militias set fire to villages in Southern Sudan and kidnap women and children and sell them into slavery. It is a blight on the conscience of the modern world that ignores the plight of the powerless!

But no one was equipped or available to stand up for the children of Israel against Pharaoh of Egypt, the almighty potentate of the world's one and only super power—no one except the God of Israel.

"Why do the biting when you have a dog?" This incorrigible tyrant ordered Hebrew midwives to kill Hebrew sons at birth. These particular dogs, however, did not oblige. The midwives, Shiphrah and Puah, refused to do Pharaoh's bidding because they feared God. They did not have enough confidence in that God to tell the truth, however, or at least refrain from lying when questioned by the King of Egypt. But in spite of that, the God in whom there is no darkness at all chose to reward them.

> The midwives said to Pharaoh, "Because the Hebrew women are not like the Egyptian women, for they are vigorous and give birth before the midwife comes to them." So God dealt well with the midwives.."
>
> Exodus 1:19-20

Rahab the harlot comes to mind—the one who lied to her King in Jericho in order to protect Joshua and his fellow spies. As a result, she was not only saved together with her family but entered into the Honour Roll of Faith in the book of Hebrews: "By faith Rahab the prostitute did not perish with those who were disobedient, because she had given a friendly welcome to the spies" (Hebrews 11:31).

Does God reward lying? Do these stories parallel the principle of Taqqiyah in Islam? The Qur'an makes a distinction between what is in your heart, which must always be true, and what you utter with your lips, which may be true or false.

> Allah will not call you to account for what is futile in your oaths, but He will call you to account for your deliberate oaths: for expiation, feed ten indigent persons, on a scale of the average for the food of your families; or clothe them; or give a slave his freedom. If that is beyond your means, fast for three days. That is the expiation for the oaths ye have sworn. But keep to your oaths. Thus doth Allah make clear to you His signs, that ye may be grateful.[77]

Whatever gloss may be put on it, this is in reality nothing but a license for deceitful dealings. Another verse makes the same point in a slightly different way:

"Allah will not call you to account for thoughtlessness in your oaths, but for the intention in your hearts; and He is Oft-forgiving, Most Forbearing."[78] When a man speaks on oath, but is called to account only on the basis of the intention of his heart, his sincerity can be discerned, obviously, only by God and not by those with whom he is dealing. The Muslim scholar, Afif Al Tabbarah, explains it in a way that hardly instils confidence:

> Lying is not always bad, to be sure; there are times when telling a lie is more profitable and better for the general welfare, and for the settlement of conciliation among people, than telling the truth. To this effect, the Prophet says: 'He is not a false person who (through lies) settles conciliation among people, supports good or says what is good.[79]

The end, according to the Holy Book of Islam, evidently justifies the means. The Bible's teaching is light-years away from this.

We have already considered the issue with regard to Abraham. The two instances of lying cited above, which received divine approval, are of women with minimal instruction in the ways of God. The first predates even the Law of Moses, and the second was a rank outsider. Both of them had very limited illumination about God, and He rewarded them for being faithful to the little they understood at great risk to their lives.

Both in the Old and in the New Testament, the Bible's teaching regarding falsehood is unequivocal. Just a couple of references will have to do:

- Lying lips are an abomination to the LORD, but those who act faithfully are his delight (Proverbs 12:22).

- But as for the cowardly, the faithless, the detestable, as for murderers, the sexually immoral, sorcerers, idolaters, and all liars, their portion will be in the lake that burns with fire and sulphur, which is the second death (Revelation 21:8).

Powerless Hebrew parents were in dire straits under the boot of Pharaoh. In a similar situation, what would a modern parent do? We have a much greater revelation of the ways of God than those whose stories we read in the Old Testament, and as Jesus says, "Everyone to whom much was given, of him much will be required, and from him to whom they entrusted much, they will demand the more" (Luke 12:48b).

St. Paul assures us that God keeps us from having to face more problems than we can handle in this life, and that He provides to each of His children just what is required when confronted with impossible dilemmas.

> No temptation has overtaken you that is not common to man. God is faithful, and he will not let you be tempted beyond your ability, but with the temptation he will also provide the way of escape, that you may be able to endure it.
>
> 1 Corinthians 10:13

He says that no trial comes to us that is not common in life. That is certainly true for the vast majority of his readers at Corinth and his readers all over the world today. But there are always the exceptions to any general rule. Some *do* face trials that are anything but common, and the situation of such people is worthy of sober reflection. It is easy to theologise in a safe environment knowing full well that this is a situation that we are never going to face. Who can be sure of how they would react in similar circumstances where telling the truth will put not only their own lives in jeopardy but the lives of others entrusted to them?

As for trials that are anything but common, take the case of thirteen-year-old Adly Shakir in Egypt, for example, and her family. This is how it was reported by Forum 18 from their office in Oslo, Norway.[80]

> In March 1997, thirteen-year-old Theresa Shakir, a Coptic Christian, was taken by her teacher, believed to be an Islamic extremist, to a nearby police station where they tried to force her to convert from Christianity to Islam. It took Theresa's family nine days to secure her release from the police station, having to approach Pope Shenouda III, head of the Coptic Orthodox Church, the office of President Mubarak and several human rights organisations in the meantime. When she was finally released, police told the family that she had changed her religion to Islam. In November of that year, Adly Shakir, Theresa's older brother, returned home late one night to find his parents and younger brother shot to death, his sister Nadia, wounded by gunshot. Theresa had also been killed, with her stomach cut open and disembowelled (a method said to be used by the extremist Islamic Group Al Gama'at Al Islamiya for those it accuses of apostasy). When he ran to the police station to report the incident, Adly was immediately arrested and accused of the murders. He was subjected to severe torture to force a confession. He was convicted and sentenced to death by hang-

131

ing. Teresa's sister, Nadia Shakir, was hospitalised for nine days for her wounds. Although Izzat, another brother, says that he asked that she be returned to him, she was released to an uncle on the condition that the surviving members of her immediate family not be allowed to see her. The uncle died shortly after and the police took custody of her. At this time, her whereabouts are not known to her family.

Freedom House is concerned that Adly Shakir may have been falsely convicted and that he had been subjected to torture. Freedom House is also deeply disturbed by the police's refusal to allow the family access to Nadia Shakir. Finally they are concerned that the police were complicit in declaring a thirteen-year-old girl a convert after holding her incommunicado.[81]

Sometimes there is an opportunity to present such cases to agencies or influential individuals who can intervene with the relevant legal authorities. Sadly, more often than not, there is only one thing we can do, and that is to commend God's people to His promise when faced with such unspeakable horrors, casting them upon the love and grace of the heavenly Father who is not ignorant of their plight.

As cruel as he was powerful, Pharaoh was not going to allow the non-compliance of the midwives to thwart his plans. He ordered all male children to be drowned in the Nile.

Anyone who has ever had a baby can imagine what it entails to hide one for three months as the mother of Moses did.

> Now a man from the house of Levi went and took as his wife a Levite woman. The woman conceived and bore a son, and when she saw that he was a fine child, she hid him three months. When she could hide him no longer, she took for him a basket made of bulrushes and daubed it with bitumen and pitch. She put the child in it and placed it among the reeds by the river bank.
>
> Exodus 2:1-3

God set out to beat "*Ajunilo*" in his own game. Almighty authority is calling the bully to account. He is going to use Pharaoh to prepare the means of his own destruction.

By a series of events that can only be explained as divine intervention, Pharaoh's daughter chose that moment to go bathing at one particular spot on the River bank and saw an infant bobbling among the reeds in a wicker basket. His older sister, who was keeping watch, had the presence of mind to recommend her mother as a suitable wet nurse. And so, Moses was brought up in Pharaoh's palace as his adopted grandson! Not surprisingly, we were later to discover "Moses was instructed in all the wisdom of the Egyptians, and he was mighty in his words and deeds" (Acts 7:22).

Apparently, he knew it, too, and set out to use his wisdom and power to liberate his real people—the Hebrews. But "the arm of flesh will fail you," as the old song[82] says, and it *did* fail Moses.

> One day, when Moses had grown up, he went out to his people and looked on their burdens, and he saw an Egyptian beating a Hebrew, one of his people. He looked this way and that, and seeing no one, he struck down the Egyptian and hid him in the sand. When he went out the next day, behold, two Hebrews were struggling together. And he said to the man in the wrong, "Why do you strike your companion?" He answered, "Who made you a prince and a judge over us? Do you mean to kill me as you killed the Egyptian?" Then Moses was afraid, and thought, "Surely the thing is known." When Pharaoh heard of it, he sought to kill Moses. But Moses fled from Pharaoh and stayed in the land of Midian.
>
> Exodus 2:11-15

Thus the naïve, self-appointed champion ended up fleeing into the desert, a fugitive murderer on the run from the law.

Question for Reflection

Although he had the advantage of growing up in the palace, why do you think Moses chose to identify with his biological rather than his adopted family?

Saying "No!" to God

God led Moses to the home of Ruel, a pagan priest of Midian who was to become his father-in-law and counsellor, and eventually, as far as we can tell, a committed follower of the God of Israel. Moses lost all his dignity and any hope of being of any service to his beloved people and now had the lowly task of shepherding the family flock of his father-in-law. He got married and settled down to a new life in a new land. Gone were the heady days of position and power and limitless ambition. Moses established for himself a comfort zone and a stable family life.

Then God invited Moses back to the task that had been on his mind since his mother explained the history of his people to him as a child—a task he had attempted to handle in his own wisdom and strength with disastrous results. He was to go back to Egypt and set free the children of Israel from oppression. This time, however, there was a different price to pay as he was now a family man.

Was it this new status, therefore, that made him resist the call of God into a role he had seen as his vocation in his younger days? Jesus Christ warns us that we should allow absolutely nothing to stand in the way when He calls us to follow, and this includes our families. He promises His followers: "And everyone who has left houses or brothers or sisters or father or mother or children or lands, for my name's sake, will receive a hundredfold and will inherit eternal life" (Matthew 19:29).

I was listening to a French preacher describing attributes of the Bible in a conference at Neuchâtel one drowsy afternoon when he used sleight of hand to wake up the congregation in a refreshingly new way. "The Bible is like…" And his Bible burst into flames! Moses could not suspect anyone of performing a magic trick when, all alone with his flock in the desert scrubland, he saw a bush on fire with the bush refusing to burn!

The burning bush was not the only miracle in God's arsenal. Using the very ordinary shepherd's crook he possessed, Moses was given the ability to do things he never before imagined.

All of that did not reconcile this chastened man to his new assignment. Very carefully, he explained to God one or two important factors the All-knowing must have overlooked:

> But Moses said to the LORD, "Oh, my Lord, I am not eloquent, either in the past or since you have spoken to your servant, but I am slow of speech and of tongue." Then the LORD said to him, "Who has made man's mouth? Who makes him mute, or deaf, or seeing, or blind? Is it not I, the LORD? Now therefore go, and I will be with your mouth and teach you what you shall speak."
>
> Exodus 4:10-11

Was he therefore persuaded? Not in the least! And his new angle?

"Oh, my Lord, please send someone else" (Exodus 4:13).

God made it clear that He most definitely did not appreciate the attitude of Moses. But here we have one of the most remarkable qualities of the Maker of heaven and earth. He could have told him who is "boss." He could have compelled or cowed him into obedience. He could have ignored him with all his ignorance and chosen someone else to do the job. No, God did none of these things. What He did was to meet Moses half way. If family issues were really his concern, He sent another member of his family to team up with him:

> Is there not Aaron, your brother, the Levite? I know that he can speak well. Behold, he is coming out to meet you, and when he sees you, he will be glad in his heart. You

shall speak to him and put the words in his mouth, and I will be with your mouth and with his mouth and will teach you both what to do. He shall speak for you to the people, and he shall be your mouth, and you shall be as God to him. And take in your hand this staff, with which you shall do the signs.

Exodus 4:14-17

God knows that pulling up stakes to answer His call and head into the unknown is not always an attractive proposition at the best of times, and even less so for a family man. He knows our frailty, and He provides all that is necessary for us to comply with His demands.

This is not to say, however, that He is in the business of soft options! For example, when He sent out His disciples two by two, Jesus Christ did not embellish the prospects. The remuneration he offered was comparable to the advertisement supposedly put out in the papers by Sir Ernest Shackleton to recruit for his 1907 Antarctic expedition:

> "Men wanted for hazardous journey. Small wages, bitter cold, long months of complete darkness, constant danger, safe return doubtful. Honour and recognition in case of success."[83]

Jesus did nothing to sugar-coat what He was demanding of His followers: "I am sending you out as lambs in the midst of wolves" (Luke 10:3). "If anyone would come after me, let him deny himself and take up his cross and follow me" (Matthew 16:24).

"When Jesus calls a man, he calls him to come and die." This was Dietrich Bonheoffer writing before his martyrdom under Hitler's Nazis in 1945.[84] We too must count the cost of discipleship today in all of our preaching and teaching, with the full understanding of the implications for our families. And then, knowing there is no better alternative, to do what God commands.

Terminal Illness!

Every family has to cope with a health crisis of one form or another. That is the normal course of life while we reside in human bodies subject to decay from the day of our birth. A terminal illness, however, brings its own peculiar challenges.

All male descendants of Abraham were supposed to be circumcised on the eighth day. The fact that Moses failed in this spiritual duty was the cause of the physical threat to his very life.

Moses was all set and ready to serve the God who had made a Covenant with his forebears except for this one small detail—he had not had his son circumcised, and this was an act of disobedience that rendered him unfit for his mission. An uncircumcised child should be cut off from among God's people. Obviously, the child was not to blame. It is the father who deserved the sentence of death.

Moses could not plead ignorance. He himself was circumcised; it was his son at issue here.

At what stage in his life was Moses circumcised? Was it when he was eight days old as Abraham was commanded? That is possible, even in the difficult circumstances surrounding his birth. He was destined to be drowned in the Nile on the orders of Pharaoh. At great risk, his parents hid him—right from the point of birth. Keeping a baby from crying is a tall order in the best of times. How much more difficult when he is subjected to the knife at circumcision and in subsequent post-operative care? But the parents of Moses could have considered it to be of sufficient importance to keep to the Abrahamic covenant even under those dire circumstances. And all through his growing years at court, this must have been a constant reminder that he was different from all the other boys in the palace.

Or was it after he had left Egypt that he chose, as an adult, to have himself circumcised? Perhaps, all things considered, his parents reasoned that having him circumcised on the eighth day would have been foolish in the extreme. And fortunately so, as it would have been an issue in Pharaoh's household where no other male was circumcised. [85] Was it then, perhaps, as an act of defiance and rebellion against his royal upbringing which he now found distasteful? Or perhaps as a token of identification with his suffering people in distant Egypt?

With children born in Midian and being raised as Midianites, the situation, obviously, was different. No one there was circumcised. It just was not the done thing. What was the point and what was the use? We do not know for sure, but, curiously, it would seem that only one of the two sons was not circumcised. Now Moses was going back to his people, not just as anyone but as their leader and teacher and example. This was the background as he set out with the blessing of his perceptive father-in-law, taking his wife and two sons with him.

And then it happened:

> At a lodging place on the way the LORD met him and sought to put him to death. Then Zipporah took a flint and cut off her son's foreskin and touched Moses' feet with it and said, "Surely you are a bridegroom of blood to me!" So he let him alone. It was then that she said, "A bridegroom of blood," because of the circumcision.
>
> Exodus 4:24-26

We have no means of knowing the way God intended to carry out this threat on the life of Moses. What is not in doubt is that he confronted a crisis which had the potential to be the last one he faced on earth—his days were about to be terminated in the prime of life.

Although we do not get to them by the same route as Moses, terminal illnesses are very much with us today and so are worthy of thoughtful consideration.

How are we supposed to handle such a crisis when it shatters the tranquillity of our ordered lives? It could be a sudden diagnosis of cancer at a metastasised stage, an accident with life-threatening injuries, or the gradual but relentless progress of some incurable condition.

One way *not* to handle it is to welcome and embrace it as a friend because it is not. Ill health is not God's original plan for us but is primarily an agent of Satan and should be recognised as such. Consequently, we must fight it with every weapon in our arsenal just like Jesus Christ and His disciples did. And we must be careful not to make the mistake of King Asa. "In the thirty-ninth year of his reign Asa was diseased in his feet, and his disease became severe. Yet even in his disease he did not seek the Lord, but sought help from physicians" (2 Chronicles 16:12).

Thankfully, our all-powerful God can turn ill health to His own end and use it to glorify His name, and we should direct our prayer toward this end. The answer could be healing or it could be death, but either way, the ultimate result will be to the praise of His glory.

But what if a long illness involves much pain and suffering with no hope of a cure? In such cases, how about euthanasia, or "mercy killing," the practice of ending someone's life deliberately and in a painless manner?

It is not difficult to see why people who are not merely ill without the hope of a cure but are in a constant state of pain and debility would prefer to die; nor why, if death delays to come naturally, they would want to hasten the process.

Even at the purely secular level, however, there is much cause for concern. Barbara Wilding, Chief Constable of South Wales Police and the most senior female police officer in the United Kingdom, articulated this concern, "From a policing perspective, we need to be very careful on this to make sure it does not become a way of getting rid of a burden."[86]

Baroness Ilora Finlay of Llandaff, independent crossbench Peer in the British House of Lords and Professor of Palliative Medicine at Cardiff University, agrees.

> You have to remember that when people are ill it is very, very easy to influence the way that they feel about themselves… If someone is made to feel that they are being a nuisance to the National Health Service, a nuisance to the state, and their families are huffing and puffing, perhaps about care costs, perhaps because they want to have a little bit of inheritance, then that person could feel that not only are they a burden but they have a duty to die.[87]

She gives two examples which should provide food for thought to the most ardent proponents of euthanasia or assisted suicide.

> I have come across instances in which an apparently firm resolve to die proves nothing of the sort. In 1991, a young man, a father of three children, was crystal clear in his repeated request to me for euthanasia. His clinical outlook was bleak. Against all predictions, he did not die. Eleven years later his wife died, leaving him to bring up their three children.
>
> In 2006, my own mother was in a hospice bed, in overwhelming pain, repeatedly saying that she wanted help to end her life. This was perhaps the greatest challenge to my view of assisted dying. But my mother was not "helped to die" (the current euphemism) by her doctors. Today, thanks to good hospice care, she lives independently at home despite her cancer and both her life and our lives are enriched.

When God forbids one human being from taking the life of another, it is a law without caveat. Only the Giver of life has the right to take it away from us. Thank God for support groups available to those facing the ordeal of terminal illness—whatever the cause. We, as members of the community of life, owe a duty of care to the most vulnerable in society, and who is more vulnerable than those who are about to die?

Conversely, it is now possible to keep a man alive hooked to various machines when he ought to be left alone to die. I believe that Dr John Stott had the right approach. He wrote a legally binding document called an "advanced directive" giving instructions concerning how he would like to be treated by doctors should he become too incapacitated to be consulted. It concludes, "However, I do not wish my life to be artificially prolonged if thereby I am left in a terminal or vegetative state. The reason that I do not wish to cling to life is that I have a living hope of a yet more glorious life beyond death, and I do not wish to be unnecessarily hindered from inheriting it."[88]

The incident raises intriguing questions about the role of Zipporah. She clearly and accurately diagnosed the cause of her husband's illness. Did she save the day by taking the initiative and having the son circumcised because her husband was foolish enough to forgo a ritual to which she had no objection?

Or was it a desperate act of an angry woman who realised that she had to go along with a distasteful ritual if she was not to lose her husband? The manner of her action, and especially her words, gives us a clue that it is most probably the latter. They do not sound complimentary either of her husband or of the ritual!

Either way, there are important lessons for us. Both parents have the responsibility to ensure that their children follow the path laid down by the Lord. And spiritual disobedience can have physical consequences.

Also, the fact that we are called into a task, however monumental, does not make us indispensable to God. He has the capacity and the prerogative, should He so wish, to eliminate us, choose some other agent, and start all over again to accomplish His purposes. On the other hand, the grace of God flows into and through our acts of simple obedience.

Question for Reflection

Are there instances today where disobedience in spiritual matters can lead to adverse physical consequences?

Sibling Rivalry

Moses, Aaron, and Miriam—what a team! It is not merely that the older siblings were in a privileged position when God appointed their brother as Head of State. God had specifically called Aaron to assist Moses in his arduous task of confronting Pharaoh. And Miriam was not just the big sister who had played a dramatic role in the survival of the great leader and prophet as an infant. In her own right, she too was a prophetess of the God of Israel.

What a privileged family! Surely we can expect them all to get along in complete harmony as they fulfilled their exalted calling at the head of the people of God. As an anonymous critic once observed, however,

> That the saints will live together
> forever happily up above—
> Oh what glory!

> That the saints will live together
> happily here below—
> Quite another story!

Sometimes there is good reason for serious disagreement within a family. Moses was on the mountain obtaining guidance for the nation, leaving Aaron to mind the store. But Aaron succumbed to the demands of the restive people who chose to rebel against the God who had done so much for them. As Philip Yancey noted in his inimitable way, they turned against God even while His miracle of manna was still digesting in their stomachs. Aaron appeased them by making a golden calf for them to worship. Not surprisingly, Brother Moses was incandescent with fury.

What he did next was a worthy example of crisis management. He did not spend time and energy berating miserable, remorseful Aaron. That could wait. Of much greater importance and immediate urgency was the need to put down the riot in the camp. This he did with decisive force at the cost of three thousand lives. He followed it up with one of the most earnest intercessory prayers the Bible records. God heard and answered by forgiving and sparing both the nation and his irresponsible deputy and brother.

> So I took hold of the two tablets and threw them out of my two hands and broke them before your eyes. Then I lay prostrate before the LORD as before, forty days and forty nights. I neither ate bread nor drank water, because of all the sin that you had committed, in doing what was evil in the sight of the LORD to provoke him to anger. For I was afraid of the anger and hot displeasure that the LORD bore against you, so that he was ready to destroy you. But the LORD listened to me that time also. And the LORD was so angry with Aaron that he was ready to destroy him. And I prayed for Aaron also at the same time.
>
> Deuteronomy 9:17-20

In this narrative, and in the major fallout Moses had with both Aaron and Miriam, there are evidently good grounds for serious disagreement within the family.

> Miriam and Aaron spoke against Moses because of the Cushite woman whom he had married, for he had married a Cushite woman. And they said, "Has the LORD indeed spoken only through Moses? Has he not spoken through us also?" And the LORD heard it.
>
> Numbers 12:1-2

GENTLE MOSES: MEEK AND MURDEROUS!

These two godly people no doubt had the best interest of their brother at heart. He already had a wife who had born him two sons. He had all the affairs of state to keep him occupied. Was this the time to invite all the distraction that marrying a new wife involves? And if he must marry, why marry a foreigner? Was there no suitable girl in all of Israel? Does not the Law expressly forbid marriage to aliens? This girl was a Cushite!

> You shall not intermarry with them, giving your daughters to their sons or taking their daughters for your sons, for they would turn away your sons from following me, to serve other gods. Then the anger of the LORD would be kindled against you, and he would destroy you quickly.
>
> Deuteronomy 7:3-4

But then, "Anyone who has listened to the two sides of a story realises that there are more than two sides to the story!" Moses would not argue his own case or defend himself. Wise man! As a friend once warned me, each time I set out to justify myself, I add God's responsibility to mine: "Who shall bring any charge against God's elect? It is God who justifies" (Romans 8:33).

The divine Author adds a parenthesis to our story, "Now the man Moses was very meek, more than all people who were on the face of the earth" (Numbers 12:3).

Several factors are worthy of consideration here.

Miriam and Aaron were talking against Moses—not to him. They were talking behind his back. He did not hear, but God did. It would seem that the New Testament church also suffered from this disease of slander and gossip. St. Paul was its target more than once, and he warned against the vice again and again. We too need to listen, (italics added):

• For I fear that perhaps when I come I may find you not as I wish, and that you may find me not as you wish—that perhaps there may be quarrelling, jealousy, anger, hostility, *slander, gossip,* conceit, and disorder (2 Corinthians 12:20).

- Let all bitterness and wrath and anger and clamor and *slander* be put away from you, along with all malice (Ephesians 4:31).

- But now you must put them all away: anger, wrath, malice, *slander*, and obscene talk from your mouth (Colossians 3:8).

- Older women likewise are to be reverent in behaviour, not *slanderers* or slaves to much wine. They are to teach what is good (Titus 2:3).

- So put away all malice and all deceit and hypocrisy and envy and *all slander* (1 Peter 2:1).

The timely warning from Jerry Bridges is worthy of attention:

> The Scriptures do not allow for any gossip or criticism, or any other form of unwholesome speech, even if what we say is true. We simply should not say anything about anyone else that we wouldn't want to reach that person's ears … Only honest criticism given from a heart of love in a spirit of humility can qualify as that which builds up the other person.[89]

Also, with whom exactly did God forbid intermarriage for the children of Israel? With the people of the land they were going to inherit, and He was specific enough to name the tribes involved. We may argue all we want about how the principle should apply to all other pagan tribes, but that is not what the Law said. Africans were not among the seven nations specifically cited in the Law against intermarriage by the people of Israel, and this girl came from the land of Cush, Southern Sudan, in today's ordering of nations.

> When the LORD your God brings you into the land that you are entering to take possession of it, and clears away many nations before you, the Hittites, the Girgashites, the

Amorites, the Canaanites, the Perizzites, the Hivites, and the Jebusites, seven nations more numerous and mightier than yourselves, and when the LORD your God gives them over to you, and you defeat them, then you must devote them to complete destruction. You shall make no covenant with them and show no mercy to them. You shall not intermarry with them, giving your daughters to their sons or taking their daughters for your sons, for they would turn away your sons from following me, to serve other gods. Then the anger of the LORD would be kindled against you, and he would destroy you quickly.

Deuteronomy 7:1-4

After all, the children of Abraham were to be a blessing to all the world and a witness and testimony to all peoples. Having their leader marry an African was perhaps part of His grand design to extend His blessing to people other than the descendants of Abraham in the flesh. We do not know this for sure, but neither did Miriam nor Aaron.

Finally, even though the Lord did forbid the children of Israel from marrying outsiders, it is within His prerogative to make exceptions. The Law is made for man, as Jesus was later to explain, and not man for the Law.

And the Pharisees were saying to him, "Look, why are they doing what is not lawful on the Sabbath?" And he said to them, "The Sabbath was made for man, not man for the Sabbath."

Mark 2:24, 27

This is what happened in the case of Samson. His parents wanted him to keep strictly to the Law and not marry a Philistine woman, one of the Canaanite peoples of the land, not suspecting that God could possibly have other ideas: "His father and mother did not know that it was from the LORD, for he was seeking an opportunity against the Philistines" (Judges 14:4).

Considering how intimately Moses walked with God, it is not inconceivable that, unknown to his brother and sister, this was a matter in which he was doing exactly what God wanted him to do. Miriam and Aaron did not take the trouble to find out but hastily judged and condemned their brother. How often we too are guilty of the same!

The Lord intervened and not only justified and defended His faithful servant Moses but chastised his sister Miriam—very severely. She was suddenly infested with leprosy, which was the most dreaded disease of the era. Horrors! What would the rank and file make of this punishment in the camp of Israel? This goes beyond washing your dirty linens in public—way beyond. Why should a man of God bring such a hideous curse on anyone just because they have a small domestic disagreement? And to his very own sister, too!

And thus could another piece of hasty judgment begin to run its course!

Fortunately, Moses was on hand to intercede for Miriam, although she had one week to cool her heels outside the camp.

> And Moses cried to the LORD, "O God, please heal her— please." But the LORD said to Moses, "Let her be shut outside the camp seven days, and after that she may be brought in again."
>
> Numbers 12:13-14

As in human families, even so in the family of God: it is not without good cause that we who will one day judge angels are cautioned against judging our fellow believers hastily.

> Judge not, that you be not judged. For with the judgment you pronounce you will be judged, and with the measure you use it will be measured to you. Why do you see the speck that is in your brother's eye, but do not notice the log that is in your own eye? Or how can you say to your

GENTLE MOSES: MEEK AND MURDEROUS!

brother, "Let me take the speck out of your eye," when
there is the log in your own eye?

Matthew 7:1-4

Taking It Further

1. What steps do you take to be informed about fellow
   Christians who live under powerful persecutors?
   What can you do to identify with their plight?

2. Have you ever had occasion to lie when in a tight
   corner? On hindsight, was it the best you could have
   done? What will help you to do better in future?

3. Have you ever had occasion to argue with God? Do
   you think that God is unhappy with us when we
   have an honest argument with Him?

4. Why do you think that God's call to service in the
   Bible often provoked panic rather than pleasure?

5. "When Jesus calls a man, he calls him to come and
   die!" (Bonheoffer). How is this born out in your
   experience or the experiences of others known
   to you?

6. Have you ever been a target of damaging gossip and
   slander? How should we react with regards to ourselves and with regard to those responsible?

JOB AND RUTH: BEREAVEMENT AND VIRTUOUS WIDOWHOOD

Job and Bereavement

In standing alongside of someone who is bereaved, most people do not know what to say, but they go ahead and say it anyway! The result is akin to the counsel of the friends of Job to whom the longsuffering saint retorted in exasperation, "I have heard many such things; miserable comforters are you all. Shall windy words have an end?" (Job 16:2-3).

Very few experience family tragedy on a scale approaching Job's, a man in whose faith and integrity the Lord God Almighty was confident enough to boast.

> And the LORD said to Satan, "Have you considered my servant Job, that there is none like him on the earth, a blameless and upright man, who fears God and turns away from evil?" Then Satan answered the LORD and said, "Does Job fear God for no reason? Have you not put a hedge around him and his house and all that he has, on every side? You have blessed the work of his hands, and his possessions have increased in the land. But stretch out your hand and touch all that he has, and he will curse you to your face." And the LORD said to Satan, "Behold, all that he has is in your hand. Only against him do not stretch out your hand." So Satan went out from the presence of the LORD.
>
> Job 1:8-19

Obviously, what Satan would most like is to crush a middle-weight child of God under a super-heavyweight trial when no one is looking, but he has three obstacles to prevent him. Firstly is that the time when no one is looking does not exist because we have a Father up above forever looking down in tender love. Secondly, He does not allow Satan to bring any trouble to us that is beyond our capacity to withstand. And finally, He provides the necessary resources for us to overcome.

Satan was careful to stay within the boundary, but he did use his latitude to the full.

> Now there was a day when his sons and daughters were eating and drinking wine in their oldest brother's house, and there came a messenger to Job and said, "The oxen were plowing and the donkeys feeding beside them, and the Sabeans fell upon them and took them and struck down the servants with the edge of the sword, and I alone have escaped to tell you." While he was yet speaking, there came another and said, "The fire of God fell from heaven and burned up the sheep and the servants and consumed them, and I alone have escaped to tell you." While he was yet speaking, there came another and said, "The Chaldeans formed three groups and made a raid on the camels and took them and struck down the servants with the edge of the sword, and I alone have escaped to tell you." While he was yet speaking, there came another and said, "Your sons and daughters were eating and drinking wine in their old-est brother's house, and behold, a great wind came across the wilderness and struck the four corners of the house, and it fell upon the young people, and they are dead, and I alone have escaped to tell you." Then Job arose and tore his robe and shaved his head and fell on the ground and worshiped. And he said, "Naked I came from my mother's womb, and naked shall I return. The LORD gave, and the LORD has taken away; blessed be the name of the LORD." In all this Job did not sin or charge God with wrong.

> Job 1:13-22

The main reason for worship in all traditional religions is to stay on the right side of the deities so that they would use their superior powers to ward off the evil that is beyond our human capabilities to avert. "If you choose not to bless me," the Yorubas habitually pray to their gods, "kindly leave me just as I am." Job's God did not, but He knew what He was doing. "Smooth seas do not make great sailors," and Job experienced "Category 12" gales on the Beaufort scale of family calamities. It was Lucy Booth, daughter of William and Catherine Booth, founders of the Salvation Army, who wrote the following, on the basis of her own field experience:

> If all were easy, if all were bright,
> Where would the cross be?
> And where the fight?
> But in hard place God gives to you
> Chances of proving what He can do![90]

"The Lord Gave and the Lord Has Taken Away"

Job's courage in his unparalleled adversity sounds like the worst form of fatalism.

We read the story of the woman the prophet Elisha encountered in Shunem. Hers was an entirely different attitude. The prophet Elisha had decided that she deserved a reward for her gracious hospitality. When she would not ask anything for herself, it was the prophet's servant who informed him that she was childless. I suspect that the prophet had not realised that none of the many well-groomed children running around the compound was actually her own and that it took Gehazi listening to the gossip among servants to ferret out the fact. God honoured Elisha's promise, and she *did* have a son. But on an excursion to the farm with his father, the child suddenly collapsed and was rushed back home to his mother where he died. The Lord gave this precious and wonderful gift without her asking. She was not of the opinion that anyone, including God Himself, should take him away from her just like that. Here was one mother who would not give up without a fight. She searched out Elisha and spat out the pent-up anguish of her soul: "Did I ask my lord for a son? Did I not say, 'Do not deceive me'?" (2 Kings 4:28).

Where is God when it hurts?

Paul Brand, the missionary doctor who gained worldwide acclaim for his research in leprosy and his pioneering reconstructive surgery to correct deformities of hands and feet caused by the disease had reason to give much thought to the question. His answer was, "God is in you—the one hurting—not in *it*—the thing that hurts."[91] It is a wrong response, therefore, always to accept tragic situations as the will of the God who feels for us and with us. Jesus demonstrated this on many occasions, especially when confronted with the sorrowful work of the grim reaper—death. He wept at the grave of Lazarus, and He was moved by the sorrow of the widow of Nain who had lost her only son:

> And when the Lord saw her, he had compassion on her and said to her, "Do not weep." Then he came up and touched the bier, and the bearers stood still. And he said, "Young man, I say to you, arise." And the dead man sat up and began to speak, and Jesus gave him to his mother.
>
> Luke 7:13-15

Elisha was sensible and sensitive enough to accord the woman of Shunem full freedom to speak her mind and would not let his servant restrain her. It is quite right to speak our mind to God. The book of Psalms is not comprised only of upbeat praise and worship. It includes many songs of lament which are models of the outpouring of anguished hearts to God in a manner utterly alien to the output of our modern song writers. What recent hymns do we have, for instance, that come anywhere close to matching David's anguished complaint in Psalm 44?

In God we have boasted continually, and we will give
thanks to your name forever.

But you have rejected us and disgraced us… You have sold
your people for a trifle, demanding no high price for them.
You have made us the taunt of our neighbors, the derision
and scorn of those around us. You have made us a byword
among the nations, a laughingstock among the peoples…

All this has come upon us, though we have not forgotten
you, and we have not been false to your covenant…

Yet for your sake we are killed all the day long; we are
regarded as sheep to be slaughtered.

Awake! Why are you sleeping, O Lord? Rouse yourself!
Do not reject us forever! Why do you hide your face?
Why do you forget our affliction and oppression?

Psalm 44:8-24

When we lived in Kenya, we were privileged to count among
our family friends a gifted evangelist working with Africa
Enterprise. He had to flee when Idi Amin's death squads were on
the rampage, taking refuge in Kenya together with his family. He
went back home to Uganda as soon as Idi Amin was deposed. He
was returning from a preaching engagement one Sunday evening
when his way was barred by bandits. They asked for the key of his
car, which he promptly surrendered while his wife scampered out
of the passenger seat. They took the key from him and started the
car and then shot him dead before they drove off!

We visited his wife soon after to console her in her grief. She
had this question for me, "When I ask why the Lord allowed this
to happen, people tell me that it is because God loves my husband and has now taken him to a better place. Does He not love
me? Why does He not take me too to that better place?" And she
continued, "But when I speak like this, people tell me I must not
question God."

I could confidently assure her that those people were wrong. She had every right to question God. Every child has the right to pose any number of questions to their father—and this God is our Father.

The Shunemite woman used her right to ask the questions, and God very graciously answered her; Elisha restored her son to life. But then it is not all the questions a child asks that the father answers! God decided not to answer the many questions of Job.

Question for Reflection

With reference to the Shunamite woman, where do we draw the line between accepting tragedies as part of the will of a loving Father and questioning His dealings with us?

Unanswered Questions

It never rains, but it pours! Here is tragedy of extraordinary proportions hatched in the pit of hell and delivered with diabolic ruthlessness to the servant of God! Material loss is one thing, but to lose one's children—not one or two but all seven—in one day? Satan reckoned it was enough to break the spirit of anyone. He was wrong.

The devil lost his wager, but he was not done. He is nothing if not tenacious, and he upped the ante by demanding to lay his wicked hands on Job himself. Confident in the unflinching devotion of His servant, the Lord again acquiesced. Job was covered in sores from the crown of his head to the soles of his feet, suffering from bodily ailments beyond the capacity of medical remedies. The devil believed that this, surely, was enough to shake his confidence in the ability or the willingness of his God to protect him, or both.

What do we do in the face of such tragedy? Job's wife had exactly the reaction that Satan desired and expected. "Then his wife said to him, 'Do you still hold fast your integrity? Curse God and die'" (Job 2:9).

Harold Kushner is an erudite Jewish Rabbi who wrote a bestseller entitled *When Bad Things Happen to Good People*.[92] Its theme is one of the principal problems of theodicy—if God is all good and all powerful, why is there so much suffering and pain in the world? He had a personal reason for dealing with that question; his fourteen-year-old son died of an incurable genetic disease called progenia. His conclusion was that he believed God to be truly good but not all-powerful because he could not reconcile himself to the idea that such a loving God would choose not to cure his son if He had the power to do so.

In his 1961 book *A Grief Observed*, C.S. Lewis described how he felt about God following the death of his wife.

> Go to Him when your need is desperate, when all other help is vain, and what do you find? A door slammed in your face and a sound of bolting and double bolting on the inside. After that, silence. You may as well turn away. The longer you wait, the more emphatic the silence will become. There are no lights in the windows. It might be an empty house. Was it ever inhabited?[93]

It is so disturbing a picture that some critics considered it to be a fictional commentary on grief in general rather than the eminent, godly writer's personal experience. Don King's commentary provides us with one of the more helpful reactions:

> He ameliorates his view later, noting "I have gradually been coming to feel that the door is no longer shut and bolted. Was it my own frantic need that slammed it in my face? … Perhaps [my] own reiterated cries deafen [me] to the voice [I] hoped to hear". Still later he adds "my mind no longer meets that locked door". The last time he refers to the door, he seems reconciled to the lack of an answer: "[It is] a rather special sort of 'No answer.' It is not the

locked door. It is more like a silent, certainly not uncom-
passionate, gaze. As though He shook His head not in
refusal but waiving the question. Like, 'Peace, child; you
don't understand'."[94]

But what do we do when such a tragedy befalls someone we
love? Job's friends were exemplary in their initial reaction. First,
they did not abandon him. They were not mere fair-weather
friends. And they did not content themselves with sending him
a quick "Get Well" card or a text message, whatever the equiva-
lents might have been in those days. They took time to go and
visit him. They did not hurry away, either, when they saw his
pitiable condition. They sat down right there with him. It was at
great risk to themselves, not knowing whether or not the disease
was contagious or infectious—so much did they love and care
for him.

Most important of all, they were sensible enough to keep their
mouths shut. "The man who remains quiet does not misspeak;
the one who contemplates silently does not offend." When you
do not know what to say, it is only sensible to refrain from saying it. This they did for seven days. And then, one after another,
they ruined it by opening their mouths and opening them much
too wide!

"A man with an experience is never at the mercy of a man with
only an argument." The case of Job demonstrates that life can be
a truly complicated affair because his experience went above and
beyond received wisdom, established philosophy, or orthodox
theology. For the next thirty-five chapters of Holy Scriptures, he
had to contend with arguments with two basic propositions:

Proposition A: When you are faithful to God, you are blessed.
Proposition B: I was; it did not work for me!

The Bible is the inerrant and infallible Word of God, trust-
worthy in all it affirms. How about when it says in Psalm 34:10,
"The young lions suffer want and hunger; but those who seek the

Lord lack no good thing"? This, for example, is a problem for honest exponents of "Prosperity Theology": who can deny the fact that many of those who seek the Lord with all their hearts *do* lack many good things?

Here is incontrovertible evidence that we need training and wisdom for handling the word of truth correctly, using the best tools of sacred hermeneutics.

Job's friends were authorities in theology and philosophy, but in the end they needed to repent of their presumption. We too, therefore, need to be careful how we open our mouths. All counselling situations call for special wisdom. It is too easy to judge others, even when we have the best intentions.

Even though all human problems have the same ultimate source, it is not likely that the personal or family troubles you and I face originate in exactly the same way as Job's. It would still be right to say, however, that "Satan went from the presence of the Lord" to bring trouble to us. This is because he cannot touch us without God's permission since He first makes sure that the enemy will not bring any trouble to us that is beyond our capacity to handle. As St. Paul says,

> No temptation has overtaken you that is not common to man. God is faithful, and he will not let you be tempted beyond your ability, but with the temptation he will also provide the way of escape, that you may be able to endure it.
>
> 1 Corinthians 10:13

C.S. Lewis has an idea on human suffering that, as usual, gives us a lot of food for thought. "God whispers to us in our pleasures, speaks in our conscience, but shouts in our pains: it is His megaphone to rouse a deaf world."[95]

This God knows exactly what He is doing, and even though it is not given to our limited human faculties always to understand the whys and wherefores, we can be sure that He is acting in our best interest in the context of His eternal love for all His creatures. No wonder, then, that He accepts full responsibility as He owns up in the words of the prophet. "I form light and create darkness, I make well-being and create calamity, I am the LORD, who does all these things" (Isaiah 45:7).

When I was at school, mathematics was not the most popular of subjects with most of the pupils. But there was one book of mathematics that was popular with everyone. It had the answers in the back! The book of Job goes one better. The answers are in the *front*. Once we read the first two chapters, we know the cause for all his troubles. But it was not given to the longsuffering saint to know these facts. He never "read" chapter one or chapter two—not even at the end of the story.

Notice the answer that God finally gave to His desperate child, Job, unbent but on the verge of despair.

> Who is this that darkens counsel by words without knowledge? Dress for action like a man; I will question you, and you make it known to me. Where were you when I laid the foundation of the earth? Tell me, if you have understanding. Who determined its measurements—surely you know! Or who stretched the line upon it? On what were its bases sunk, or who laid its cornerstone, when the morning stars sang together and all the sons of God shouted for joy?
>
> Job 38:2-7

Job's experience impresses it on us that we must have the humility to accept that the problems we face are not always open to logical reasoning out. If we are subject to the loving Father who rules our lives, we will sometimes have to accept His unquestionable love as the only valid explanation. Alistair McGrath comments, "The message boils down to this: Until you know a little more about running the physical universe, Job, don't tell me how to run the moral universe."[96]

McGrath continues with a quote from Frederick Buchner who goes even further. "God doesn't explain. He explodes. He asks Job who he thinks he is, anyway. God doesn't reveal His grand design. He reveals Himself."

As the African proverb quips, "Where were you when God put water in the coconut?"

Do you sometimes say to yourself, "This is one question I will ask God when I get to heaven"? I believe there will be no need for questions when we get there because the very sight of Christ will provide all the answers. We should take encouragement, therefore, from the words of the hymn by Esther Kerr Rusthoi:

> It will be worth it all when we see Jesus,
> Life's trials will seem so small when we see Christ;
> One glimpse of His dear face all sorrow will erase,
> So bravely run the race till we see Christ.[97]

One of these glorious days, we will see Christ. The light of His countenance will shine on all the unanswered questions of our family problems. That is when we shall realise that we really do not have to know the reason now! For the present, we hold on to Him in faith.

Question for Reflection

What are the most common problems in seeking to help friends who face tragedies in their lives?

Naomi and Single Parenthood

Bethlehem, which means the "House of Bread," was the town that Elimelech left together with his wife and two sons, driven by an acute famine to the land of Moab. When he died, his widow did not see fit to return to Bethlehem and to hunger but instead prolonged her sojourn. Her two sons, meanwhile, were not idle; they were employing their time productively to court and to marry local girls. Tragedy struck, alas, as first one young husband and then the other died, thus reducing the family to three disconsolate widows. But we are getting ahead of ourselves.

In Ruth 1:3, we read the melancholy obituary. Elimelech, the husband of Naomi, died, and she was left with her two sons. Divine wisdom ordains for each child who comes into the world to do so at the instigation of two sponsors, a father and a mother, and in the context of a supportive community, for parenting is such a big, big job! Sadly, however, it sometimes happens that the child is deprived of the care of one or other of the two parents, perhaps through death, divorce, extramarital pregnancy, or some other misfortune, and then there is only the father or the mother to carry the heavy responsibility. Relatively rare in primitive societies, lone parenthood is a phenomenon that is growing at geometric progression in the rampant divorce culture of the enlightened West. The most recent available statistics indicate that there are about three million one-parent families in the United States—over eighty percent of them are headed by women.

For the United Kingdom, the one-parent families' charity "Gingerbread" sets out the following gruesome statistics on its website:[98]

- Nearly a quarter of households with dependent children are single parent families, and there are 1.9 million single parents in Britain today.

- There are three million children living in a single parent household (24 percent of all dependent children).

- Single parents are predominantly women, although 8 percent of single parents are fathers.

One memorandum submitted by One Parent Families to the UK Parliamentary Select Committee on Works and Pensions as recorded in Parliamentary Business states that,

> "Fifty-four percent of children in one-parent families are poor—1.7 million of them—compared with just over a

fifth (22 percent) of children with two resident parents. 45 percent of all poor children now live in one-parent families. Of the 2.6 million children who live in families with no-one in paid work, 1.8 million (69 percent) live in one-parent families.[99]

The main issue governments attempt to address is economic, based on its fundamental belief that if that single issue were addressed, all the others would fall into place; financial security makes housing affordable in good neighbourhoods away from bad influences and provides access to good education that leads to better jobs, happiness, and security. If only it were so straightforward!

Two heads, under normal circumstances, are better than one, as the saying goes. Every due credit to all the lone parents who have raised admirable crops of healthy, happy, richly-fulfilled, and eminently-successful children, but when a family is deprived of one parent, it is very much an uphill task for the one who has to shoulder the responsibility all alone.

Fortunately, help is usually available in the wider society. According to the African proverb popularised by Hilary Clinton, "It takes the entire village to raise a child." Growing up in Africa, I knew that every adult in the community was responsible for my welfare. They did not merely have the freedom but the responsibility to call me to order and, if necessary, punish me for wrong behaviour. In the more individualistic cultures of the Western world, there are compensatory voluntary and governmental support agencies to assist the lone parent and so make their task less onerous. Some churches are more sensitive to this need than others. As a community of God's people, surely, every church should aim to be an example to the rest of society in the way we provide the necessary support and assistance to those of our members who have to bear such a heavy load.

For their part, such single parents can be encouraged by the fact that God is on their side. The One who helped and enabled

Naomi is still alive and at work and can be trusted to give to them all that is required to make a success of single parenthood.

As an alien woman in a foreign land, Naomi could not have had too much by way of communal support as she was left to bring up her two boys on her own after the sad decease of her husband. Evidently, she had the support of her God, as her sons grew up not only to be eligible bachelors but actually got married in their adopted home. But worse was to befall Naomi as first one and then her second son fell ill and died.

Question for Reflection

Can anything be done to tackle the main causes of single parenthood in your community?

The Challenge of Widowhood

Naomi said to her two daughters-in-law, "Go, return each of you to her mother's house. May the LORD deal kindly with you, as you have dealt with the dead and with me. The LORD grant that you may find rest, each of you in the house of her husband!" ...Then they lifted up their voices and wept again. And Orpah kissed her mother-in-law, but Ruth clung to her. And she said, "See, your sister-in-law has gone back to her people and to her gods; return after your sister-in-law." But Ruth said, "Do not urge me to leave you or to return from following you. For where you go I will go, and where you lodge I will lodge. Your people shall be my people, and your God my God. Where you die I will die, and there will I be buried. May the LORD do so to me and more also if anything but death parts me from you."

Ruth 1:8-9, 14-17

Thankfully, the famine abated in Bethlehem, and Naomi could at last return to her native home and people. Ruth decided to cast her lot with the older widow, above and beyond the call of duty we might say, since the marriage vow terminates on the death of the spouse. What awaits her in her new home other than penury and insecurity? In a rabidly masculine culture, who was there to guarantee the welfare of two widows with no fixed address and no visible means of livelihood, especially the younger woman who was a stranger in a strange land?

Resolved neither to dissipate her energy with pathological mourning nor to gad about making a spectacle of herself, Ruth proved to be an indefatigable worker who commended herself to all and sundry with her industry, her character, and her love and care for her ageing mother-in-law. She would not let the two of them become a charity case, opting rather to go garnering after harvesters in the field, acting in line with a provision in the Law of Moses that she must have learned in her effort to identify with the religion of her new community. God evidently guided her footsteps, as she ended up in the fields of Boaz, one of the most eligible bachelors in the land, and her potential "kinsman-redeemer" to boot.

Writing in *Christianity Today*, Miriam Neff expresses the plight of modern day widows admirably, and it is not a pretty story:

> Who are we? We are the invisible among you—the widows. Studies show that widows lose 75 percent of their friendship network when they lose a spouse. Sixty percent of us experience serious health issues in that first year. One third of us meet the criteria for clinical depression in the first month after our spouse's death, and half of us remain clinically depressed a year later.[100]

The North American Mission Board of the Southern Baptist Convention provides the following help to grieving members under the title, "Widowhood: Guidelines for Coping." It is an apt summary of the gamut of emotions that widowhood entails.

> In moving toward that reality, it can be helpful to be aware of the stages of grief. These stages are not necessarily sequential; they may occur—and reoccur—in any order, at varying degrees of intensity and frequency.
>
> First there is shock and disbelief. A kind of numbness dominates your mental and physical reactions. This is God's gift to you, his spiritual sedative which allows you to walk through this time of anguish. The next phase is often anger—anger with the circumstances which brought about the death, anger with the loved one for leaving you, anger with yourself for things you did or failed to do, anger with God for letting it happen. In tragic death, there is anger against the person responsible. Guilt is usually a component of grief. You may feel guilty for failures in the relationship in the past, or for the feelings you are experiencing in the present. Depression occurs at many stages of the process, sometimes just a feeling of sadness or loneliness, but sometimes moving into a full-scale clinical depression. If these feelings persist, it is always wise to get the help of a mental health professional or pastor trained in counselling.
>
> Finally, the grief process begins to end, and you come to the point of acceptance. You are able to view the past with gratitude rather than pain, and you can begin to think of the future. The pain may never go away completely, but you do get control.[101]

In many cultures around the world, far from receiving the sort of support indicated by such informed advice, a widow has a very raw deal indeed. In addition to the distress of bereavement, she sometimes has to contend with societal expectations that are far from helpful. Relatives of the husband would sometimes emerge from the woodwork, helping themselves to his possessions while the widow's eyes were blinded with tears. Ancient tradition *does* provide for a system by which some next of kin assumes responsibility for the widow and her children, but far too often what transpires stems from a mercenary greed that is both ancient and modern.

The case of Virginia Edith Wambui in Kenya falls into a class of its own. When Mr. Silvanus Otieno, a high-flying criminal lawyer, died in Nairobi, all his wife wanted was to give a decent Christian burial to the man to whom she had borne fifteen children—exactly the way he wanted. But the elders of his Umira Kager clan of the Luo tribe objected. To bury him with Christian rites and out of Luoland, they insisted, would incite malevolent spirits to haunt the tribe, causing accidents and deaths and who knows what else? The enlightened widow would have none of it and dragged the tribal elders to court. It took 154 days of legal wrangling before judgement was pronounced in their favour. Mr. Otieno was buried at Nyamila in Nyanza province according to Luo tribal rites. Beaten but unbowed, Wambui earned herself a name among the champions of feminine rights in Africa.[102]

John Schoofs, a social researcher, writes,

> Like many cultures in Africa, the Luo practice widow inheritance. When a husband dies, one of his brothers or cousins marries the widow. This tradition guaranteed that the children would remain in the late husband's clan— after all, they had paid a dowry for the woman—and ensured the widow and her children were provided for. When the guardian takes the widow, sexual intercourse is believed to "cleanse" her of the devils of death. A woman who refuses to take a guardian brings down chira—ill fortune—on the entire clan.[103]

The Jewish tradition of levirate marriage was not a million miles removed from the Luo stipulation for widow welfare. Inheritance normally passed through the male line, but the law taught them that daughters could inherit if there was no male child. Complications arise when there is no female child either but there is a widow. Instructing the Israelites to take a position millennia ahead of its time, God ordained that inheritance could pass through such a widow, too. According to the law of inheritance laid down by Moses, a kinsman could inherit Elimelech's estate, but only on condition of inheriting the widow along with it.

> If brothers dwell together, and one of them dies and has no son, the wife of the dead man shall not be married outside the family to a stranger. Her husband's brother shall go in to her and take her as his wife and perform the duty of a husband's brother to her. And the first son whom she bears shall succeed to the name of his dead brother, that his name may not be blotted out of Israel.
>
> Deuteronomy 25:5-6

With feminine astuteness enhanced by age and experience, Naomi guided the younger widow into a decisive course of action. Ruth went to approach Boaz at the threshing floor where he was spending the night:

> And when Boaz had eaten and drunk, and his heart was merry, he went to lie down at the end of the heap of grain. Then she came softly and uncovered his feet and lay down. At midnight the man was startled and turned over, and behold, a woman lay at his feet! He said, "Who are you?" And she answered, "I am Ruth, your servant. Spread your wings over your servant, for you are a redeemer." And he said, "May you be blessed by the LORD, my daughter. You have made this last kindness greater than the first in that you have not gone after young men, whether poor or rich.
>
> Ruth 3:7-10

Ruth's virtues of industry and chaste comportment recommended her highly to this illustrious gentleman who was her potential guardian and husband as kinsman-redeemer.

In the New Testament, St. Paul did not have much time for a certain kind of younger widow and would not have the church enlisting them in its charitable offerings. He instructed the young pastor, Timothy,

> Honour widows who are truly widows. But if a widow has children or grandchildren, let them first learn to show godliness to their own household and to make some return to their parents, for this is pleasing in the sight of God. She who is truly a widow, left all alone, has set her hope on God and continues in supplications and prayers night and day, but she who is self-indulgent is dead even while she lives. Let a widow be enrolled if she is not less than sixty years of age, having been the wife of one husband, and having a reputation for good works: if she has brought up children, has shown hospitality, has washed the feet of the saints, has cared for the afflicted, and has devoted herself to every good work... So I would have younger widows marry, bear children, manage their households, and give the adversary no occasion for slander.
>
> 1 Timothy 5:3-6, 9-14

Straight as an arrow, Boaz's nobility of character qualifies him to be an exemplary burkinabé from the African country of Burkina Faso.[104] He did everything by the book.

> Now Boaz had gone up to the gate and sat down there. And behold, the redeemer, of whom Boaz had spoken, came by. So Boaz said, "Turn aside, friend; sit down here." And he turned aside and sat down. And he took ten men of the elders of the city and said, "Sit down here." So they sat down. Then he said to the redeemer, "Naomi, who has come back from the country of Moab, is selling the parcel of land that belonged to our relative Elimelech. So I thought I would tell you of it and say, 'Buy it in the presence of those sitting here and in the presence of the elders of my people.' If you will redeem it, redeem it. But

if you will not, tell me, that I may know, for there is no one besides you to redeem it, and I come after you." And he said, "I will redeem it." Then Boaz said, "The day you buy the field from the hand of Naomi, you also acquire Ruth the Moabite, the widow of the dead, in order to per-petuate the name of the dead in his inheritance." Then the redeemer said, "I cannot redeem it for myself, lest I impair my own inheritance. Take my right of redemption yourself, for I cannot redeem it.

Ruth 4:1-6

Evidently, Boaz did not mind impairing his own inheritance to preserve the name of another. It is this willingness to lose him-self that inserted his name forever into Holy Writ. Before the council of elders the matter was signed and sealed with due deco-rum, and Boaz became the husband of Ruth. The post-script to the story is that he became the great-grandfather of King David, the most illustrious of all the kings of Israel.

How fortunate for the people of Israel that their laws and customs derived directly from the all-wise God. This is not the case with the Luos or any other tribe on earth. As a result, all of our cultures need redeeming on the basis of the Word of God. Wambui Otieno is a poignant example. Nobody from the tri-umphant Luo clan who took away her husband for burial subse-quently lent a hand in raising her children. But the Luo Elders have served notice that whenever and wherever she died, they would come to claim her body in order to bury it beside her hus-band in Luoland. Their culture poses a challenge to the Kenyan Church. How will it rise to the test in the book of James because, as much as anything else, our religion will one day be judged on the basis of how we treat our orphans and widows! "Religion that is pure and undefiled before God, the Father, is this: to visit orphans and widows in their affliction, and to keep oneself unstained from the world" (James 1:27).

Taking It Further

1. Have we had the experience of well-meaning people saying the most unhelpful things in their efforts to console us in times of bereavement? Give examples that will help us avoid such mistakes in future.

2. What is your reaction to Isaiah 45.7?

3. What traditional support is available to widows in your culture? In what ways should the church improve upon it?

4. What support is available to single parents in your church and what improvements are required?

5. Does your church have contact with aliens, refugees or asylum seekers? What is being done or what more can be done to make them feel welcome?

SAMSON: PHYSICAL GIANT, MORAL DWARF

A Marriage Made in Heaven

Before the outpouring at Pentecost, God's Holy Spirit came upon the people of God in a selective manner to enable and empower special people for special tasks. Samson was one such privileged individual.

> There was a certain man of Zorah, of the tribe of the Danites, whose name was Manoah. And his wife was barren and had no children. And the angel of the LORD appeared to the woman and said to her, 'Behold, you are barren and have not borne children, but you shall conceive and bear a son. Therefore be careful and drink no wine or strong drink, and eat nothing unclean, for behold, you shall conceive and bear a son. No razor shall come upon his head, for the child shall be a Nazirite to God from the womb, and he shall begin to save Israel from the hand of the Philistines.
>
> Judges 13:2-5

Manoah and his wife believed God and did as they were told. The child, Samson, was born and dedicated a Nazirite from birth. The Law of the Nazirites was very strict.

> When either a man or a woman makes a special vow, the vow of a Nazirite, to separate himself to the LORD, he shall separate himself from wine and strong drink. He shall drink no vinegar made from wine or strong drink and shall not drink any juice of grapes or eat grapes, fresh or dried.

171

> All the days of his separation he shall eat nothing that is produced by the grapevine, not even the seeds or the skins. All the days of his vow of separation, no razor shall touch his head. Until the time is completed for which he separates himself to the LORD, he shall be holy. He shall let the locks of hair of his head grow long. All the days that he separates himself to the LORD he shall not go near a dead body. Not even for his father or for his mother, for brother or sister, if they die, shall he make himself unclean because his separation to God is on his head. All the days of his separation he is holy to the LORD.
>
> Numbers 6:2-8

For Samson, the Nazirite vow was not for some days or even months or years; it was for life. Everything went according to plan until Samson was old enough to marry, and he made a particularly distressing request of his parents.

> [Samson] came up and told his father and mother, "I saw one of the daughters of the Philistines at Timnah. Now get her for me as my wife." But his father and mother said to him, "Is there not a woman among the daughters of your relatives, or among all our people, that you must go to take a wife from the uncircumcised Philistines?" But Samson said to his father, "Get her for me, for she is right in my eyes."
>
> Judges 14:2-3

Only a handful of mysteries baffled the wise man in the book of Proverbs, and the last of them is amply illustrated by the story of Samson. "Three things are too wonderful for me; for I do not understand: the way of an eagle in the sky, the way of a serpent on a rock, the way of a ship on the high seas, and the way of a man with a virgin" (Proverbs 30:18-19).

The way the good Lord guides His children in this regard is unfathomable. Here He chose to make an exception to the general rule. He had forbidden the children of Israel from intermarrying with the people of the land. Samson's parents could therefore be forgiven for their hesitation to comply with the fraught request of their enamoured son.

Inter-marriage between people of different races and cultures, of course, *does* pose challenges of understanding between the couple, unless the two have grown up or lived for long enough to imbibe the values of a common culture whose norms they both understand and share. It requires harder work, but that is not to say that there is anything wrong with such inter-marriage. Whether one is a Chinese Mandarin from Nanking and the other a Quechua Indian from Argentina does not matter in the least. What is clear is that God wants His children to marry within the household of the Faith. For example, St. Paul says in 2 Corinthians 6:14, "Do not be unequally yoked with unbelievers. For what partnership has righteousness with lawlessness? Or what fellowship has light with darkness?"

Admittedly, Paul was writing in a context where to be an unbeliever implied being part and parcel of the prevailing culture of idolatry and its consequent disregard for the laws of God. And in 1 Corinthians 7:39, "A wife is bound to her husband as long as he lives. But if her husband dies, she is free to be married to whom she wishes, only in the Lord."

It is not the most generous way of putting it, but the bland logic of one cynic comes to mind. "If you do not marry a child of God, you are marrying a child of the devil. And if you marry a child of the devil, you have Satan for your father-in-law!"

Question for Reflection

Our adult children sometimes come up with ideas we are sure cannot be of God. What should we do or not do in such a case?

A Matter of Choice

The ten-million-dollar question is how we arrive at the final decision. Choosing the right life partner is certainly not an exact science. A marriage made in heaven is very rarely a straight-forward affair.

Since the days of Adam, human hearing has deteriorated to a remarkable degree. It is incomparably harder to hear what God is saying to us, and to find out His mind with regard to the question of marriage demonstrates this as much as any other human experience.

It really ought to be simple enough. After all, marriage is God's initiative. He knew Adam needed a wife, and He took it upon Himself to prepare just the right girl for him. Adam's part was to repose complete confidence in God and get on with living the ordinary life of everyday, eating and working and sleeping. He did not over-sleep either. God woke him up when the time was ripe and his bride was ready.

The way it tends to work for most of us is more like the story of the little girl who went shopping with her father when he promised to buy her the very best toy available in the city. He warned her they were going to visit many stores because they had a lot of other shopping to do. At the very first store, she went to the toy department and picked the best on display.

"Not here, and certainly not that one," the father objected. The same scene was repeated at the next store and then the next. She noted that each time the best on offer was indeed an improvement on the ones before. But then they came to a store where she found one that was by far superior to all she had previously admired. With shining eyes, she thanked her father for not letting her settle on any of the earlier ones, but he still insisted that even this one was not the best, at which she burst into tears. Daddy stood his ground in spite of her tantrum. To her utter amazement, her father's choice was a composite toy which combined the best features of all the ones she had seen before.

Why is it so very hard for us to really, really believe that our loving, heavenly Father will work out what is right for us and that He knows and cares and will give to us the very best? If only we would wait on Him. There is a saying in Africa that what the toad will eat, God will not leave hanging on a tree. Surely He can be trusted not to put beyond our reach the boy or girl specially prepared for us in His love and grace. And we can always be sure that it is another child of God just like us.

There are exceptions to the rule that we can only conclude have God's directing hand on them.

One such example was Sarah, a young Congolese convert seeking the Lord's leading on the most important decision in her life. If a girl makes the wrong decision in her choice of a job, she can always resign and look for another job. If she chooses the wrong person to marry, however, or to tell it more like it is, if she allows herself to be chosen by the wrong person, she is stuck for life. Sarah required no other incentive to pray earnestly—and her mother along with her.

When a man of the same tribe turned up and said he had been working as a Lutheran pastor in the neighbouring country of Tanzania, Sarah wondered if this was God's answer to her prayers. She told her mother of his interest, and they did some more praying together before the families went ahead with the match.

Glowing with excitement, Sarah headed for Tanzania together with her groom, with a view to labouring side by side with him in the business of the gospel of the Lord Jesus Christ. Imagine her bewilderment to discover that she was in fact the second wife of this missionary, for he was indeed an accredited missionary, but not of any Christian church or group. He was a missionary of the Islamic League, having studied for five years in Saudi Arabia, specialising in Islamic apologetics and propagation! He had no qualms about his ruse in trapping Sarah. He explained how, according to the principle of "Taqqiyah," it is admissible to lie for the promotion of Islam. Talk of marrying a child of the devil! As far as Sarah was concerned, what Jesus said in the gospel of St. John obviously applies:

> You are of your father the devil, and your will is to do your father's desires. He was a murderer from the beginning, and has nothing to do with the truth because there is no truth in him. When he lies, he speaks out of his own character, for he is a liar and the father of lies.
>
> John 8:44

The heartbroken young bride went back to break the news to her mother at the first opportunity, and after copious tears and serious prayers, the two ladies concluded that Sarah was truly married to this man in the eyes of God and man and that his deceit did not constitute enough grounds for divorce. There was only one thing to do, therefore, and that was to pray for his conversion, which they did with solemn resolve.

Meanwhile, assiduous as ever, and stopping at nothing to win Christians to Islam, the gentleman decided to study the Bible so as to become more adept in subverting Christians to his cause. He even requested an Anglican bishop to recommend a man with whom he could discuss the Bible. This was the path that led him to accept Jesus Christ as his Lord and Saviour. His first wife decided to leave and, only too predictably, he had to flee for his life as his erstwhile fellow religionists plotted his termination with extreme prejudice. He received good training while under cover in three countries, ending up as a minister of the Gospel he once sought to destroy.

This was not the first exception to the general rule, and it would not be the last. Samson's parents reluctantly acceded to their son's request. We are told in a helpful parenthesis, "His father and mother did not know that it was from the LORD, for he was seeking an opportunity against the Philistines. At that time the Philistines ruled over Israel" (Judges 14:4).

It is possible, then, for God to guide us along unusual paths. We have to be sure that it is truly God who is doing the guiding and not the desires of our fickle hearts, for it is with good reason that the Scriptures describe our hearts as deceitful. "Blessed is the man who trusts in the LORD, whose trust is the LORD... The heart is deceitful above all things, and desperately sick; who can understand it?" (Jeremiah 17:7, 9).

When it is a matter that has everything to do with our human emotions, therefore, we should go out of our way to use all the means available to us to gain that assurance that it is indeed the Lord we are trusting. Far too often, unfortunately, it is a moral revolt that precedes and prompts theological justification of our actions.

That God once guided us in one unusual way does not mean that He will always guide us in unusual ways. It was God's Spirit who enabled Samson to kill a lion with his bare hands, but considering his Nazirite calling, he had no business turning aside to see the carcass of the lion on a subsequent journey—and in a vineyard, too! And he certainly had no business with the prostitute of Gaza, nor with the woman in the Valley of Sorek, Delilah, who was his ultimate undoing.

Samson was entrusted with a business that was more than enough to keep him engaged body, mind, and soul, but he allowed himself to be diverted by the common lust of his sinful heart. God's chosen champion against the enemies of his nation, Samson had proved to himself and to everyone what he was capable of doing under the power of the Spirit of God, but he did not continue to live like that.

For reasons we cannot fathom, God does not give His gifts only to those who would use them appropriately and to His glory. This is the story of Mozart which was so magnificently depicted in the multi-Oscar-winning film *Amadeus*. Antonio Salieri renounced the pleasures of the flesh and promised eternal piety before God in exchange for the gift of music. Instead of him, however, it was a "giggling, dirty-minded creature," Wolfgang Amadeus Mozart, that God decided to favour. Mozart was effortlessly brilliant while Salieri was ponderously mediocre, and no amount of wishing or praying or hard work would change it. That was why Salieri turned on God. As he burned his crucifix, he gave the Almighty a piece of his mind.

> From now on, we are enemies, you and I, because you choose for your instrument a boastful, lustful, smutty, infantile boy and give me only the ability to recognise the incarnation. Because you are unjust, unfair, unkind, I will block you, I swear it. I will hinder and harm your creature on Earth as far as I am able.[105]

From time to time, we encounter the problem in one form or another. We set the saints on their knees praying and fasting for months on end for the sickly baby in our church and nothing seems to happen. On the other hand, there could be an evangelist we do not have any reason to admire but who has an undeniable gift and an amazing ministry of healing! Most obviously, he does not merit it. That, presumably, is why it is called a "gift," and as Paul says in Romans 11:29, "the gifts and the calling of God are irrevocable."

To use a modern expression, Samson was a man who did not know how to button his pants. There were many sober, sensible, God-honouring young men in Israel at the time, no doubt, but it was to this irresponsible philanderer that God chose to give the gift of prodigious strength. Samson tore a lion apart with his bare hands and destroyed a battalion of soldiers with the jawbone of a donkey only to go and sell himself cheaply under the skirts of godless sex.

Some men are addicted to sex, an addiction that experts say is characterized by obsessive sexual behaviour regardless of the growing negative consequences for the person or their relationships. Samson seems to have been one of them. It is identical to all other forms of addiction in that the sex addict cannot help himself. Try as he may, he cannot desist from the habit despite destructive results and deep feelings of shame.

"Lust is like eczema—the more we scratch it, the more it itches." Any relief is only temporary; in the long term, the desire simply increases. The American writer Frederick Buechner puts it this way; "Lust is the craving for salt of a man who is dying of thirst."

It is easier to criticise the fallen than to own up to our own hypocrisy. The "Samson Society," founded by Nate Larkin, seeks to help men who are addicted to sexual lust to be honest with themselves and turn their lives around, and his clients are not convicted paedophiles or registered sex offenders but respected church members, businessmen, and seemingly model husbands. One of his co-workers, David Zailer, comments,

> Nothing else will go really well in our recovery until we get as honest as we can. A guy may show up because he feels guilty, his wife demanded it, or he may have good intentions. But if he's not broken, he won't stay. Our pro-gramme is for *desperate* men.[106]

This was the sort of help that Samson needed in his days, but there was no one to give it to him.

Question for Reflection

Have you ever encountered God's leading in a way that can truly be regarded as an exception to the general rule? How can we be sure that it is indeed God's leading?

"To Love and to Cherish"

What exactly did marriage mean to Samson? If the psalmist compares the glory of sunrise to a bridegroom coming out of his chamber,[107] we can only imagine what it would be for such a he-man as Samson. He could not have been too pleased to have to interrupt his honeymoon to sort out "payment" for losing his ill-advised bet to his local wedding guests. He had made a wager that they could not solve a riddle he told to them, but his bride prevailed upon him to reveal it:

> She wept before him the seven days that their feast lasted, and on the seventh day he told her because she pressed him hard. Then she told the riddle to her people. And the men of the city said to him on the seventh day before the sun went down, "What is sweeter than honey? What is stronger than a lion?" And he said to them, "If you had not plowed with my heifer, you would not have found out my riddle." And the Spirit of the LORD rushed upon him, and he went down to Ashkelon and struck down thirty men of the town and took their spoil and gave the garments to those who had told the riddle. In hot anger he went back to his father's house. And Samson's wife was given to his companion, who had been his best man.
>
> Judges 14:17-20

Oh yes, Samson had cause to be angry, but my, what a temper the man had! He took the garments off thirty able-bodied and well-to-do men of Ashkelon, first making sure they no longer needed their clothes by the simple expedient of killing them. With this, he was able to pay his wager and at the same time avenge himself on some of those hated oppressors of the people of God.

But what did he do next?

"In hot anger he went back to his father's house" (Judges 14:19).

Right from the first wedding, God had set down the essential procedure that marriage entails: "Therefore a man shall leave his father and his mother and hold fast to his wife, and they shall become one flesh" (Genesis 2:24).

Samson, it would seem, missed that lesson in his pre-marital counselling and so he deserted his wife as he scurried back to his mother, right in the middle of his honeymoon! And the wife he had vowed to love and to cherish? He simply left her with her parents as if they had not been married. "The bee does not start a new house with honey." That is true enough, but what kind of a start was this one?

Married but Not Engaged is the title of a book by Paul and Sandy Coughlin. That would seem to be an apt description of Samson! He was married but failed to engage with his wife in the intimate union that God ordains in marriage. To varying degrees, how many of us married men and women disengage from our spouses to scurry off, maybe not to Mother, but to some other person or interest?

There are indeed those for whom the problem is the father or mother who will not let go. This leads to the interfering mother- or father-in-law. There are those too who have an emotional dependence on their father or mother and are loathe to sever the link sufficiently to be engaged in their own independent family life. Either way, the obligation is on the man or woman to break the older bond in order to establish the new. The husband in particular should be a man. He should leave his father and mother and cling to the wife of whom he is now the head.

It might not be father or mother or another person at all. Sometimes it is legitimate work or some otherwise innocent pursuit. Someone coined the term "computer widow" in the early days of the personal computer when it was the "must have" gadget that occupied the time of enterprising, upwardly mobile men and choked wife and family out of their lives.

When God calls us into family life, he calls us into a big job. No other work, not even full time Christian service, takes a higher priority. The man must always give the time necessary to his wife and the woman to her husband. Is it not of particular significance that one tenet of the Law of Moses was that a newly married man is excused military service for a whole year? "When a man is newly married, he shall not go out with the army or be liable for any other public duty. He shall be free at home one year to be happy with his wife whom he has taken" (Deuteronomy 24:5).

No, Samson did not forget all about his wife. He *did* go back to pay her a visit "later on, at the time of the wheat harvest." He even took a present with him, but she was no longer there to receive him. With the active connivance of his father-in-law— she had made off with his best man!

It is important not to judge people too harshly when their marriages break up. It could just as easily happen to any of us. It brings to mind the words of the imprisoned saint as he witnessed a group of fellow prisoners being led to their execution, "There but for the grace of God goes John Bradford!"[108]

The causes of marital problems are rarely simple. Samson was wrong to leave his wife with her parents, but how does that excuse their giving her to another man or her agreeing to this arrangement?

Question for Reflection

"Therefore shall a man leave his father and mother and hold fast to his wife." Why do you think this is addressed to the man and not to the woman?

Flee Fornication!

"Flee fornication" is how the King James Version of 1 Corinthians 6:18 begins. Samson did not. Instead, his main preoccupation in life was absolutely up to date in the worst tradition of our sex-obsessed, hedonistic generation. Specially chosen and exceptionally endowed by God though he was, the strong man of Israel would do anything to crawl under the next Philistine skirt that came his way.

Sometimes gifted leaders are poor learners. Samson told the meaning of his riddle to his wife during their honeymoon. She went and told it to her people, and he lost his bet. But that experience did not stop him from playing the same game with Delilah, who was not even his wife. This time, however, it was not a game but a deadly wager with his life as the prize. Samson broke one very important rule of life: "Keep your own secret!" If you cannot, why should you expect anyone else to keep it?

> When Delilah saw that he had told her all his heart, she sent and called the lords of the Philistines, saying, "Come up again, for he has told me all his heart." Then the lords of the Philistines came up to her and brought the money in their hands. She made him sleep on her knees. And she called a man and had him shave off the seven locks of his head. Then she began to torment him, and his strength left him. And she said, "The Philistines are upon you, Samson!" And he awoke from his sleep and said, "I will go out as at other times and shake myself free." But he did not know that the LORD had left him. And the Philistines seized him and gouged out his eyes and brought him down to Gaza and bound him with bronze shackles. And he ground at the mill in the prison.
>
> Judges 16:18-21

Delilah has always had a bad press. She is often confused with the prostitute with whom Samson spent the night in Gaza. No, she was not a prostitute. She simply was a woman with whom the champion fell in love in the Valley of Sorek. We do not know how she managed to gain his attention. Was she the sort of girl who did not dress attractively but rather to attract, wafting around men in a cloud of provocative perfume? Even then, no more blame attaches to this femme fatale than to any other patriotic secret agent ready to sacrifice her honour and even her life to destroy an enemy military commander in a honey trap.

Samson deserved full credit for all his troubles in choosing the path of plain and flagrant disobedience of God's law by his sexual misadventures. In the battle against the forces of evil, the child of God must heed the warning in the book of Hebrews. "Let us also lay aside every weight, and sin which clings so closely, and let us run with endurance the race that is set before us" (Hebrews 12:1).

We have to cast off the sin that entangles us, which is what Samson failed to do, but that is not all. We must also dispense with every weight that hinders, even if it is not sinful. The illustration here is of a long distance race. There are rules that govern the marathon, for example. It includes not starting before the gun and not departing from the set route. Anyone who breaks the rules will be disqualified. That is what happened to Fred Lorz at the St. Louis Summer Olympics in 1904. The American runner was the first to return to the stadium to rapturous applause, but he had travelled eleven miles of the course by car! If Fred Lorz had run all the way in his top hat and Wellington boots, however, he would not have been disqualified because the rules do not include the type of dress the competitors choose to wear—or the kind of shoes. But no one does that for the sole reason that it will hinder them from winning. For us, too, there are things that are not sin, but we should still be careful to avoid them because they will hinder us from fulfilling the tasks that God has set for us.

"Others May, You Cannot," was the title of a tract by a Methodist minister based in Los Angeles in the mid 1800s. Its message is as pertinent today as ever:

> If God has called you to be really like Christ in all your spirit, He will draw you into a life of crucifixion and humility and put on you such demands of obedience, that He will not allow you to follow other Christians, and in many ways He will seem to let other good people do things that He will not let you do.[109]

This is wise counsel that has been appreciated by many, among whom was James Hudson Taylor, founder of the China Inland Mission, who apparently hand-copied it for his own benefit when he was about forty-two years old—a dated, hand-written copy having been found among his treasured papers after his death. The moral, then, is that we should go beyond not following Samson's bad example. We should also beware of the harmless pursuits that can hinder us from being the best that we can be and fulfilling God's highest purposes in our lives.

Taking It Further

1. Are there incidents of marriage breakup among believers in your community? What avenues of help are available to couples who are having the first signs of trouble in their marriage?

2. Would you agree that there is more incitement to sexual temptation today than ever before? If so, what can parents do and what should the church do to help its young people?

3. It has been said that money, sex, and power are the three main tools that Satan uses to bring down prominent men of God. What steps can leaders and those who actively support them take to guard against these stumbling blocks?

4. "Others May, You Cannot!" What reasons do you have to agree or to disagree with this concept from Revd Watson?

5. Are older couples sometimes guilty of making it appear as if it is all plain sailing and they have no serious problems in their marriage? How can they be of more help to younger couples?

6. Are there some secrets couples should keep from their spouses? What are your reasons?

ELI AND SAMUEL: GODLY PARENTS OF GODLESS OFFSPRING

Immoral Priests

Imagine this scene.

You are standing in a rather large, sparsely-furnished, dimly-lit room. Straight in front of you and all around, you can see the hangings. Tapestries hand-woven by the very best artisans in the entire world and of the richest natural fabric you have ever seen and are ever likely to see, all in royal colours of blue and purple. You look up, and your eyes feast on a rich and tasteful ceiling of natural fur from non-endangered species.

On the ground, exquisite utensils of pure gold are carefully arranged on gold-plated furniture.

And under your feet—desert sand.

You are standing, of course, in the Tent of Meeting, the Tabernacle constructed according to God's instructions. It was the handiwork of Bezalel and Oholiab, master craftsmen who, it is safe to surmise, could attain to this degree of expertise only because they had plied their trade at the topmost level imaginable—in the service of the Pharaohs in Egypt. You would not be in that room if you were not a Levite and a priest. Even at that, there is an inner room you cannot enter unless you happen to be the reigning High Priest of Israel. This is the most holy place where only he can enter—only once a year.

Colour does not come up very often in the Bible, and half of all references to colour are to do with that tent of meeting or the temple that was later to serve the same purposes of worshiping the Lord in the beauty of holiness.

At the centre of all the ceremonies are the priests of the God of Israel. This was the role of the family of Eli as High Priest, assisted by his two sons, Hophni and Phinehas.

Thus, these two young men were born into privilege. As members of the tribe of Levi, they were set apart for God and His service. Unlike men of other tribes, they did not have land or animals or farms or any other businesses of their own.

Priests had the normal upbringing of the children of Israel, which taught them to know and observe the Law of Moses. In addition, they were trained to represent the people to God and to represent God to the people. Their duties included offering prescribed sacrifices before the Lord, tending the Ark of the Covenant with worshipful propriety; and they were responsible for its transportation when required. For all these tasks, they were amply rewarded.

> The Levitical priests, all the tribe of Levi, shall have no portion or inheritance with Israel. They shall eat the Lord's food offerings as their inheritance. They shall have no inheritance among their brothers; the Lord is their inheritance, as he promised them. And this shall be the priests' due from the people, from those offering a sacrifice, whether an ox or a sheep: they shall give to the priest the shoulder and the two cheeks and the stomach. The firstfruits of your grain, of your wine and of your oil, and the first fleece of your sheep, you shall give him. For the Lord your God has chosen him out of all your tribes to stand and minister in the name of the Lord, him and his sons for all time.
>
> Deuteronomy 18:1-5

God did not make a provision for those who served at his altar that was merely *adequate*. It was generous in the extreme! Had He not prescribed, in Deuteronomy 24:4 as part of the Law that His people should not muzzle an ox that threshes the corn? How much more then should His own honoured servants who facilitated the worship and adoration of the faithful be allowed to eat their fill! And so, whenever the people brought their sacrifices, the priests had a right to much more meat than they could possibly consume.

But all that was not enough for Hophni and Phinehas. They wanted more—much more—and whatever they wanted they took, including unwarranted liberty with women who came to worship the Lord.

> Now the sons of Eli were worthless men. They did not know the LORD. The custom of the priests with the people was that when any man offered sacrifice, the priest's servant would come, while the meat was boiling, with a three-pronged fork in his hand, and he would thrust it into the pan or kettle or cauldron or pot. All that the fork brought up the priest would take for himself. This is what they did at Shiloh to all the Israelites who came there. Moreover, before the fat was burned, the priest's servant would come and say to the man who was sacrificing, "Give meat for the priest to roast, for he will not accept boiled meat from you but only raw." And if the man said to him, "Let them burn the fat first, and then take as much as you wish," he would say, "No, you must give it now, and if not, I will take it by force."
>
> 1 Samuel 2:12-16

It is often suggested that government functionaries in poor countries take bribes and indulge in all sorts of corrupt practices because they are very poorly paid. Bribery and corruption, it is argued, is merely a logical response to their debilitating poverty and abject powerlessness. Hence, to reverse the famous saying by

Lord Acton, "Powerlessness corrupts, and absolute powerlessness corrupts absolutely!"

That is what they too would like the world to believe. "They pretend they are paying us," they claim, "and we *too* pretend we are working." But how much they are paid has nothing to do with it. Otherwise, how does this explain those who steal billions to be transferred into Swiss accounts where it does neither they themselves, their family, nor anyone else in their country any good? Even after stashing away obscene quantities of ill-gotten wealth, they continue to spend their lives conjugating the verb "to bribe." For the overwhelming majority, the only reason they steal is because they are thieves. It is greed, not poverty that is the real cause of corruption.

God detests all sin. When someone perverts the worship of the holy God into sinful usage, however, it would seem that they touch a particularly raw nerve in the Almighty. Hence the severity with which He deals with the sin of idolatry in the history of Israel. It is little wonder that Jude had such unpleasant things to say about those he described as, "ungodly people, who pervert the grace of our God into sensuality …" (Jude 4b). Hophni and Phinehas fit into that category. It is heart-breaking to hear of paedophile priests who abuse children. They betray a sacred trust and deserve the condemnation of society and ought rightly to be subjected to the full rigour of the law of the land. Why the church turned a blind eye and tolerated it for decades is beyond explanation. Sometimes, even when discovered, such priests were given neither the punishment they deserved nor the help they needed. Instead, they were merely transferred to another situation where they could continue to molest children. Monetary reparations are a poor recompense, even if they bankrupt the church!

In the sordid annals of the betrayal of sacred trust, none can be more despicable than what is recorded on film in the documentary by Scott Solary and Luci Westphal entitled *All God's Children*.[110]

Mamou Alliance Academy in Guinea, West Africa, is a Christian and Missionary Alliance (C&MA) boarding school for missionary kids. There, in the 1960s and '70s, dozens of children were beaten, abused, and even raped by teachers and overseers. As if that was not enough, they were told that if they ever revealed what went on, they would be defeating their parents' work and damning millions of potential African converts to hell. The poor victims bottled up their indescribable sufferings for more than thirty years before they summoned the courage to band together to confront the demons of their past, seek justice, and, in some cases, offer forgiveness. Brandon Fibbs writes in "Christianity Today,"

> *All God's Children* is a harrowing tale. Including firsthand interviews and footage of children at the school (though showing no abusive situations), the film offers a glimpse into the long-term mental and spiritual ramifications of violence practiced against the innocent. Many of the former students have left the faith, some struggle with their sexuality, and others battle depression and suicide. One ex-student could not conceive of a world in which anyone would want children, while another finds hymns nauseating because they were the soundtrack of his abusive childhood. Yet another felt compelled to show the world that his experiences were a perverted aberration of God's will and is now a minister. [111]

And their parents?

> The filmmakers interviewed several of the parents, many of whom are as haunted by the past as their children are. They thought those looking after their children were friends and fellow labourers in the field. They had no reason for distrust until it was too late. While none of the

former students interviewed here blame their parents outright, their feelings of helplessness and abandonment are
obvious.[112]

It is one of those unfathomable mysteries of God's grace that
He can forgive even such sinners when they repent. They should
thank God I am not in His position... because I wouldn't!

Question for Reflection

Hophni and Phineas perverted the worship of God's people and it cost them their lives. Do similar issues sometimes
arise in the Church today? How can they be prevented?

A Father's Rebuke

Evil reports of the monstrous deeds of his sons came to Eli, and the
ageing High Priest was not amused. He knew what was right, and he
did what was right. He was decidedly uncompromising in condemn-
ing the sins and in rebuking the culprits as we see in verses 22-25.

> Now Eli was very old, and he kept hearing all that his sons
> were doing to all Israel, and how they lay with the women
> who were serving at the entrance to the tent of meeting.
> And he said to them, "Why do you do such things? For I
> hear of your evil dealings from all the people. No, my sons;
> it is no good report that I hear the people of the LORD
> spreading abroad. If someone sins against a man, God will
> mediate for him, but if someone sins against the LORD,
> who can intercede for him?' But they would not listen to
> the voice of their father.
>
> 1 Samuel 2:22-25

"The dog that must get lost," as the saying goes, "does not hear
the hunter's whistle." Hophni and Phinehas did not heed parental warning. In any case, the damage was done. The holy God of
Israel had had enough, and He pronounced His judgement.

I gave to the house of your father all my offerings by fire from the people of Israel. Why then do you scorn my sacrifices and my offerings that I commanded, and honor your sons above me by fattening yourselves on the choicest parts of every offering of my people Israel?' Therefore the LORD, the God of Israel, declares: 'I promised that your house and the house of your father should go in and out before me forever,' but now the LORD declares: 'Far be it from me, for those who honor me I will honor, and those who despise me shall be lightly esteemed. Behold, the days are coming when I will cut off your strength and the strength of your father's house, so that there will not be an old man in your house....And this that shall come upon your two sons, Hophni and Phinehas, shall be the sign to you: both of them shall die on the same day.

1 Samuel 2:28-31, 34

What was that? In the name of all that is fair! It is all right to punish these wicked sons for their sins? We may even dare to wish that making them both die on the same day is only the first instalment. They merely got what was coming to them, all in line with the warning to come from the pen of the wise man in the not too distant future. "He who is often reproved, yet stiffens his neck, will suddenly be broken beyond healing" (Proverbs 29:1).

But spare a thought for their miserable father! It is tragic enough for any man to lose two sons together. But for all these other horrible things to happen to a poor old man who did not approve of what his children did and who rounded on them so forthrightly for their waywardness? There is something in the book of the Law about visiting the sins of the fathers upon their children, which we can perhaps explain in terms of the scars of sin that remain indelible. But to visit the sins of children on their innocent father is a totally different matter! It actually contradicts what God was later to say through the Prophet Ezekiel.

The soul who sins shall die. The son shall not suffer for the iniquity of the father, nor the father suffer for the iniq-

> uity of the son. The righteousness of the righteous shall be upon himself, and the wickedness of the wicked shall be upon himself.
>
> Ezekiel 18:20

Strangely inconsistent, is it not, coming from the One who is the same yesterday, today and forever? But that is not the end of the puzzle.

Compare Samuel

Comparing the sons of Eli with Samuel is comparing chalk with cheese.

First we meet with Samuel's godly mother groaning inwardly as she uttered her wordless prayers in the temple. Eli, the High Priest, was evidently tired of intemperate behaviour by some of those who come for the annual festivities in the holy sanctuary. To him, here was another one of those drunken women.

> And Eli said to her, "How long will you go on being drunk? Put your wine away from you." But Hannah answered, "No, my lord, I am a woman troubled in spirit. I have drunk neither wine nor strong drink, but I have been pouring out my soul before the LORD. Do not regard your servant as a worthless woman, for all along I have been speaking out of my great anxiety and vexation."
>
> 1 Samuel 1:14-15

"The stomachs of all lizards are flat on the ground," the elders observe, "but we do not know which ones are aching." How could Eli guess at the heartache of this childless woman in deep communion with the One who knows and cares and is able—able to do "exceeding abundantly above" all we can ask or imagine. (Ephesians 3:20, KJV).

God heard and answered. Hannah kept the vow she made long before her son developed into an embryo by handing him over to the Lord as soon as he was weaned.

> And when she had weaned him, she took him up with her, along with a three-year-old bull, an ephah of flour, and a skin of wine, and she brought him to the house of the LORD at Shiloh. And the child was young. Then they slaughtered the bull, and they brought the child to Eli. And she said, "Oh, my lord! As you live, my lord, I am the woman who was standing here in your presence, praying to the LORD. For this child I prayed, and the LORD has granted me my petition that I made to him. Therefore I have lent him to the LORD. As long as he lives, he is lent to the LORD."
>
> 1 Samuel 1:24-28

It was not accidental, therefore, that this child, Samuel, turned out to be arguably the most faithful of all the rulers in the history of the nation. Not one negative thing is recorded against him in all of Scripture. But his *own children* were a different kettle of fish.

> When Samuel became old, he made his sons judges over Israel. The name of his firstborn son was Joel, and the name of his second, Abijah; they were judges in Beersheba. Yet his sons did not walk in his ways but turned aside after gain. They took bribes and perverted justice. Then all the elders of Israel gathered together and came to Samuel at Ramah and said to him, "Behold, you are old and your sons do not walk in your ways. Now appoint for us a king to judge us like all the nations." But the thing displeased Samuel when they said, "Give us a king to judge us." And Samuel prayed to the LORD. And the LORD said to Samuel, "Obey the voice of the people in all that they say to you, for they have not rejected you, but they have rejected me from being king over them. According to all the deeds that they have done, from the day I brought them up out

of Egypt even to this day, forsaking me and serving other
gods, so they are also doing to you. Now then, obey their
voice; only you shall solemnly warn them and show them
the ways of the king who shall reign over them."

1 Samuel 8:1-9

Just one generation removed, Samuel's Joel and Abijah played
in the same League as Eli's Hophni and Phineas, although they
did not wear the same jerseys. The fact that they were not priests
but judges is immaterial. Having had the same opportunities in
life and enjoyed the same privileges, they abused their positions
in exactly the same unspeakable manner and to the same unim-
aginable degree.

Two verdicts are of particular interest in this story. First is that
God decided not to punish either Samuel or his sons. As a rule,
God punishes sin. Eli's sons were punished for their sins, and
Eli was punished for the sins of his sons, even though he called
them to account. Why then were Samuel's sons not punished for
their sins? And why was Samuel not punished for the sins of his
sons? Going strictly by what is recorded, we might say that he is
even more deserving of punishment than Eli since it is not stated
anywhere that he chastised Joel and Abijah in the same way as we
saw Eli rebuke his sons. The focus of his response on hearing the
complaints against them was on a different issue. "But the thing
displeased Samuel when they said, 'Give us a king to judge us.'
And Samuel prayed to the LORD."

Second is that God took the people of Israel to task for making a justifiable request. Samuel's children were unworthy of their
high calling to be rulers. Why should they be allowed to continue
as Judges, when "they took bribes and perverted justice"? Are
these the sort of leaders God wants over His people? Is this not
the same God we know, in the words of the Apostle Peter, as
the Righteous Father "who judges impartially according to each
one's deeds"? (1 Peter 1:17)

Question for Reflection
Like the children of both Samuel and Eli, the children of godly leaders such as Billy Graham sometimes enter into their parents' ministry today. What are the pros and cons?

Train Up a Child...

Adulthood comes early to the children of Israel. The coming of age ceremony is at age twelve for girls, Bat Mitzvah, while the Bar Mitzvah is at age thirteen for boys.[113] The terms mean, literally, "Daughter/Son of the Commandment." Until that day, the father bore responsibility for the sins of his son or daughter. One prayer a father makes during this ceremony is to thank the Lord that from that moment he ceases to carry the burden of the sins of the child.

Following this ceremony, the young man has a civil personality in his own right. He is adjudged qualified to bear full responsibility for Jewish law, tradition, and ritual. He can pronounce the traditional blessing, be a witness in a court of law, or be part of the quorum that constitutes a synagogue. He is considered as someone who knows all that is essential to know about the Law of Moses—and with good reason.

> Hear, O Israel: The LORD our God, the LORD is one. You shall love the LORD your God with all your heart and with all your soul and with all your might. And these words that I command you today shall be on your heart. You shall teach them diligently to your children, and shall talk of them when you sit in your house, and when you walk by the way, and when you lie down, and when you rise. You shall bind them as a sign on your hand, and they shall be as frontlets between your eyes. You shall write them on the doorposts of your house and on your gates.
>
> Deuteronomy 6:4-9

At age three, Jewish children raised in the traditional manner are taught the Jewish alphabet. Formal education in Jewish culture and tradition begins in the synagogue at age four. Bible stories commence at age five, and rabbinical commentary starts at age ten. The Bar Mitzvah ceremony comes after three further years of this intensive and relentless training.

By the time he is thirteen, a child instructed in this manner is bound to know the Law inside out and upside down. Besides, he would have had the Law not only explained and expounded but modelled in the family. And he would have experienced its implications in society through the cycle of rituals that accompany the seasons and the years. Every week takes him through a Sabbath (Leviticus 23:3), and every year takes him through a Passover festival, (Leviticus 23:5), a feast of Unleavened Bread (Leviticus 23:6), of the First Fruits (Leviticus 23:9-11), of Weeks (Leviticus 23:15-16), of Trumpets (Leviticus 23:23-25), of the Day of Atonement (Leviticus 23:27-28), and of Tabernacles (Leviticus 23:34-36). And he would experience at least one, and perhaps two, "seventh year" when the land is given its Sabbath. All of these are object lessons to enable the child not merely to understand but to enter into the life of the Law.

It is the duty of every father to ensure that he does, and God holds him responsible if he fails in this duty. And, in the process, the parent needs to take care not to overdo the religious bit and exasperate or alienate the child—or worse, as Paul was later to caution, "Fathers, do not provoke your children to anger, but bring them up in the discipline and instruction of the Lord" (Ephesians 6:4).

It goes without saying, therefore, that all of this requires massive investment in time and is accompanied with appropriate, loving discipline. Thankfully, it is not that parents are encumbered with a distasteful burden. Rather, they are endowed with a tremendous opportunity to shape a life. This is how a knowledgeable pair of francophone writers put it in a book replete with admirable sociological, theological, and practical insights:

What a child learns at school will accumulate in the form of knowledge more or less valid, but what he learns in infancy will leave an indelible imprint on his personality. A growing child is marked for life not only in his mental attitudes but right up to the very configuration of his brains by the milieu which takes charge of him or else abandons him to himself… This is nothing new. All oppressive systems have sought to take advantage of it to institute the new societies of which they dreamed. Huguenot children raised in convents, children of Australian aborigines, or of gypsies, torn from their parents, to cite but a few examples…[114]

If loveless outsiders can inscribe their ideologies on these receptive minds, how much more should loving, caring parents seek to imprint the law of God on such tender lives!

We can safely conclude that it was this early opportunity that was missed by Eli, the High Priest of Israel. He did rebuke his children when he heard bad reports about them. That is true enough, but it was his *adult* children he was rebuking—a classic case of too little, too late.

It is a problem with many godly men who are rendering exemplary service to God and to His church. They do not give the necessary time to their children. It is not as if they do not love or care for these precious gifts in other ways. They would often go to great expense to provide them with toys and gadgets to keep them happy or keep up with the Joneses, and they would not hesitate to provide them with the best education that money can buy. Instead of spending time with their kids, however, they are too busy to give them anything other than "quality time," as if that was possible without spending "quantity" time with them!

One of my friends was going to work one morning when his little daughter ran up to him. "Daddy, good night!" she said.

Scooping her up into his arms he corrected her amiably, "'Good night'? You mean, 'Good morning,' sweetie."

"No, Daddy! Good night! You are going to work, and I am going to school. From work you will go to Committee meetings and prayer meetings and then go to visit with friends. By the time you return home, I will be asleep in bed. I want to be sure I say my good night to you today!"

A family friend remarked to a young man about his godly father. The young man's response was, "It is good that you know my father so well. He is always busy doing God's work along with other godly people like you. That is why I never got to know him like you do!"

And, sometimes, fathers would delegate all the caring to the mother. Thank God for the input of courageous, indefatigable mothers in the lives of their children, but this is a responsibility for both parents in which the father should take the lead. "But if anyone does not provide for his relatives," according to St. Paul, "and especially for members of his household, he has denied the faith and is worse than an unbeliever" (1 Timothy 5:8).

It is true that St. Paul was referring to physical provisions when he wrote to Timothy, but the teaching can safely be extended to include the much more important provision for the spiritual welfare of our offspring.

On this score, evidently, the High Priest Eli was one leader whose example is to be avoided at all costs.

We have a responsibility and a promise in the book of Proverbs 22:6. "Train up a child in the way he should go; even when he is old he will not depart from it." Children are given us in sacred trust by God. If we do not put their feet on the road of faith, who is to blame if they travel on the highway that leads to destruction?

Question for Reflection

How real is the danger in your experience of godly parents not giving due time to their family? Why do you think this is so?

Away from Home

What a child does on leaving home could turn out to be a rude shock or else a glorious testimony to the lessons they had learned at home. There was a poor, innocent girl who was captured during an incursion of the Syrian army into the land of Israel. She became a slave in the household of the enemy's military Commander. How did her upbringing reveal itself?

> Naaman, commander of the army of the king of Syria, was a great man with his master and in high favour because by him the LORD had given victory to Syria. He was a mighty man of valour, but he was a leper. Now the Syrians on one of their raids had carried off a little girl from the land of Israel, and she worked in the service of Naaman's wife. She said to her mistress, "Would that my lord were with the prophet who is in Samaria! He would cure him of his leprosy." So Naaman went in and told his lord, "Thus and so spoke the girl from the land of Israel." And the king of Syria said, "Go now, and I will send a letter to the king of Israel."
>
> 2 Kings 5:1-5

Despondent and hateful this girl had every reason to be, but far from it, she actually cared for the welfare of her distinguished enslaver. She had observed his helplessness in the face of an incurable disease and seen the powerlessness of the gods of her captors. She also knew it was different in her homeland; and she pointed Naaman to the prophet of the God of Israel, who alone had the power to heal!

"When two elephants fight, the grass gets hurt." This unnamed girl was not the only youthful victim of war of whom we read in the Bible. Also transported from their native land, Daniel and his three friends had opportunity to live out what they had learned from their parents.

> The king commanded Ashpenaz, his chief eunuch, to bring some of the people of Israel, both of the royal fam-

ily and of the nobility, youths without blemish, of good appearance and skillful in all wisdom, endowed with knowledge, understanding learning, and competent to stand in the king's palace, and to teach them the literature and language of the Chaldeans. The king assigned them a daily portion of the food that the king ate, and of the wine that he drank. They were to be educated for three years, and at the end of that time they were to stand before the king. Among these were Daniel, Hananiah, Mishael, and Azariah of the tribe of Judah.

Daniel 1:3-5

These four bright, young men were among the fortunate few who made it through the rigorous qualifying examination to enter the Imperial College for Civil Administration set up by King Nebuchadnezzar in Babylon. They had demonstrated exceptional scholastic aptitude combined with a charming and commanding personality. All they had to do now was apply themselves to their studies, and the sky was the limit as to how far they could rise in the Civil Service of the vast empire. To begin with, there was the menu at the refectory, the same as the king's in the palace. How much better could life ever get for the children of slaves? But that, exactly, was where the problem started. They were being expected to eat what they had learned was not lawful for Jews to eat. Under no circumstance were they going to disobey the Law of their God, and they did not. Together with his three friends, "Daniel resolved that he would not defile himself with the king's food or with the wine that he drank" (Daniel 1:18). Evidently, they must have impressed the Head sufficiently to put his head on the block for them because he agreed to their proposal of an alternative, kosher diet.

Surely, these were not the only four Hebrew young men at the college. Why were they the only four who did not partake of the king's rich food?

It is not unusual that children behave one way at home and a different way away from home. Sometimes it is because they are over-protected at home. They are not exposed to any of the wrong choices that are to be found in the world at large. Such young people arriving at university, for example, discover that there is no one to stop them from doing whatever they choose to do, and there are many more choices than their former world availed.

The two issues involved were once brought home to me in a shocking way—the need to equip young people to live in the real world and then to release them to do so. I was guest in the home of a minister when his teenage daughter called me aside in the best tradition of sharing with an African Elder. Her father, she confided, was too strict in the way he regulated her life out of fear that she would misbehave and bring disgrace on him and his ministry. She knew and loved the Lord and felt she should be trusted to live out her life freely in the public arena. I believed she had a point and had a quiet word with her father. He agreed that she was right and accorded her the freedom she so very reasonably requested.

But it did not work out positively. It took all of three months before she became pregnant! Quite obviously, she had not been adequately prepared for such a life. Or is there another possible reason?

Question for Reflection

What aspect of traditional Jewish training do you think needs to be adopted in your own culture?

Children's Responsibility

Let us take another look at that text in the book of Proverbs. "Train up a child in the way he should go; even when he is old he will not depart from it" (Proverbs 22:6).

This is God's Word. But how about all those children who grow up and then decide to turn away from the faith of their parents? Is it always because they have not been well trained in the way of truth?

Some think that defective upbringing is invariably to blame. For those who would find fault with parents in the manner of the friends of Job, Leslie Leyland Fields urges caution, and she uses the most telling illustration imaginable. We have to be careful not to employ criteria which would fail the perfect heavenly Father Himself! She writes in Christianity Today,

> If our supposition—that we can measure the success of our parenting by the outcome of our children—is scripturally based, we should be able to apply the test to God himself. After all, God is not only the author of our Scriptures, he is also himself a parent, one who identifies himself as our Father. The Old Testament in particular provides a long, deep look into the Father's heart. When we look at his children, however, the news is not good. The descent into rebellion began with his very first children, Adam and Eve, and continued through the days of Noah, ending in global destruction. Then a new family was birthed, the nation of Israel, whom God tenderly calls "my firstborn son" (Ex. 4:22). But that relationship, too, is torturous, marked by constant rebellion and the breaking of God's father-heart. Our own record as his children is not much better...[115]

Evidently, the matter is far from being straight-forward. King Solomon, who inscribed this teaching into Scripture, was himself a very poor example of it in that he *did* turn away from the path along which his godly father directed his tender feet; it was his many wives who turned away his heart from the way of God. Fields continues.

> The great hall of faith in Hebrews 11 provides us with a list of men and women who through extraordinary faithfulness "conquered kingdoms, administered justice,

and gained what was promised; who shut the mouths of lions, quenched the fury of the flames"—believers of such immense faith that 'the world was not worthy of them' (11:32-38). Yet these spiritual giants were raised in anything but model homes, and many of them were themselves highly flawed parents. Abraham sired a child with a maidservant, then agreed to banish the son to the desert. Isaac and Rebekah were locked in parental favouritism over Esau and Jacob. Rebekah led her son to commit an unthinkable travesty: stealing his brother's birthright. Jacob learned his lessons from his mother well and continued on the path of deceit and, later, of destructive favouritism among his sons. Moses was given the young, pagan, unmarried daughter of Pharaoh as his mother. Jephthah was the son of a prostitute, and killed his only daughter because of an impetuous vow. Many more examples from Scripture confound our parenting expectations, but two more must be mentioned. Jonathan, David's closest friend, was a paragon of righteousness and purity in stark contrast with his murderous father, King Saul. And the boy king Josiah, singularly commended as one who served the Lord "with all his heart and with all his soul and with all his strength" (2 Kings 23:25), was the son of Amon, a man who "did evil in the eyes of the Lord" (2 Kings 21:20).[116]

Clearly, happy results do not always accrue when we might suppose they would be obvious, and God's grace would sometimes take over in the most unexpected circumstances!

We hear very much of children's rights these days but hardly anything of children's responsibilities. Children too, however, are responsible agents before the Lord. "You can lead a horse to the river, but you cannot force it to drink." Some children have the training all right but refuse to follow it. For them, the parents certainly cannot be held to account. In fact, the Law has a way of dealing with such children, and it is not pretty.

> If a man has a stubborn and rebellious son who will not
> obey the voice of his father or the voice of his mother,
> and, though they discipline him, will not listen to them,
> then his father and his mother shall take hold of him and
> bring him out to the elders of his city at the gate of the
> place where he lives, and they shall say to the elders of his
> city, "This our son is stubborn and rebellious; he will not
> obey our voice; he is a glutton and a drunkard." Then all
> the men of the city shall stone him to death with stones.
> So you shall purge the evil from your midst, and all Israel
> shall hear, and fear.
>
> Deuteronomy 21:18-21

Samuel's children, evidently, did not attain to the sort of
extreme which would have necessitated such terminal judgement. If he had failed to teach them as the Law required, however, God would certainly have held him responsible as surely
as He held Eli responsible for his failure. The fact that He did
not would therefore point to them as the culprits who failed to
heed instruction.

What is a father or a mother to do when a child decides to follow
his own way in spite of all the teaching and training and model-
ling they have provided to the best of their ability? They can pray,
earnestly crying to the One who loves that child more than they
do and who is not willing that any should perish. He is able to
answer gloriously in his own manner and at his own time. Oh,
the agony of heart that many godly parents endure because of
their children!

Dr. Billy Graham is one of God's special gifts to our generation. For many years, his first son, Franklin, decided to go his
own way. Christians from all over the world joined the parents
in making earnest intercession to God. God looked down in
mercy from on high and answered most gloriously in His own
time. This is the same Franklin who ran the Samaritan Purse

before succeeding his father as President of the Billy Graham Evangelistic Association.

God did not punish Samuel, and He was displeased with the request of the nation to replace his sons as Judges.

While it is true that Samuel's sons were terrible judges, the point here is that God had not yet written them off when the people did. Not all terrible people are beyond redemption. Israel's main problem was impatience, not waiting for God to complete the work of grace He was doing in these wicked lives. God knew the kind of leaders the people should have, and He was quite capable of turning their seemingly hopeless judges around.

We must never lose sight of the longsuffering nature of the love of God. It is only those who have committed the sin against the Holy Spirit who are beyond redemption, but none of us can dismiss anyone as having committed the unforgivable sin while they are still alive. What grounds would we have for losing hope for any of our children, however far they may stray, or indeed for anyone whatsoever? To do so would be to make the same mistake as the children of Israel. Some, like the thief on the cross, are saved at the last moment. Thus, we can prayerfully entertain hope even for the salvation of people such as Duncan Bannatyne who came to a deliberate decision that he was not yet ready to respond to God's claim on their lives. This is the successful Scottish entrepreneur, philanthropist, and best-selling author who is most famous for his work as a "business angel" investor helping new enterprises on the BBC TV programme Dragons' Den. His philanthropic interest includes orphanages, and it was when visiting "Casa Bannatyne," which he had built in Romania that he had a poignant encounter with God. This is how he describes it in his autobiography:

> For me the tears came at about ten o'clock that night. I went out and found a quiet place at the side of the house. I couldn't stop the tears. I had no choice but to let the tears flow; and they just kept pouring out of me and wouldn't

stop. After many minutes, I began to get the feeling that I wasn't alone. It was there and then that God said hello. It was unmistakable; I knew who had come, and I also knew why. It wasn't a spiritual thing; it was a Christian thing. It was profound, and I stood there stunned, considering the offer and thinking about what it would mean. I knew I wanted to keep building up my business, and I wanted to keep making money, and I also knew I wanted to carry on doing all the things I wasn't proud of—I knew I was never going to be this totally Christian guy going to church on Sundays. So I said, "No, I'm not ready." And God said, "Okay," and disappeared.[117]

The people of Israel, unfortunately, would not wait for God's good time. They had their own agenda and expected God to subscribe to it. They wanted a king, and they wanted him right then.

And what was their reason for wanting a king? So that they could be like other nations—exactly the opposite of what God wanted for them! He did not want them to be like other nations but to be a people apart and a model for the rest of the world. This is what He had told them way back in the desert as soon as they got out of Egypt.

> Now therefore, if you will indeed obey my voice and keep my covenant, you shall be my treasured possession among all peoples, for all the earth is mine; and you shall be to me a kingdom of priests and a holy nation.
>
> Exodus 19:5-6

The king they wanted would fight their wars in the manner of the kings of other nations when God had promised and was ready to fight for them. They wanted a king to lead them instead of God who had made the offer to their forefathers to be their leader.

No wonder God was not pleased with them! It was a re-enactment of the history of the nation, as the older translation describes their action and its consequences: "[They] lusted exceedingly in the wilderness, and tempted God in the desert. And he gave them their request; but sent leanness into their soul" (Psalms 106:15-16, KJV).

How often do we, too, want to be like the people around us when God has called us to be a people apart? We are anxious for the world to see us as "normal" people just like them, which is all right up to a point, because we do not want to turn people away from the gospel by acting weird. This does not remove the fact, however, that when we turn from our old ways to Christ, we are different. We are specially chosen as priests to represent God to others and so are "a peculiar people." In the words of the old rendering, "But ye are a chosen generation, a royal priesthood, an holy nation, a peculiar people; that ye should show forth the praises of him who hath called you out of darkness into his marvellous light" (1 Peter 2:9, KJV).

Israel did have their king. His name was Saul. He started well but took the wrong turning along the way; and so began the fulfilment of Samuel's dire prophecy about kingship in Israel.

We never heard anything further about the sons of Samuel. But is it too much to expect that one day we shall discover that God did turn them around? That we shall see them among the redeemed in heaven? And so with many other wayward children for whom anguished parents lift up holy hands!

St. Paul reminds us about God's special attribute of faithfulness in his second letter to Timothy. "If we are faithless, he remains faithful—for he cannot deny himself" (2 Timothy 2:13).

Taking It Further

1. Do you agree with the reason given above for the difference in the way God dealt with Eli and with Samuel? Do you think this is still valid for today?

2. What do you think were the causes of child abuse within the Church and why do you think it went on for so long before anything was done about it?

3. What sacrifices do parents have to make in Christian ministry in your experience, and what effect do these have on their children?

4. What special pressures do the children of Christian leaders experience and how can they best be helped through them?

5. What are the pros and cons of the unrelenting emphasis on children's rights? Do you feel that some actions of governments make godly parenting more difficult? If so, what can be done about them?

6. Are children from Christian homes sometimes overly sheltered and therefore ill-equipped for real life? If so, how can this best be remedied?

KING DAVID AND HIS LUSTFUL CLAN

The Danger of Success

David's first marriage came about in an unusual way. His royal bride was given to him by King Saul as his reward for killing Goliath, the giant, enemy champion who was defying the armies of Israel. His popularity with all the people resulted in pathological hatred from his father-in-law who made several attempts on his life. He had to flee into the wilds at the head of a band of nationalists who were offering protection to isolated farmers vulnerable to attacks by Philistine raiders and rival lawless gangs. It was one wife's timely intervention to counter the arrogance of an ungrateful farmer that paved the way for wife number two for David when Abigail's husband suffered a heart attack.

God protected David against his enemies, and he was eventually enthroned after both the King and his heir apparent, Jonathan, died in battle. Then as ruler of the Chosen Race, he basked in the radiance of divine favour. God give him victory after victory in numerous conflicts against surrounding nations.

And then he got too big for his boots. It is as juicy a scandal as has ever emanated from any royal court in history.

Here is a blow-by-blow account of how the drama unfolded.

Act 1, Scene 1: Idle Hands

In the spring of the year, the time when kings go out to battle, David sent Joab, and his servants with him, and

all Israel. And they ravaged the Ammonites and besieged
Rabbah. But David remained at Jerusalem.

2 Samuel 11:1

David should have been out there fighting the battles of his
God against the enemies of Israel. That is what was expected
of him as a King. There are some tasks for which delegation of
authority are not appropriate. Here was one of them. It is not
as if there was some urgent matter of state to detain the king in
Jerusalem. He was simply taking an ill-advised holiday.

"An idle head is the devil's workshop, and idle hands are his
tools." If we choose to busy ourselves doing our own will and
serving our own purposes when we should be serving God, we
could readily find that we are actually lending ourselves for use
by the devil of Hell.

> It happened, late one afternoon, when David arose from
> his couch and was walking on the roof of the king's house,
> that he saw from the roof a woman bathing; and the
> woman was very beautiful. And David sent and inquired
> about the woman. And one said, "Is not this Bathsheba,
> the daughter of Eliam, the wife of Uriah the Hittite?" So
> David sent messengers and took her, and she came to him,
> and he lay with her. (Now she had been purifying herself
> from her uncleanness.) Then she returned to her house.
> And the woman conceived, and she sent and told David,
> "I am pregnant."
>
> 2 Samuel 11: 2-5

David did not climb unto that roof to look for trouble, but
trouble was lying in wait for him in the shapely figure of a woman
in her bath. What was wrong with Bathsheba taking her bath in
the privacy of the courtyard of her married home?

It is necessary for us to understand the setting. Bathrooms
were an outhouse with four walls but without a roof. A roof was
not needed since all the neighbours were at ground level and

there was no danger of inadvertent exposure. This particular house happened to be in the vicinity of the king's palace, and, not surprisingly, the king's house was taller than everybody else's. It also had a roof on which the king could relax in the cool of the evening. This is exactly what he was doing when he happened to see a woman bathing at the back of her home.

Pure and simple, it was an accident of time and place. No harm done. No apologies needed, even. It happens all the time—an overly suggestive billboard, a nude image in an innocent magazine, an unsolicited page arriving as spam on the Internet. "The difference between looking and lusting is about six seconds."[118] The immediate reaction of a true gentleman is to look away and to switch off, but this king was not a gentleman. Not now, at any rate. He looked and kept on looking, and he re-adjusted the focus. And he discovered that this was a woman well worth the look. Her beauty entered into his heart, and he wanted to see more and know more. It turned out that she was a married woman. Well, that was that.

No, not for King David.

He had been sexually aroused by the incident and had to do something about it. Fortunately, he had a choice of two wives at his beck and call. But there was also a third option—an option clearly forbidden by the seventh commandment of the Law of his God. This was the path chosen by the most illustrious king of Israel, the same man who excelled so brilliantly in fulfilling his special mission from God.

> He chose David his servant and took him from the sheep-folds; from following the nursing ewes he brought him to shepherd Jacob his people, Israel his inheritance. With upright heart he shepherded them and guided them with his skillful hand.
>
> Psalms 78:70-72

"If your neighbour's beard is on fire, you douse your own with water." If such an illustrious man could be inflamed with lust to such an extent, the likes of you and I should take every precaution in the Book to reduce our vulnerability!

Question for Reflection

There has always been sexual sin in the world, but why do we seem to be more obsessed with sex than our forebears? Would you say that easy access to birth control and abortion has made our generation more promiscuous? If so, what can be done to effect a change?

Act 1, Scene 2: Digging Deeper

Adultery might be generally accepted in society, and no one would stand up to condemn a king for taking another man's wife, but when it turns out to be the wife of a soldier on active service in his army, even a king has to draw the line. No, not this king.

The wise man in the book of Proverbs paints a frightening picture of a husband's revenge:

> Can a man carry fire next to his chest and his clothes not be burned? Or can one walk on hot coals and his feet not be scorched? So is he who goes in to his neighbor's wife; none who touches her will go unpunished... He who commits adultery lacks sense; he who does it destroys himself. He will get wounds and dishonor, and his disgrace will not be wiped away. For jealousy makes a man furious, and he will not spare when he takes revenge. He will accept no compensation; he will refuse though you multiply gifts.
>
> Proverbs 6:27-9; 32-35

Untouchable in his exalted office, a ruler, of course, can safely exclude himself from that level of common justice. Or can he?

It was on 21 January, 1998, when the Washington Post broke the news that the president of the United States was having an affair. Bill Clinton was turning a twenty-two-year-old White House intern into a mistress in training. Unlike the kings of Israel, presidents in a modern Western democracy can be called to account, and the press corps latched on to the story like a divorce lawyer to an angry spouse. President Clinton was obliged to respond. Standing demurely by his side was Hillary, the wife he had married the year before the young intern was born, as he looked through the lens of the camera into the eyes of watching millions around the world and made the bold-faced denial, "I did not have sexual relations with that woman, Miss Lewinsky." But he did, and he had not seen off his tormentors.

King David had his way with the woman, and that was that. Except that that was not that—for the woman became pregnant. Alas, Bathsheba was not on the Pill before the act, and RU-486, "the Morning After" remedy, was not yet an option.

Abortion was clearly a possibility. But, thankfully, abortion was not a standard procedure considered to be the "right" of a woman in that generation. Nobody had yet thought of the "Pro-choice" agenda. In any case, that solution did not appeal to his degenerate majesty.

What to do?

> So David sent word to Joab, "Send me Uriah the Hittite." And Joab sent Uriah to David. When Uriah came to him, David asked how Joab was doing and how the people were doing and how the war was going. Then David said to Uriah, "Go down to your house and wash your feet." And Uriah went out of the king's house, and there followed him a present from the king. But Uriah slept at the door of the king's house with all the servants of his lord, and did not go down to his house. When they told David, "Uriah did not go down to his house," David said to Uriah, "Have you not come from a journey? Why did you not go down to your house?"
>
> 2 Samuel 11:6-10

How flattering it must be for a lowly officer to be invited from the battlefield for consultation with the commander-in-chief! One or two nights in the comfort of his home and under the sheets with his wife, and it does not matter what questions are whispered when the baby arrives nine months later, resembling the man next door and not its father.

Even the cleverest plans do not always work. This one did not. Unlike the King's, this soldier's devotion to duty was such that he would not take his holiday in the middle of a military campaign.

> Uriah said to David, "The ark and Israel and Judah dwell in booths, and my lord Joab and the servants of my lord are camping in the open field. Shall I then go to my house, to eat and to drink and to lie with my wife? As you live, and as your soul lives, I will not do this thing."
>
> 2 Samuel 11:11

Not even the consumption of alcohol at the devious insistence of the wily king could break down his resolve. Or was it that he was too drunk to find the way to his home?

King David was a very clever man. It did not take him long to figure out another way to cover up his misdeed. As Richard Nixon was to discover with Watergate, to cover a little lie requires a bigger lie. That American president was not the first powerful ruler who failed to understand the very first lesson about holes: "When you are already in one, stop digging!" Something considerably bigger was now required to pull off the king's cover up.

> In the morning David wrote a letter to Joab and sent it by the hand of Uriah. In the letter he wrote, "Set Uriah in the forefront of the hardest fighting, and then draw back from him, that he may be struck down, and die."
>
> 2 Samuel 11:14-15

The field commander obeyed the order of the commander-in-chief, and Uriah was killed in action; without doubt, he must have been buried with full military honours. His widow was free to remarry, and she married the king. End of story.

Well, not quite, for there is a God in heaven. He rules over the affairs of men and calls even mighty kings to account.

Question for Reflection

Have you ever had the experience of covering up some serious error? What did the experience do for you in the short term and in the long term?

Act 1, Scene 3: The Day of Reckoning...and Repentance

In his own case, President Clinton was brought to trial by the Legislature as required by law. He was impeached by the House of Representatives but acquitted by the Senate on all charges—allegations of perjury and obstruction of justice regarding the affair and lying under oath in a civil lawsuit. The Senate vote fell short of the two-thirds majority required for conviction and removal from office under the Constitution. Polls of the American electorate taken at this time showed that up to seventy percent were against pursuing the allegations.

President Clinton eventually made some sort of public confession. After having had the truth dragged out of him by a federal grand jury, he finally came clean in a television address to the nation.

> I know that my public comments and my silence about this matter gave a false impression. I misled people, including even my wife. I deeply regret that. ... Indeed, I did have a relationship with Ms. Lewinsky that was not appropriate. In fact, it was wrong. It constituted a critical lapse in judgment and a personal failure on my part for which I am solely and completely responsible...[119]

By means of a parable, the prophet Nathan got the king to pass judgment on his own loathsome act. Then God pronounced His divine sentence, assuring King David he would get his just deserts.

> Thus says the LORD, "Behold, I will raise up evil against you out of your own house. And I will take your wives before your eyes and give them to your neighbor, and he shall lie with your wives in the sight of this sun. For you did it secretly, but I will do this thing before all Israel and before the sun."
>
> 2 Samuel 12:11-12

It is not for nothing that David is called the man after God's own heart. Caught red-handed, he did not attempt to stonewall, to hide, or to make excuses. He repented without hesitation or reservations and sought forgiveness from the Lord.

He began by making an unequivocal statement owning up to his guilt. "Then David said to Nathan, 'I have sinned against the Lord'" (1 Samuel 12:13a).

And he really, really meant it, as is evidenced by his full confession, recorded for posterity in Psalm 51—a model for all our confessions of sin.

First is the basis of that confession. He could not appeal to anything he had ever done right or done for God. God did not "owe him one." He had no favours to call in. He did not attempt to minimize the gravity of what he had done. This was not a minor indiscretion. When people commit adultery, they say they "have an affair." When Kings commit atrocities, they seek to hide behind some "reason of state." For this chastened king, there was no posturing and no euphemism. He called sin by its proper, ugly names. All he could plead was the mercy of God.

> Have mercy on me, O God, according to your steadfast love; according to your abundant mercy blot out my trans-

gressions. Wash me thoroughly from my iniquity, and cleanse me from my sin! For I know my transgressions, and my sin is ever before me... Deliver me from blood-guiltiness, O God, O God of my salvation, and my tongue will sing aloud of your righteousness.

Psalm 51:1-3, 14

He made one significant error in his confession: "Against you, you only, have I sinned and done what is evil in your sight, so that you may be justified in your words and blameless in your judgment" (verse 4).

All sin is ultimately against God, but some sins are also against our fellow human beings. David was so taken up with a sense of his responsibility to God that he seemed to forget this other important angle. That he sinned against God is beyond question, but just as surely, he also sinned against Uriah and against the woman Bathsheba, too. Even if she was a willing participant, which cannot be discounted, she might not have been so compliant had he not been the monarch. And finally, he sinned against the people who held him in sacred trust as their King.

David's confession continued with a deep theological truth—the doctrine of original sin. This is not to say that he sought to minimize his culpability by blaming his action on what is inborn and inherited as part of our fallen human nature or defective genes. God holds us responsible to live an upright life from the inside out, but this we fail to do. As a result, we are not only sinners by birth but also by choice. He continues:

> Behold, I was brought forth in iniquity, and in sin did my mother conceive me. Behold, you delight in truth in the inward being, and you teach me wisdom in the secret heart.

Verses 5-6

What, then, is the way out?

What follows is an earnest plea for cleansing, that the muck of the past might be totally expunged, giving way to a new beginning. This goes beyond "turning over a new leaf" in that it is not the same filthy scribe who would again write on a new page the dictates of his polluted heart and mind. His life from now on would be the product of a pure heart and a steadfast spirit, the fruit of a renewed creation. His fallible human flesh had failed him. God's holy presence would henceforth prompt him to do what is right, and the Holy Spirit would now strengthen, encourage, ennoble, and enable him. He sought God's cleansing in the verses that follow:

> Purge me with hyssop, and I shall be clean; wash me, and I shall be whiter than snow. Let me hear joy and gladness; let the bones that you have broken rejoice. Hide your face from my sins, and blot out all my iniquities. Create in me a clean heart, O God, and renew a right spirit within me. Cast me not away from your presence, and take not your Holy Spirit from me.
>
> Verses 7-10

This leads to a new-found confidence that turns around the life of the culprit and opens new vistas of service to the God whose laws he had so blatantly spurned. In order to accomplish this, however, he required a special measure of grace, and it is on this theme of grace he concludes the psalm:

> Then I will teach transgressors your ways, and sinners will return to you… O Lord, open my lips, and my mouth will declare your praise. For you will not delight in sacrifice, or I would give it; you will not be pleased with a burnt offering.
>
> Verses 13, 15-16

He fulfils the conditions, and so he can boldly approach the altar of God's mercy with a confident expectation of forgiveness and renewal:

The sacrifices of God are a broken spirit; a broken and contrite heart, O God, you will not despise. Do good to Zion in your good pleasure; build up the walls of Jerusalem; then will you delight in right sacrifices, in burnt offerings and whole burnt offerings; then bulls will be offered on your altar.

Verses 13-19

There would be time enough to spell out those details later. As immediate response to the prophet Nathan, the simple and artless words in the pregnant, heavy whisper to the prophet would have to do: "I have sinned against the Lord" (1 Samuel 12:13a).

The God who searches the heart knew it was all there long before David applied his poetic skill to set it down for us in this celebrated psalm. Not surprisingly, therefore, the prophet did not hesitate to communicate the mind of God to him.

"The LORD also has put away your sin; you shall not die. Nevertheless because by this deed you have utterly scorned the LORD, the child who is born to you shall die."

2 Samuel 12:13b-14

This response to David's confession is a valuable lesson on the effects of sin and the scars it leaves behind. There are several strands to God's forgiveness.

First and foremost, it means that David would not die—death being the first and also the ultimate result of sin. The prophet put it starkly, "Behold, all souls are mine; the soul of the father as well as the soul of the son is mine: the soul who sins shall die" (Ezekiel 18:4).

And Romans 6:23 leaves us in no doubt, "For the wages of sin is death, but the free gift of God is eternal life in Christ Jesus our Lord."

To pay anyone their salary is invariably the correct thing to do. Not to pay it is to fail to do what is right and proper. Any and every sin deserves its wretched pay. But when God forgives a sinner, He pays their shameful wages to their Friend instead.

This Friend dies the death that is due to them. That was the first meaning of God's forgiveness for David and also for all sinners who cry to Him with sincerity from their hearts.

There is something else. He does not only forgive but also cleanses. This is how John puts it in his Epistle: "If we say we have no sin, we deceive ourselves, and the truth is not in us. If we confess our sins, he is faithful and just to forgive us our sins and to cleanse us from all unrighteousness" (1 John 1:8-9).

Take for example the case of a domestic helper I catch stealing from me. There are several interesting ways I can deal with her in order to ensure that it never happens again. But if she expresses her regrets convincingly enough, I could decide to forgive her and continue to keep her in my employ. But it would be uncommonly foolish of me to leave my valuables lying around where she could once again get her thieving hands on them! I have forgiven her, true, but every time I look at her, I see a thief. I have forgiven her, but I have not cleansed her. God goes that one step farther. That is the point that John makes in his letter—God forgives and also purifies us.

St. Paul uses a special word, "justification," to describe something else which God does for the sinner He forgives. He treats them "just as if they had never sinned." He says in his letter to the church in Rome: "Therefore, since we have been justified by faith, we have peace with God through our Lord Jesus Christ" (Romans 5:1).

Thus, God not only forgave King David but also cleansed and justified him. Each time we read his story, we link him not only with his great deeds but also with his great failures and failings. Not God. All those failures and failings no longer exist in His reckoning. That is why he is God's chosen role model for others. "David my servant" is how the Lord fondly refers to him, and more than once others are contrasted with him as such. "His heart was not wholly true to the LORD his God, as the heart of David his father" (1 Kings 15:3).

Question for Reflection

Nathan confronted King David and helped him to admit his guilt. Why do we find it difficult to help our leaders, or even our friends, in a similar way today?

Act 1, Scene 4: Ugly Scars

Unfortunately, while the effects of sin are completely erased in the heavenly realm, the consequences here on earth remain. God forgives a rapist who repents, but the victim remains forever raped. If a man commits adultery and catches a sexually transmitted disease as a result, his repentance does not remove his suffering, and if it is an HIV/AIDS infection, that suffering could mean suffering unto death. If a woman were to become pregnant as a result of rape, God's forgiveness for the rapist does not abort the foetus. The resulting child is a full-fledged human being just like any other.

Through this incident in the life of the man after God's heart, God demonstrates to us the sinfulness of sin and the fact that consequences remain even when sin is forgiven. David confessed, repented, and was forgiven, cleansed, and justified, yet every aspect of the sentence pronounced on him and on his household was fulfilled to the letter.

"I will raise up evil against you out of your own house."

The King's marriage to Bathsheba brought a new element to the succession. Absalom was a prince who was not going to brook competition with her favoured offspring. He sought to pre-empt that possibility by organising a *coup d'état*. "A new oak does not grow under the shade of an older one," and so the old must give way for the new. This indeed was calamitous for the venerated, old soldier who had to flee for dear life. And it was calamity out of his very own house.

But that was not all.

> I will take your wives before your eyes and give them to your neighbor, and he shall lie with your wives in the sight

of this sun. For you did it secretly, but I will do this thing before all Israel and before the sun.

2 Samuel 12:11-12

One could be inclined to suggest that dear old Nathan was being a little melodramatic in giving such free rein to his prophetic imagination. How could such public ignominy possibly befall the consorts of the king—and in broad daylight! Well, here is how it happened.

> Then Absalom said to Ahithophel, "Give your counsel. What shall we do?" Ahithophel said to Absalom, "Go in to your father's concubines, whom he has left to keep the house, and all Israel will hear that you have made yourself a stench to your father, and the hands of all who are with you will be strengthened." So they pitched a tent for Absalom on the roof. And Absalom went in to his father's concubines in the sight of all Israel.

2 Samuel 16:20-22

"A new broom sweeps clean, but the old broom knows the corners." King David had the wherewithal to survive the insurgency. But his sorrows were far from over. Remember what the prophet said? "I will raise up evil against you out of your own house."

This was only the beginning. How about rape and murder within the royal family? In every gruesome detail, we have a tabloid report screaming at us in 2 Samuel 13. Let us take a close look at the sequel, which we could describe as Act 2 to this tragic drama in order to learn its lessons.

Question for Reflection

David was forgiven, but the punishment pronounced on him was fulfilled to the letter. Do you agree with the reason given above or do you have other ideas to explain the facts?

Forbidden Love

Now Absalom, David's son, had a beautiful sister, whose
name was Tamar. And after a time Amnon, David's son,
loved her. And Amnon was so tormented that he made
himself ill because of his sister Tamar, for she was a virgin,
and it seemed impossible to Amnon to do anything to her.
But Amnon had a friend, whose name was Jonadab, the
son of Shimeah, David's brother. And Jonadab was a very
crafty man.

2 Samuel 13:1-3

What is wrong with Amnon falling in love with his half-sister,
Tamar? Nothing, and everything. Nothing, in that it was acceptable practice within the culture. Besides, he was only following the
example of the arch-patriarch of the family of Israel, Abraham,
who had married his half-sister, Sarah. Everything, as this was
now a different era in the history of the people of God with every
aspect of life regulated by the Law given through Moses. And
this was a no-go area as far as that Law was concerned.

If a man takes his sister, a daughter of his father or a
daughter of his mother, and sees her nakedness, and she
sees his nakedness, it is a disgrace, and they shall be cut off
in the sight of the children of their people. He has uncov-
ered his sister's nakedness, and he shall bear his iniquity.

Leviticus 20:17

Still, it began innocently enough as the consequence of a totally
understandable human attraction. After all, a man or a woman is
capable of being attracted by any other man or woman to the
point of falling head over heels in love. It is irrelevant if nobody
else sees how it could possibly happen—it still remains a physical
and emotional possibility. This is the way we are made. Within
every man and woman the image of God is never completely
erased. There could be something of that divine image that only

this man or woman could see, and that factor could overcome all the defects that repel all other human beings. "Beauty is in the eye of the beholder."

Love—true human love—can be blind as the blindest bat that ever lived. We are horrified when a girl claims to fall in love with a man the age of her grandfather. We are sure it cannot be true and reckon that she falls in love only with the money she would inherit at his not-too-distant demise. That may well be true in the majority of cases, but there are instances of genuine love regardless of a huge disparity in age. Or a godly man may fall in love with a married woman. It does not matter that in the eyes of others she may be as undesirable as poison and as ugly as sin.

But Tamar was anything but ugly. Indeed, those alluring physical characteristics that set the offspring of David apart seem to have come together in this stunning, young lady to an exquisite degree. There are only four or five women in Scripture specifically described as 'beautiful,'[120] and Tamar was one of them.

The question is not the physical or emotional fact of "falling in love." The question is what we do with it.

Question for Reflection

Do you agree that it is easily possible to fall sincerely in love with the wrong person? If so, what can help us not to do the wrong things as a result?

The Friend from Hell

Amnon did a very sensible and practical thing. He confided in his friend. That is always to be recommended. "A friend loves at all times, and a brother is born for adversity" (Proverbs 17:17). "Without counsel plans fail, but with many advisers they succeed" (Proverbs 15:22).

The story of the selfless friendship that David shared with Jonathan in his youth was the stuff of legends. When he had an intractable problem with his very life at risk, he knew what to do. He confided in his friend who acted on the basis of truth and honour, even though he had to stand both against his father and against his own princely interests.

In his immensely practical exposition of 2 Corinthians, Jonathan Lamb talks of accountability "through a small prayer triplet where we meet with two other close friends, praying for our shared concerns and being open with each other about our struggles and temptations as well as our hopes and our joys."[121]

As young Christians, we were counselled to develop this sort of friendship among ourselves—prayer partners[122] with whom we share our most intimate concerns. We shared together our joys and our sorrows for praise and prayer, and it was all with the assurance that our story would not be shared "in confidence" with another brother to be shared "in confidence" with yet another! Exclusively, we shared with each other and then with God. We were also committed to encouraging and rebuking and holding each other accountable before the Lord. It was a lesson that has endured the test of time—a lesson we can confidently recommend to younger generations. To have and to be a faithful friend is not enough, for there is need for faithfulness not only to man but also to God.

The trouble was that Jonadab was a child of the devil only too ready to lead his friend astray with the counsel from hell. How important it is to choose our friends with care! No wonder the evangelists warn us again and again not to keep company with the people of this world or even with believers who live in sin. Positively, as the elders observe, "Leaves used to wrap up soap for long enough turn to soap." Negatively, St. Paul gives the warning, "Do not be deceived: 'Bad company ruins good morals'" (1 Corinthians 15:33).

Question for Reflection

What do you think of the concept of friends to whom we are accountable? How can this idea be promoted, especially among the youth in your church?

Resist the Devil

Amnon took the advice of his shrewd friend, and poor Tamar fell into the cunning trap he tended for her.

> So Amnon lay down and pretended to be ill. And when the king came to see him, Amnon said to the king, "Please let my sister Tamar come and make a couple of cakes in my sight, that I may eat from her hand." Then David sent home to Tamar, saying, "Go to your brother Amnon's house and prepare food for him." So Tamar went to her brother Amnon's house, where he was lying down. And she took dough and kneaded it and made cakes in his sight and baked the cakes. And she took the pan and emptied it out before him, but he refused to eat. And Amnon said, "Send out everyone from me." So everyone went out from him. Then Amnon said to Tamar, "Bring the food into the chamber, that I may eat from your hand." And Tamar took the cakes she had made and brought them into the chamber to Amnon her brother. But when she brought them near him to eat, he took hold of her and said to her, 'Come, lie with me, my sister."
>
> 2 Samuel 13:6-11

Hitherto, Tamar had done nothing wrong. It was not her fault that she was beautiful or that everyone in the large family was aware of her "A+ grade" in the cookery class. God gives natural gifts, and every gift is a matter for praise to the Giver. To Him be the glory when we are able to develop a valuable skill. Whatever special gifts God gives to us, and whatever particular skills we develop, however, the enemy would seek to subvert them for his own purposes. The beautiful face we see in the mirror, nimble feet on the soccer pitch, and those dexterous fingers at the piano—all of them should be dedicated to the Giver for use in His service.

It was when she tried to reason with a man who had lost all reason that Tamar made her one mistake. What she had to say was reasonable, but this was neither the time nor the place. Cool logic is but straw for fire to a man consumed with the passion of lust.

God promises not to let us be tempted beyond what we can bear and with each temptation to provide a way of escape. But the old proverb cautions us not to put ourselves in harm's way. "The one who trusts himself to God does not climb the palm tree using ropes made from banana stalk."

Amnon ordered all his attendants out of the room, leaving him alone with Tamar. They could not have been too far away to hear a scream, but she did not scream for help. We have no way of knowing whether such a scream would have had a positive effect or whether Jonadab would have ensured that it did not. What we *do* know, however, is that she should have learned this as part of her upbringing in the Law of Moses. Harsh as it may seem to us, if she had already been betrothed in marriage, she would have merited a sentence of death on the basis of the Law for not screaming out.

> If there is a betrothed virgin, and a man meets her in the city and lies with her, then you shall bring them both out to the gate of that city, and you shall stone them to death with stones, the young woman because she did not cry for help though she was in the city, and the man because he violated his neighbor's wife. So you shall purge the evil from your midst. But if in the open country a man meets a young woman who is betrothed, and the man seizes her and lies with her, then only the man who lay with her shall die. But you shall do nothing to the young woman; she has committed no offense punishable by death. For this case is like that of a man attacking and murdering his neighbor because he met her in the open country, and though the betrothed young woman cried for help there was no one to rescue her.

> Deuteronomy 22:23-27

Tamar was not yet betrothed to any man. The requirement of the Law was different. She should be properly married to her rapist.

> If a man meets a virgin who is not betrothed, and seizes her
> and lies with her, and they are found, then the man who
> lay with her shall give to the father of the young woman
> fifty shekels of silver, and she shall be his wife because he
> has violated her. He may not divorce her all his days.
>
> Deuteronomy 22:28-29

That is little comfort, we would readily agree, but in that day
and age, it would transfer the shame from her to him. And by her
own admission, Tamar was not averse to marrying Amnon. Still,
none of these shift the responsibility from him to her. She was
the victim of a diabolical, pre-meditated, and incestuous assault.

Very Great Hatred

The forbidden fruit, Amnon suddenly discovered, is not as sweet
as it is cranked up to be.

> Then Amnon hated her with very great hatred, so that
> the hatred with which he hated her was greater than the
> love with which he had loved her. And Amnon said to her,
> "Get up! Go!" But she said to him, "No, my brother, for
> this wrong in sending me away is greater than the other
> that you did to me." But he would not listen to her. He
> called the young man who served him and said, "Put this
> woman out of my presence and bolt the door after her."
>
> 2 Samuel 13:15-17

Poor Amnon! All the pent-up passion and all the wistful long-
ing, the hours spent dreaming and scheming, and finally—this?
With his objective attained, of what further worth is the object?
Where is the flush of joy at the conquest when the summit turns
out to be a blind alley with no vista beyond? "A waste of shame"
is how Shakespeare describes it.

> The expense of spirit in a waste of shame Is lust in action …
> Enjoy'd no sooner but despised straight, Past reason hunted,

and no sooner had Past reason hated, as a swallow'd bait...
All this the world well knows; yet none knows well
To shun the heaven that leads men to this hell.[123]

When a boy declares his love, how can a girl really be sure that it does not carry Amnon's brand and cost? One thing we can say for sure is that "true love waits." That love that is not ready to wait until marriage before sex has every chance of turning into passionate hatred.

Not all cases of premarital sex are predicated by Amnon's type of devious premeditation. It could be a case of a young man who is genuinely in love, enjoying the company of the girl he loves. They begin by expressing that love in little, tender ways. For reasons only the Maker can explain, the time comes when he begins to make her uncomfortable with his touch. Perhaps it is because she has the most to lose if things go wrong, but the woman does not usually lose control as quickly as the man. She still has her wits about her, and when the warning signs appear, she can and should call a halt by demonstrating in no uncertain terms that she is not available. If she fails to call a halt, she too increasingly loses control.

One thing leads to another, and if they end up where they did not intend, the boy may not necessarily express himself as wantonly as Amnon did. At minimum, however, he most definitely does not have the same respect for either himself or the girl as he had before. And it is possible for his love to turn to hate as decisively as Amnon's.

As far as Amnon was concerned, it was all Tamar's fault. The foolish girl had somehow been guilty of being there—being there *and* being beautiful—and there was nothing he could do about it. Until now!

In its right place, sex is one of the most wonderful things in all of God's creation. In the wrong place it is one of the most ugly and most destructive.

"When King David heard of all these things, he was very
angry. But Absalom spoke to Amnon neither good nor
bad, for Absalom hated Amnon because he had violated
his sister Tamar."

(2 Samuel 13:21-22).

Amnon satisfied his incestuous lust and ruined his sister's life.
The thing was not done in a corner. King David had every reason
to be furious, having himself been a tool in Amnon's scheme.
There was little he could do to salve Tamar's wounds of body,
mind, and soul, but he could at least punish the culprit, or else he
could compel him to marry her as the Law said he should. King
David did neither.

How aware are we of the Tamars in our churches and communities of women, young and not so young, who have been trauma-
tised and scarred for life by the ugly crime of rape?

Oprah Winfrey, herself a victim of rape in her younger days, has
set up a fund for victim support. She writes on her website, "Rape
is used as a weapon of war to destroy a woman's life all around the
world. In some areas, women who have been raped are seen as unfit
to marry or become outcasts, struggling to survive. See what a difference you can make in the life of a rape survivor."[124]

One important aspect of providing support is to dispel general
public ignorance and explode disingenuous myths that surround
this topic. Angelfire Ministries sees this as a pressing concern.
Carol Martin makes a very helpful list of such myths and provides relevant facts on each.

MYTH: It is impossible for a husband to sexually
assault his wife. Regardless of marital or social relationship, if a woman does not consent to sexual activity, she is being sexually assaulted. In fact, 14 percent of

women are victims of rape committed by their husband.

MYTH: A person who has really been assaulted will be hysterical. Survivors exhibit a spectrum of emotional responses to assault: calm, hysteria, laughter, anger, apathy, shock. Each survivor copes with the trauma of the assault in a different way.

MYTH: Sexual assault is an impulsive act. Seventy-five percent of all assaults are planned in advance. When three or more assailants are involved, 90 percent are planned. If two assailants are involved, 83 percent are planned. With one assailant, 58 percent are planned.

MYTH: Assailants are usually crazed psychopaths who do not know their victims. As many as 80 percent of all assaults involve acquaintances. An assailant might be someone you know intimately. He may be a co-worker, a friend, or a family member.

MYTH: Gang rape is rare. In 43 percent of all reported cases, more than one assailant was involved.

MYTH: Many women claim that they have been sexually assaulted because they want revenge upon the man they accuse. Only four to six percent of sexual assault cases are based on false accusation. This percentage of unsubstantiated cases is the same as with many other reported crimes.

MYTH: Persons who dress or act in a "sexy" way are asking to be sexually assaulted. Many convicted sexual assailants are unable to remember what their victims looked like or were wearing. Nothing a person does or does not do causes a brutal crime like sexual assault.

MYTH: In most cases, black men attack white women. In most sexual assault cases, the assailant and his victim are of the same racial background.

MYTH: All women secretly want to be raped. Women, like all human beings, want a life of dignity and safety. Sexual assault robs a person of dignity and a sense of personal safety. No one wants the physical and emotional pain caused by sexual assault.

MYTH: Only young, pretty women are assaulted. Survivors range in age from infancy to old age, and their appearance is seldom a consideration. Assailants often choose victims who seem most vulnerable to attack: old persons, children, physically or emotionally disabled persons, substance abusers, and street persons. Men are also attacked.

MYTH: It is impossible to sexually assault a man. Men fall victim for the same reasons as women: they are overwhelmed by threats or acts of physical and emotional violence. Also, most sexual assaults that involve an adult male victim are gang assaults.

MYTH: As long as children remember to stay away from strangers, they are in no danger of being assaulted. Sadly, children are usually assaulted by acquaintances—a family member or other caretaking adult. Children are usually coerced into sexual activity by their assailant and are manipulated into silence by the assailant's threats and/or promises, as well as their own feelings of guilt.[125]

We must not forget male victims of this degrading crime. Victim Support, UK, estimates that as many as 5 percent of men have been assaulted by rape at least once in their lives, and they find it no less traumatic and embarrassing than women do. They seem to be stating the obvious, but these are facts which ought to propel us to action.

> Being a victim of any kind of crime can be frightening and upsetting. But rape and sexual assault are particularly distressing crimes for the victim, and the effects can last for a long time. And men can find this kind of attack difficult to deal with because this is widely, but wrongly, thought of as a crime that only affects women.[126]

Question for Reflection

Do you agree with the assessment of Jonadab, Amnon, and Tamar in the story or would you put a different value judgement on the actions of any of them?

God Punishes Sin!

If Amnon could get away with doing this to a royal princess, whose daughter was safe from rape? In the company of his evil genius of a friend, Jonadab, he was free to congratulate himself for getting away with it. There was one important fact they both forgot: God punishes sin. This is a principle factored into the fabric of human existence. God punished sin in Genesis at the beginning; He will punish sin in Revelation at the end, and He punishes sin all the way between. He punishes sin in this world, and He will punish sin in the world to come. This is a fact for every "Amnon" to bear in mind. They always have to reckon with the Judge who is invariably a Witness to their crime.

> Let no one say when he is tempted, "I am being tempted by God," for God cannot be tempted with evil, and he himself tempts no one. But each person is tempted when he is lured and enticed by his own desire. Then desire when it has conceived gives birth to sin, and sin when it is fully grown brings forth death.

James 1:13-15

The first year passed… and then the second. For Amnon, the bitter let-down that accompanied the sexual pleasure he took with his tearful victim was a distant memory. That was when retribution, brewing ominously in Absalom's devious mind, matured and sprang into action. Tamar's father could ignore her trauma of body and spirit. Her brother did not. Was this perhaps the origin of the word of the Wise Man, "A friend loves at all times, and a brother is born for adversity"? (Proverbs 17:17).

Amnon had a friend who, in his own way, loved him in the time of his lustful distress. Tamar had a brother who, in his own way, would do something about her adversity.

Evil continued to stalk the family of King David, and he was once again an unwitting participant in foul intrigue. He gave his royal assent to a seemingly gracious invitation from Absalom for his brothers to come for a feast, only to discover it was merely a ploy to murder Amnon for raping his sister.

"I will raise up evil against you out of your own house" (2 Samuel 12:11).

Here is incentive enough for all who have eyes to see and ears to hear to avoid the first approaches to sin of any description—particularly the sin of sexual immorality. God does provide the way of escape, but we need to do our part and not linger on the threshold of evil. "Pray to God, and row away from the rocks!"

Question for Reflection

"God punishes sin." Compare the ways He does so in the Old Testament, the New Testament, and today.

The Wisest of Them All, and the Richest

The champion of champions in King David's adulterous clan is his son and successor, King Solomon, all the more unfortunate in view of his very promising beginning. Being the son of the wife who was married through the channels of adultery and murder, God's favour on him is a marvellous example of His gracious dealing with repentant sinners and innocent victims of sin.

King David was forgiven, and even though the direct fruit of his adultery died as a baby, this subsequent product of their union was an object of some of the most generous divine favours ever bestowed on man. Even granted that he had no hand in the dalliance of his parents before his birth, why should he be preferred above six older half brothers,[127] products of more normal marriages, to succeed his father as king?

> Ask, ask, ask, and it shall be given you!
> Seek, seek, seek and ye shall find!
> Knock, knock, knock and it shall be opened unto you—
> For your heavenly Father is so kind!
> And He knows what is best for His children,
> In body, soul, and mind.
> So
> Ask, ask, ask!
> Knock, knock, knock!
> Seek, and ye shall find!

So goes a chorus we learned in Sunday School. "God, please make me as beautiful as Princess Diana, as rich as Bill Gates, and as clever as Albert Einstein!" Thankfully, He most emphatically does not, for He knows what is best for His children in body, soul, and mind!

In our personal and family lives, we are often tempted to think that if only we could have enough of this or that our problems would be solved. King Solomon's personal and family life is the proof that this is not the case. Indeed, far from being the solution, those very things could be the problem. According to the elders, "Other creatures deride the scorpion for having no head. His retort was that it is because they have heads that they have headaches."

Take the story of a Kentucky couple who won a lottery jackpot of thirty-four million dollars in 2000. They bought the usual fancy cars and mansions and entered into a life of luxury while they rapidly lost everything that really mattered along the way—then they divorced. It was not long afterward that he died of alcohol-related illness. She too died soon afterward—all alone in her new house. It all happened a mere five years after they cashed the winning ticket![128]

Of course, we are sure we could not possibly be as stupid as these misguided specimens of wretched humanity. But what is the guarantee? Even if, along with all that money, we also had the knowledge, the intelligence, and the wisdom, of Solomon? King Solomon was the one man who had it all, literally, and yet he could only truthfully declare at the end, "Vanity of vanities, says the Preacher, vanity of vanities! All is vanity" (Ecclesiastes 1:2).

His ultimate prayer was,

> Give me neither poverty nor riches; feed me with the food that is needful for me, lest I be full and deny you and say, "Who is the LORD?" or lest I be poor and steal and profane the name of my God.
>
> Proverbs 30:8-9

This is King Solomon writing in mature, old age to instruct all who will listen, and he was writing from sober experience. He began his kingly reign by committing himself to doing the will of God, who in turn appreciated his request for "an understanding mind to govern your people, that I may discern between good and evil" (1 Kings 3:9). In a manner typical of His awesome generosity, "God gave Solomon wisdom and understanding beyond measure, and breadth of mind like the sand on the seashore" (1 Kings 4:29).

A Renaissance man two and a half thousand years ahead of his time, Solomon learned all there was to be learned on every subject under the sun, and people sought out his wisdom from near and far. He was also a judge with uncanny insight into human psychology, a visionary military strategist, a wise investor, an astute businessman, and an enthusiastic builder of great structures. The temple that he took thirteen years to build was a tourist attraction. The work of the world's most accomplished artisans in masonry and wood and precious metals, it imposed its breath-taking splendour on Jerusalem's skyline. It was only one of many such edifices erected by this multitalented monarch. There were also magnificent palaces for him and his wife, and he built new cities and defensive strongholds all over the land.

In addition to all these, through his investment in the import-export business, through custom and excise duties paid by the business community, and through tributes from subject peoples, King Solomon made the country rich.

Question for Reflection

When you look at all what gave to Solomon, what are those things in particular for which you praise the Lord when you count your own blessings?

The Height of Folly

However wise he may have been in all these and other domains—and God declares him to be the all-time champion—King Solomon did not make a success of his family life because he was extremely foolish when it comes to the matter of sex.

God's instructions as to the dos and don'ts of kingship were ever so clear in the Law, and no king could plead ignorance for two reasons. First was that the Law was taught to him from childhood as to any other child in the land. Second was that he should have a copy made for himself on accession to the throne and then consult it unfailingly and incessantly.

Only he must not acquire many horses for himself or cause the people to return to Egypt in order to acquire many horses, since the LORD has said to you, "You shall never return that way again." And he shall not acquire many wives for himself, lest his heart turn away, nor shall he acquire for himself excessive silver and gold. And when he sits on the throne of his kingdom, he shall write for himself in a book a copy of this law, approved by the Levitical priests. And it shall be with him, and he shall read in it all the days of his life, that he may learn to fear the LORD his God by keeping all the words of this law and these statutes, and doing them.

Deuteronomy 17:16-19

Instructions against returning to Egypt were clear enough, but Egypt was precisely where King Solomon began his indiscriminate adventure with women by making a marriage alliance with Pharaoh. It can be argued that marrying an Egyptian wife was not expressly forbidden, and a marriage alliance was a commonly acceptable "reason of state" in that time and place. If only King Solomon had chosen to limit himself to this questionable alliance, the course of history might have been different—but he did not.

Now King Solomon loved many foreign women, along with the daughter of Pharaoh: Moabite, Ammonite, Edomite, Sidonian, and Hittite women, from the nations concerning which the LORD had said to the people of Israel, "You shall not enter into marriage with them, neither shall they with you, for surely they will turn away your heart after their gods." Solomon clung to these in love. He had 700 wives, princesses, and 300 concubines. And his wives turned away his heart. For when Solomon was old his wives turned away his heart after other gods, and his heart was not wholly true to the LORD his God, as was the heart of David his father. For Solomon went after Ashtoreth the goddess of the Sidonians, and after Milcom the abomination of the Ammonites. So Solomon did what was evil in the sight of the LORD and did not wholly follow the LORD, as David his father had done. Then Solomon built a high place for Chemosh the abomination of Moab, and for Molech the abomination of the Ammonites, on the mountain east of Jerusalem. And so he did for all his foreign wives, who made offerings and sacrificed to their gods.

1 Kings 11:1-8

No reason in the world, and certainly no reason of state, can provide satisfactory explanation for such excess by any sexual athlete. A Yoruba saying takes note that "the fact that he finds it affordable does not make the wealthy man increase the salt in his food." Why on earth does a man want a different woman for every day in the calendar year and more?

One option God chose to forgo was to provide more than one wife for Adam. Starting from Lamech, there has been no shortage of men who believe the all-wise Creator got that one wrong. This Lamech was a bad example in more ways than one. The sum total of his life history, in fact, amounted to a legacy of polygamy, vengeance, and murder:

Lamech said to his wives: "Adah and Zillah, hear my voice; you wives of Lamech, listen to what I say: I have killed a man for wounding me, a young man for striking me.

Genesis 4:23

We can cite other characters, otherwise outstanding in many respects, who followed Lamech's foolish example. King Solomon's own father, David, was a great man who fell flat on his face at this hurdle. The consequences for him hardly recommend the practice, as Solomon knew only too well. There was no love lost between the children of rival wives of his father, and just as the Law had warned, for all his wisdom, the many wives of Solomon turned his heart away from God.

Even though there is not a single instance where polygamy is mentioned with any hint of approval, its unfortunate lessons continue to be lost on future generations among the people of God, and the practice evidently survived in the early church. This is the only valid reason we can give for Paul insisting, as concerns the leadership of the church, that polygamists were to be excluded, in his letter to Timothy and also to Titus. "Let deacons each be the husband of one wife, managing their children and their own households well" (1 Timothy 3:12).

People offer many reasons for polygamy, but we can be sure that our good and gracious God considered all of the options before setting up what He knows to be best for us: one husband, one wife.

King Solomon ignored the Law of God with perverse resolve. But God's laws are not suggestions. They are not some good ideas to consider before we make our own decisions. They are there to be obeyed. No one can break them with impunity. And so King Solomon's sins were judged like everyone else's, and the kingdom was torn apart at the end of his reign. Not being wise enough to obey God's Law in the matter, not even *he* was wise enough to prevent the consequences.

The law in most Western countries forbids polygamy, but no law can stop men and women from behaving badly. If men may not marry two or more wives, then they go for mistresses, King Solomon had three hundred of them in addition to his seven hundred wives.

But it is simultaneous polygamy the law forbids—not serial polygamy. If it is forbidden to have two or more wives or husbands at the same time, how about having them one after another? Consequently, men and women are free to divorce and then re-marry legally and to do so as often as they have the inclination and the means! Hence, the celebrated actress Elizabeth Taylor had eight marriages to seven spouses (re-marrying one of those from whom she was earlier divorced), and so far Larry King, the iconic talk host of "Larry King Live" on CNN, has equalled the record exactly. They are far from being the only products of our culture of multiple divorce and remarriage.

Such unbridled adultery as Solomon's is sure to take its physical and emotional toll on anyone. Having dissipated the strength of his youth in sexual delinquency, King Solomon eventually provides us with this heart-felt warning from bitter experience:

> Let your fountain be blessed, and rejoice in the wife of your youth, a lovely deer, a graceful doe. Let her breasts fill you at all times with delight; be intoxicated always in her love. Why should you be intoxicated, my son, with a forbidden woman and embrace the bosom of an adulteress?
>
> Proverbs 5:18- 20

As the proverb puts it, "The damage which the insensate does to himself is worse than the harm he does to others." When we go astray, the thought of this self-inflicted injury is a particular cause of grief to those who love and care for us, and no one loves or cares for us more than our heavenly Father—God. But, mercifully, we can once again revert to the theme of Grace. As King Solomon's father wrote,

> The LORD is merciful and gracious, slow to anger and abounding in steadfast love. He will not always chide, nor will he keep his anger forever. He does not deal with us according to our sins, nor repay us according to our iniquities.
>
> Psalm 103:8-10

The proof of Solomon's repentance in old age is preserved in the records for us—notably in the book of Ecclesiastes. God is still able and willing to forgive and to restore those who stray from His plan in this as in other ways—if only they would turn back to Him from the path of sin.

Taking It Further

1. What should the church be doing to equip our young people to face the challenges of their generation concerning sexual purity? What can we do especially to prevent our Christian girls from becoming easy prey to men with dishonourable intentions?

2. David repented, and yet not only was *he* punished, but many people suffered along with him. What does this tell us about God's view of leaders, and how should it influence our attitudes to them?

3. How can your church be proactive in helping the "Tamars" among its members?

4. Read Psalm 51 through, slowly. How do you feel at the beginning, in the middle, and at the end of the exercise?

5. Paul did not seek to put an end to polygamy in the early church but only that it should not be found among the leadership. Why do you think this was so?

HOSEA: THE PROSTITUTE'S HUSBAND

Submit to One Another!

When we looked at the story of Abraham we went into great detail about a wife's responsibility to submit to her husband. The story of Hosea gives us an opportunity to take a close look at what is required of the husband.

St. Paul once dropped a bombshell on the church at Ephesus. Specifically addressing the relationship between husband and wife, he wrote to them, "Submit to one another out of reverence for Christ" (Ephesians 5:21).

If those words were meant for an all male or an all female audience, nobody would bat an eyelid. But to direct it to men and women together, especially in particular to husbands and wives in that period of history, was explosive stuff!

A concept of a husband submitting to his wife in any shape or form does not come naturally to any man anywhere—at any time. Only the Spirit of God can make it happen, and what Paul says about husband and wife submitting to one another is in the context of His work. In his contribution to the New International Version Study Bible, Walter L. Liefeld, Professor Emeritus of New Testament at Trinity Evangelical Divinity School in Deerfield, Illinois, makes the point that this mutual submission is associated with the infilling of the Holy Spirit. He writes, "The command 'be filled' in v.18 is followed by a series of participles in the Greek: speaking (v.19), singing, (v.19) making music, (v.20) and submitting, (v.21)."[129]

It is not enough to say that it does not come naturally. The idea of mutual submission was preposterous in a culture that treated women as chattels. But Paul was dealing in revolutionary concepts. Keen to ensure that he was not misunderstood or misrepresented, he went on to clarify the implications of his words first for the wife and then for the husband. He pulled no punches:

> Husbands, love your wives, as Christ loved the church and gave himself up for her, that he might sanctify her, having cleansed her by the washing of water with the word, so that he might present the church to himself in splendor, without spot or wrinkle or any such thing, that she might be holy and without blemish. In the same way husbands should love their wives as their own bodies. He who loves his wife loves himself. For no one ever hated his own flesh, but nourishes and cherishes it, just as Christ does the church because we are members of his body. "Therefore a man shall leave his father and mother and hold fast to his wife, and the two shall become one flesh."
>
> Ephesians 5:25-31

He said that husbands should love their wives. That too was new. What exactly does it mean to love your wife? Where was the example to follow? Jesus Christ was the model he laid before his readers. Husbands were to love their wives as Christ loved the church, and gave Himself up for her. That immediately tells us many things about the nature, the quality, and the extent of the love he had in mind.

Most definitely, Christ does not love the church because the church does anything to deserve His love. Here is how it is put in Paul's letter to the Romans:

"For one will scarcely die for a righteous person—though perhaps for a good person one would dare even to die— but God shows his love for us in that while we were still sinners, Christ died for us" (Romans 5:7-8).

Or again as he says in his letter to Titus:

For we ourselves were once foolish, disobedient, led astray, slaves to various passions and pleasures, passing our days in malice and envy, hated by others and hating one another. But when the goodness and loving kindness of God our Savior appeared, he saved us, not because of works done by us in righteousness, but according to his own mercy, by the washing of regeneration and renewal of the Holy Spirit, whom he poured out on us richly through Jesus Christ our Saviour, so that being justified by his grace we might become heirs according to the hope of eternal life.

Titus 3:3-7

In an inexplicable divine fiat, the God of grace looks at people who are altogether undeserving, and He lavishes His love upon them in an extraordinarily bountiful manner. But they requite Him with disdain. This is a phenomenon illustrated time and again in Old Testament history. It was the message painstakingly elaborated in chapter sixteen of the book of Ezekiel. God betroths Israel, the naked and orphaned teenager, and washes her and dresses her in the finest of robes. Israel's response was the epitome of criminal ingratitude.

I clothed you also with embroidered cloth and shod you with fine leather. I wrapped you in fine linen and covered you with silk. And I adorned you with ornaments and put bracelets on your wrists and a chain on your neck. And I put a ring on your nose and earrings in your ears and a beautiful crown on your head. Thus you were adorned with gold and silver, and your clothing was of fine linen and silk and embroidered cloth. You ate fine flour and honey and oil. You grew exceedingly beautiful and advanced to royalty. And your renown went forth among the nations because of your beauty, for it was perfect through the splendor that I had bestowed on you, declares the Lord GOD. But you trusted in your beauty and played the whore because of your renown and lavished your whorings on any passerby; your beauty became his. You took some of your garments and made for yourself colorful shrines, and on them played the whore. The like has never been, nor ever shall be.

Ezekiel 16:10-16

It is the incredible story of love bestowed on an undeserving people. God likened them to a bride richly endowed by a loving spouse, but her response was one of flagrant betrayal. The gifts with which her husband lovingly adorned her were what she used to market herself in prostitution to strangers! The fullest illustration of this phenomenon is the acted parable which is the tragic, real life story of the prophet Hosea.

Question for Reflection

Do you agree with the statement that to submit to a wife "does not come naturally to any man anywhere"? What is the reason for your answer?

Naked and Unashamed

An arranged marriage was not unusual in Hosea's culture— and what higher privilege than that God Himself should do the arranging?

Those who trust Him to choose a spouse for them had better take warning—He sometimes goes out of His way to be unconventional. And the more confidence He has in you the more unconventional He might get!

God evidently knew that Hosea had the quality to pull this one off, because His choice for the prophet was none other than a common prostitute. It brings a new twist to the concept of a marriage made in heaven, but what better way to illustrate God's sufferance with the nation's unfaithfulness and His unrelenting, unrequited love?

When the LORD first spoke through Hosea, the LORD said to Hosea, 'Go, take to yourself a wife of whoredom and have children of whoredom, for the land commits great whoredom by forsaking the LORD.

Hosea 1:2

Love, we are told, is blind, and there are good reasons for the wise saying. The marriage bond, however, is a voluntary accord to be contracted with more than both eyes open. It calls for the involvement of something beyond the critical faculties of two people already blinded by passion. It is only sensible to employ the counsel of family and friends who still have their wits about them. For, once sealed, this contract has room for no third party, and it is meant to be binding until death but *without* taking on the characteristics of a noose!

Hosea, evidently, knew what he was doing. Having heard the word from the Lord, he searched out and married Gomer, lifting her out of a life of shame to the level of high honour as the spouse of a prophet of the God of Israel. She now had a legal framework in which to be naked and unashamed. And she became the envy of all who had despised her before. Even her former clients now had to show some deference, according her the respect the status of her husband commanded. "Therefore a man shall leave his father and his mother and hold fast to his wife, and they shall become one flesh" (Genesis 2:24).

"One flesh!" That is what Hosea chose to become with Gomer. Not only in body but in all other areas of their lives the husband and wife, being one, have nothing to hide from each other—or do they? If all the truth were known, there is some cause for shame somewhere in the life of most of us, issues we wish we could hide in the deepest recesses of our guilty, remorseful, or simply embarrassed consciences. God's purpose in marriage is that the couple be wholly transparent in full acknowledgement of their fallen human conditions.

It took surgical intervention to sever us from the umbilical cord that had linked us physically with mother in the womb. That was the source of life and nourishment until an independent existence began at birth. That independence lasts until marriage when we are again joined to another person—this time by a bond much stronger than the umbilical cord. St. Paul spells out one of the implications when he indicates that, at marriage, the body of each partner comes under joint management, "For the wife does not have authority over her own body, but the husband does. Likewise the husband does not have authority over his own body, but the wife does" (1 Corinthians 7:4).

The "one man, one wife" arrangement is God's chosen context for the most intimate possible physical interaction between human beings—the sexual pleasure that should be freely and fully shared by husband and wife. Indeed, St. Paul warns against unwarranted restraint on the matrimonial bed:

> Do not deprive one another, except perhaps by agreement for a limited time, that you may devote yourselves to prayer; but then come together again, so that Satan may not tempt you because of your lack of self-control.
>
> 1 Corinthians 7:5

So Gomer did not deserve the love of a husband in the first place, but God gave her one—and what a husband! What is more, she had first one child and then another and yet a third. She could now settle down to enjoy life to the full, bringing up her sons and daughter to eschew the errors of her younger days.

But how did the ex-prostitute requite this love so graciously lavished on her?

Gomer went to extravagant extremes to spurn and to forfeit this amazing grace and favour. She did not merely commit adultery in the discreet way common to adulterers. She went into flagrant prostitution. This was not because she had some human need that drove her into undesirable alleyways nor because some devious pimp lured or coerced her into a life of sin. It was entirely of her free volition.

Old habits die hard, and like the proverbial dog returning to its vomit, Gomer abandoned her husband and family and went right back into the street corners to hunt for clients. Attired in the fineries her husband lovingly provided, she took up where she had left off and recommended renting her body to strangers.

Her husband and even her children pleaded with her to no avail. Gomer had to learn her lesson all over again—and learn it the hard way.

It did not take her too long to discover that she was no longer in the bloom of her youth and was now unable to attain to the fees she once commanded. Business was bad—very bad. In fact, she went into debt, and her debts mounted. Pursued by her creditors, this prodigal housewife did not have the sense to retrace her steps and return to the arms of her longsuffering husband. She blundered on, wasting her opportunity and her life until she ended up under the auctioneer's hammer in the slave market.

Question for Reflection

Describe your likely reaction if faced with the sort of response from someone you love as described in Ezekiel 16 above.

"I Hate Divorce"

Sometimes, for whatever good or bad reason, a Christian spouse comes to the conclusion that they made a mistake in marrying their particular wife or husband. They could indeed be right. Sincere Christians can and do make wrong decisions, and this area of life is no exception. Mercifully, the good Lord can, and very often does, prevent us from making wrong choices, but in His unsearchable wisdom, He does not always exercise that option. When we become convinced of such a terrible error, the question is what to do about it. Surely, on realising we have taken a wrong turning, the right thing to do is to retrace our steps; is it not? Not always, and certainly not where marriage is concerned. Two wrongs do not make a right. Divorce would constitute a second and even more serious mistake.

Until recently, a driver in a strange city would find their way around by taking a street map with them. Now we install a

Satellite Navigation system in the car to do all the work for us. It tells us where to turn right or left or go straight ahead. Sometimes we fail to do as it says, and it advises us to turn around. But we do not *have* to. In that case, it then re-calculates our position and plots an alternative route to take us to the desired destination.

Bearing in mind the difference that SatNavs are fallible while He is not, God's guidance in the marriage situation operates something like that. When we seek to honour Him in the context of that marriage to the supposedly wrong spouse, His grace "re-plots" our position and re-directs our lives within that marriage still to arrive at the destination of His purpose for our lives.

In Hosea's case, an honourable divorce would more than satisfy the demands of God's justice, not only according to the tenets of Old Testament religion in which she lived but also of the New Testament in which we live. But Jesus Christ does not deal with His Church on the basis of justice. He does not give us what we truly deserve, just as Hosea did not give to Gomer what she truly deserved. Israel as God's people in the Old Testament did everything to cause Him to abandon them many times over, and we His church in the New Testament era are exactly the same. But God held on to them tenaciously, and, in spite of ourselves, He loves us just the same. For Him, divorce was not and is not an option. This is the basis of His message to us today, "Husbands, love your wives as Christ loved the church…"

The Pharisees rendered us a good service once when they set a trap for Jesus. They posed a leading question based on Scripture: "Is it lawful to divorce one's wife for any cause?" (Matthew 19:3).

It gave the Teacher an opportunity to set the record straight.

To begin with, they had quoted the Scripture inaccurately, as is often the practice with people nursing unwholesome intentions. Moses did not allow divorce "for any cause." Here is what the relevant passage says:

> When a man takes a wife and marries her, if then she finds
> no favour in his eyes because he has found some indecency
> in her, and he writes her a certificate of divorce and puts it
> in her hand and sends her out of his house ....
>
> Deuteronomy 24:1

Thus, the Law refers to a woman who becomes displeasing to her husband not for just any cause whatever, but only because he finds "some indecency" in her.

In His response, Jesus first explains that marriage is a Creation ordinance, and for life.

> He answered, "Have you not read that he who created
> them from the beginning made them male and female,
> and said, 'Therefore a man shall leave his father and his
> mother and hold fast to his wife, and the two shall become
> one flesh'? So they are no longer two but one flesh. What
> therefore God has joined together, let not man separate."
>
> Matthew 19:4-6

He then clarifies that particular indecency to which Moses referred, making it clear that it is unfaithfulness to the marriage bed.

> They said to him, "Why then did Moses command one
> to give a certificate of divorce and to send her away?" He
> said to them, "Because of your hardness of heart Moses
> allowed you to divorce your wives, but from the beginning
> it was not so. And I say to you: whoever divorces his wife,
> except for sexual immorality, and marries another, com-
> mits adultery."
>
> Matthew 19: 7-9

As far as Jesus is concerned, therefore, the married couple should remain faithful to each other, and it is only for them and for them alone that the sexual act does not bring shame or guilt. Failure here and here alone constitutes the indecency that provides grounds for rupture in the union but only as a concession—not as a given.

Don Durham makes several interesting points in his book with the thought-provoking title *Happily Ever After (and Other Myths About Divorce)*.

> Unfortunately, many people have moved beyond the idea of adultery as a problem so serious as to prompt divine permission to divorce to the assumption that divorce is virtually required when a partner is unfaithful.[130]

Sometimes the law of the land stipulates a mandatory sentence for a particular crime. For instance, a life sentence may be required for someone found guilty of murder. In such a case the judge cannot use his discretion to give any other sentence but what is prescribed. We sometimes behave as if Jesus Christ stipulates divorce as mandatory whenever a spouse commits adultery. He did not!

There is yet another issue at stake here. *Divorce and Remarriage in the Church* is a book written by David Instone-Brewer, Senior Research Fellow in Rabbinics and the New Testament at Tyndale House, Cambridge. Painstakingly researched from rabbinic sources, it has an interesting and very helpful perspective on the Old Testament background to Christ's teaching on divorce and remarriage. It is best to use his own summary, as presented in an article for Christianity Today, October 2007. First, focusing particularly on the concept of "any cause," he comments on the question the Pharisees asked in Matthew 19:3, "Is it lawful for a man to divorce his wife for any cause?" he wrote:

> The "any cause" divorce was invented from a single word in Deuteronomy 24:1. Moses allowed divorce for "a cause of immorality," or, more literally, "a thing of nakedness." Most Jews recognised that this unusual phrase was talking about adultery. But the Hillelite rabbis wondered why Moses had added the word "thing" or "cause" when he only

needed to use the word "immorality." They decided this extra word implied another ground for divorce—divorce for "a cause." They argued that anything, including a burnt meal or wrinkles not there when you married your wife, could be a cause! The text, they said, taught that divorce was allowed both for adultery and for "any cause".

Another group of rabbis (the Shammaites) disagreed with this interpretation. They said Moses' words were a single phrase that referred to no type of divorce "except immorality"—and therefore the new "any cause" divorces were invalid. These opposing views were well known to all first-century Jews. And the Pharisees wanted to know where Jesus stood. "Is it lawful to divorce your wife for any cause?" they asked. In other words: "Is it lawful for us to use the "any cause" divorce?" …

Jesus agreed firmly with the second group that the phrase didn't mean divorce was allowable for "immorality" and for "any cause," but that Deuteronomy 24:1 referred to no type of divorce "except immorality." [131]

What the Pharisees were advocating is akin to what is usually described as "no fault divorce" these days in that it brought a swift end to marriages by dispensing with the need to prove any serious wrongdoing. Clearly, this was the exact opposite of what Jesus Christ intended, as He made abundantly clear to the Pharisees and so to us!

There is a passage on the subject in Exodus 21 which is much less well-known: "If he takes another wife to himself, he shall not diminish her food, her clothing, or her marital rights. And if he does not do these three things for her, she shall go out for nothing, without payment of money" (Exodus 21:10-11).

Again based on his scholarly research, Instone-Brewer has a very helpful comment on it, and it deserves to be quoted at length:

Although the church forgot the other cause for divorce, every Jew in Jesus' day knew about Exodus 21:10-11, which allowed divorce for neglect. Before rabbis introduced the "any cause" divorce, this was probably the most common type. Exodus says that everyone, even a slave wife, had three rights within marriage—the rights to food, clothing, and love. If these were neglected, the wronged spouse had the right to seek freedom from that marriage. Even women could, and did, get divorces for neglect—though the man still had to write out the divorce certificate. Rabbis said he had to do it voluntarily, so if he resisted, the courts had him beaten till he volunteered!

These three rights became the basis of Jewish marriage vows—we find them listed in marriage certificates discovered near the Dead Sea. In later Jewish and Christian marriages, the language became more formal, such as "love, honour, and keep." These vows, together with a vow of sexual faithfulness, have always been the basis for marriage…[132]

Gomer flouted all aspects of the Law concerning marriage many times over. She had shown no love for her husband and had certainly not honoured him; she had not fulfilled the duties incumbent on her as a wife, and had been guilty of brazen adultery. She deserved to be cast away with ignominy.

This is where we come to the climax of the fascinating story of Hosea's noble love for Gomer. "Grace" is the only word that describes what he decided to do.

"The threaded needle is not easily lost." The thread of this husband's love remained attached to the wayward wife wherever she strayed. A worthy servant of the God who declared through the prophet Malachi that He hates divorce, Hosea went to the slave market, outbid all comers, paid the full price, and brought his wife back home with him.

And the LORD said to me, "Go again, love a woman who is loved by another man and is an adulteress, even as the LORD loves the children of Israel, though they turn to other gods and love cakes of raisins." So I bought her for

fifteen shekels of silver and a homer and a lethech of bar-
ley. And I said to her, "You must dwell as mine for many
days. You shall not play the whore, or belong to another
man; so will I also be to you."

Hosea 3:1-3

The plaintive invitation to her can be summarised as, "Come
home, my beloved, and sin no more!" It is the same as God's to us.
The "Hound of Heaven" is what Francis Thompson calls the
Lover who pursues the errant, fleeing beloved in his famous poem,

> I fled Him, down the nights and down the days;
> I fled Him, down the arches of the years;
> I fled Him, down the labyrinthine ways
> Of my own mind; and in the midst of tears
> I hid from Him, and under running laughter...
> From those strong Feet that followed, followed after...
> ... with unhurrying chase,
> And unperturbèd pace,
> Deliberate speed, majestic instancy[133]

J.R.R. Tolkien comments helpfully on the poem:

> As the hound follows the hare, never ceasing in its run-
> ning, ever drawing nearer in the chase, with unhurrying
> and imperturbed pace, so does God follow the fleeing soul
> by His Divine grace. And though in sin or in human love,
> away from God it seeks to hide itself, Divine grace follows
> after, unwearyingly follows ever after, till the soul feels its
> pressure forcing it to turn to Him alone in that never end-
> ing pursuit.[134]

This is what the story of Hosea and Gomer reflects as it illus-
trates the love of God for His wayward chosen people, Israel,
and ultimately the love of Jesus Christ for His church. Gomer
portrays the church as surely as she portrayed the nation of Israel.
Alister McGrath has this to say on the subject:

> The Epistles were written to a motley crew of converted angel worshippers, thieves, idolaters, backbiters, and prostitutes—those were the people in whom God took up residence. Read Paul's description of the supposed "ideal church" in a city like Corinth: a raucous, ornery bunch that rivals any church in history for their un-holiness. And yet Paul's most stirring depiction of the church as Christ's body appears in a letter to them…Just as he committed his name to the nation of Israel and had it dragged in the mud, he now commits his Spirit to flawed human beings.[135]

God went one step further than what Hosea did or could do. The price He paid was not reckoned in cash and kind. It was His very life blood.

This, if we dare to believe it, is how God asks husbands to love their wives.

In the first place, it is not tied to the merits of the wife. It has nothing to do with her beauty, her intelligence, her dowry, her hard work in the home, her care for the children, her love for the husband, or anything else she brings or fails to bring into the relationship.

In the second place, it is not reduced or removed by the way she behaves or does not behave in or out of her married home.

And third, it is not restricted, circumscribed, or otherwise limited by anything, whether good or bad, that this life has to offer—not even by the threat of death. Only death itself brings a legitimate end to this commitment.

The traditional marriage vow captures it well enough with the pledge, "…to have and to hold, from this day forward, for better, for worse, for richer, for poorer, in sickness or in health, to love and to cherish 'till death do us part."

That death, if need be, would be the man giving his life for his wife. It is the same apostle who requires godly wives to submit to husbands in all things who lays the godly burden on husbands: "Husbands, love your wives, as Christ loved the church and gave himself up for her."

Taking It Further

1. How do you understand the concept of the bodies of husband and wife coming "under joint management"?

2. Some researchers indicate that Evangelical Christians are no different from the rest of society in their rate of divorce and remarriage.[136] Why do you think this is so, and what should we be doing about it?

3. Christians often place much more emphasis on the wife's responsibility in marriage than the husband's. How can the church help husbands better to fulfil their role?

4. What help does your church offer to couples whose marriage is in trouble?

5. In your experience, who suffers the most in a divorce? What help and support can the church give to divorcees?

JOSEPH AND MARY: BEYOND HUMAN UNDERSTANDING

Teenage pregnancy

The sexual revolution of the '60s opened the floodgates to sexual irresponsibility and the social acceptance of "unwed pregnancies." I once heard of how in England before the Second World War a bank clerk lost his job for making his girlfriend pregnant before the wedding day. Banking is a profession requiring the highest level of personal integrity, and such an act of indiscipline made the young man unfit for the job.

How different from our present world! The sexual act in pre-war England was much more likely to lead to pregnancy since contraceptive devices were not commonly available like today, and abortion was not legally an option.

Turn back the clock two thousand years and consider the plight of Mary in her rural Palestine village.

> Now the birth of Jesus Christ took place in this way. When his mother Mary had been betrothed to Joseph, before they came together she was found to be with child from the Holy Spirit. And her husband Joseph, being a just man and unwilling to put her to shame, resolved to divorce her quietly. But as he considered these things, behold, an angel of the Lord appeared to him in a dream, saying, "Joseph, son of David, do not fear to take Mary as your wife, for that which is conceived in her is from the Holy Spirit.

She will bear a son, and you shall call his name Jesus, for he will save his people from their sins." Matthew 1:18-21

Our sexually permissive world may be tolerant of moral laxity, but thankfully, Christians do not regulate their lives by what the world approves. We expect our young people to follow the teachings of the Bible and keep sex for the marriage bed. But sometimes they fail; then how do we react? Or even before they fail, what help do we give them by way of proper sex education in order to counter the teachings and examples they see all around so as to ensure that they do not fail? Far too often all we give in the church is the negative injunction: "Don't!"

What is even worse, having failed to give to them the preparation and equipping necessary to help them stand, when they fall, we do not provide the encouragement and active assistance required to help them rise up again within the Christian fold but treat them as lost and gone forever. How apt the title of Dwight Carlson's book, *Why Do Christians Shoot Their Wounded?* (IVP 1994)! Thank God for every exception to the rule—may their tribe increase!

Everyone knew everyone else in the rural Judean village, and there was nowhere for Mary to hide. It was not a matter of public disgrace to her only but to her parents too, and sometimes godly parents are more concerned with their own reputation than with the welfare of their children. In any case, even if Mary's parents believed her story of the angel and the vision, how were they going to convince the general public in a censorious traditional community?

Let us call her "Debby." She was the daughter of an African evangelist. When she became pregnant in Secondary School, she tried a "backstreet abortion" without success. Debby then did what she should have done in the first place. She went to her parents and owned up to what she had done. Her father, however, could not handle the shame she had brought to him as a man of

God. His reaction made her realise she had come to the wrong person for help! Decidedly, Debby was not reformed, and she got pregnant a second time. Is it surprising that this time she took care not to go anywhere near her father?

Mary's fiancé, Joseph, was as decent a gentleman as they come. The text spares us any impression of the shock and dismay he must have felt at the discovery that her beloved and trusted Mary was pregnant. Tony Jordan makes a realistic dramatic effort to portray it for us in his 2010 BBC1 TV series, "The Nativity." This is how he dramatises the exchange between the two as it might happen in the modern world:

> "Who is he?"
> "Who?"
> "The father."
> "There isn't one. Not in the way you mean."
> "What?"
> "I haven't betrayed you."
> "For God's sake, you are pregnant. And I know it isn't mine!"
> "This isn't my doing."
> "You were raped?"
> "No!"
> "Then what?"
> "A messenger came to me."
> "What?"
> "From God. The messenger. He told me I would bear a son. That the Holy Spirit…would enter me. And give me a child."
> "This is what you want me to listen to?"
> "It is the truth! And I am still a virgin!"
> "You are saying that a messenger came from God and told you that you would bear a son."
> "Yes!"
> "While you were in Judah?"
> "No, before I left."

"Before you left! But you didn't think to mention it?"
"I tried but I couldn't find the words. I was frightened and confused."
"You are carrying God's son?"
"Yes!"
"Or is the truth that you went to Judah and had a few too many glasses of wine and ended in bed with someone?" [137]

In the ordinary course of life, the honourable thing for Joseph to do was a quiet disengagement from a girl who had proved herself to be unworthy of his hand in marriage, and that was his plan. Sometimes the "honourable" thing to do, however, may not be the right thing to do. When such a situation arises, God has His own way of nudging us in the right direction.

God knew that Joseph needed special help to understand that he was part of an earthshaking event, and it came in the form of a dream. From then on he never looked back but provided for Mary and her child all the dutiful support and unstinting love of husband and father.

"Betty" was another girl I got to know quite well since I was a frequent visitor to the Fellowship of Christian Students in the Teachers' Training College she attended. She was already engaged to "Kenny" when she started experiencing repeated demonic attacks for which she sought medical and psychiatric help, to no avail. And then, mysteriously, she found herself in the family way—"mysteriously" because she simply had never gone to bed with any man! In fact, the only time she had ever been on her own with a man in the past twelve months was for prayer sessions with a spiritual counsellor. She had turned to her priest for help, and when that also failed, she sought help from a "Prayer House" of the Cherubim and Seraphim Church. It had involved a period of fasting and praying into the night together with the church leader, and she could not always keep her eyes open during the long prayer sessions.

Of course, no one would believe her, and the honourable thing for Kenny to do was to break off the engagement. Betty was so convinced that the "man of God" was the only possible candidate for father to her unborn child that she dragged him to a court of law. He ended up confessing that he had raped Betty and that she could not have been aware of the fact because he had first put her into a hypnotic trance before the act!

Kenny did agree to go ahead with the wedding and accept the baby as his own. This was obviously easier to do after Betty had been proved innocent in a court of law and her rapist was sent to jail.

Mary did not have this sort of legal vindication, and Joseph did not have any possibility of public endorsement for accepting her story. In a situation completely beyond human understanding, theirs was a remarkable testimony of faith and love in action.

Says the Rev. Dr. John Stott:

> We need the humility of Mary. She accepted God's purpose, saying, "May it be to me as you have said"....We also need Mary's courage. She was so completely willing for God to fulfil his purpose, that she was ready to risk the stigma of being an unmarried mother, of being thought an adulteress herself and of bearing an illegitimate child. She surrendered her reputation to God's will.[138]

Question for reflection

Mary's pregnancy as an unmarried teenager would be more readily accepted today. What are your reasons for considering this either a good or a bad thing?

Aliens and Refugees!

Mary carried her pregnancy to full term and gave birth to a bouncing baby boy. It was not in the most auspicious of circumstances. The couple had to make do with a stable when they could not find more convenient lodgings at the end of a tiring journey to comply with government regulations to take part in a national census. That discomfort was nothing, however, compared to an incident some two years later after a well-heeled group of strange visitors arrived from distant lands to congratulate the family on the birth of their son.

> Now after Jesus was born in Bethlehem of Judea in the days of Herod the king, behold, wise men from the east came to Jerusalem, saying, "Where is he who has been born king of the Jews? For we saw his star when it rose and have come to worship him." When Herod the king heard this, he was troubled, and all Jerusalem with him; and assembling all the chief priests and scribes of the people, he inquired of them where the Christ was to be born. They told him, "In Bethlehem of Judea, for so it is written by the prophet: 'And you, O Bethlehem, in the land of Judah, are by no means least among the rulers of Judah; for from you shall come a ruler who will shepherd my people Israel.'" Then Herod summoned the wise men secretly and ascertained from them what time the star had appeared. And he sent them to Bethlehem, saying, "Go and search diligently for the child, and when you have found him, bring me word, that I too may come and worship him."
>
> Matthew 2:1-8

"Wise men from the east" is what these noble visitors are called, and they were no doubt very wise in discerning the movement of the stars, but streetwise they most certainly were not! What wisdom is there in calling on a reigning tyrant to find out about the birth of another King in his domain?

They located the child they came to seek and paid Him due homage, following which they were warned in a dream not to report their finding back to Herod. Then the story took a sinister turn.

> Now when they had departed, behold, an angel of the Lord appeared to Joseph in a dream and said, "Rise, take

the child and his mother, and flee to Egypt, and remain there until I tell you, for Herod is about to search for the child, to destroy him." And he rose and took the child and his mother by night and departed to Egypt and remained there until the death of Herod.

Matthew 2:13-15

Thus Jesus became a refugee in an alien land. It is an experience that millions were later to share with him, particularly in Africa, and particularly in our generation. How comforting to know that the God of heaven and earth understands their plight, not only as an act of divine knowledge but experientially in His Son!

As a result of their generous hospitality, some have "entertained angels unawares" (Hebrews 13:2). What a privilege Egypt had to be host to the King of kings and Lord of lords in His hour of need! The Coptic Orthodox Church can be forgiven for capitalising on it by developing a tradition of "Holy Family Locations," comprising the many exotic places up and down the country that Joseph and Mary are purported to have visited together with the baby Jesus and where they were evidently received with the most gracious Coptic hospitality—in the lucrative tradition of modern tourism![139]

What is important for us today is this. How do we treat the aliens and refugees among us? Both as individuals and as Christian communities, what is our attitude to them? For sure, there are the illegal migrants who have not only arrived illegally but are living their illegal existence by plying illegal activities. It is right that the law of the land should deal with them appropriately. But we must never lose sight of God's injunction to the children of Israel as it is applicable to us: "Do not ill-treat an alien or oppress him, for you were aliens in Egypt" (Exodus 22:21, NIV).

Sadly, this is an area where we are often found wanting today. For example, a March 2008 report following a two-year investigation by the British Independent Asylum Commission described the system as being "tainted with inhumanity."

The system still denies sanctuary to some who genuinely need it and ought to be entitled to it, is not firm enough in returning those whose claims are refused and is marred by inhumanity in its treatment of the vulnerable...The policy of using destitution as a lever to encourage voluntary return of refused asylum seekers risks forcing some extremely vulnerable people—who might have qualified for sanctuary had their cases been well handled—to face persecution in their country of origin.[140]

Quite rightly in the light of the sheer number of asylum-seeking refugees, our governments set up institutions to process applications. As in the case cited here, such institutions do not always carry out their duties with due compassion. Sadly, rather than working hard to establish the factors which led them to flee their homes, the emphasis is very often to find reasons why they should not be accepted. Converts to Christianity from Islamic Republics have sometimes been denied asylum because they could not recite the Lord's Prayer or the Ten Commandments.[141] Surely, their persecutors would not wait until they learn these lessons before beheading them!

Meanwhile, back in Bethlehem, Herod had all children less than two years old murdered, all because of the indiscretion of the Wise Men. Why God chose to warn them of Herod's intention *after* they had visited him and not before is another one of those mysteries beyond human understanding. It is the same with many of the tragedies that turn home owners into refugees all of a sudden. Why does God allow people such as Herod to exist at all? We can list that too among the issues we cannot explain, but the adage is not entirely facetious: "Do not blame God for creating the viper but thank Him for not giving it wings!" All the Herods of this world have their limitations, and they too will one day give account to the only One we have to fear:

"I tell you, my friends, do not fear those who kill the body, and after that have nothing more that they can do. But I will warn you whom to fear: fear him who, after he has killed, has authority to cast into hell" (Luke 12:4-5).

These issues that we cannot explain are not the real problem. How we react to the reality before us is all that counts. Ours is to confront tyrants in order to bring godly influence to bear on their policies whenever possible and also to bring succour to their victims in every way we can. In so doing, we shall remain faithful to the Just Judge of all the earth.

Thirty years later or thereabouts, Jesus Christ came to the end of His life as a result of doing exactly that. Were some of the parents of those murdered children in the crowds that applauded Him by shouting "Hosanna!"? Were they with the mob a week later baying for His blood with shouts of "Crucify Him!"? Where we stand is a pertinent question for us today.

Question for Reflection

Jesus Christ had firsthand experience of what it means to flee from His homeland for safety. How should this inform our attitude to refugees?

The Lost Son

Four-year-old Madeline McCann is arguably the best known lost child in history. At the time of writing, our prayers continue to go up for her and her distraught parents. Madeline had disappeared from her bedroom in a Portuguese holiday resort while her parents were elsewhere in the grounds having a relaxing evening with friends.

When the news broke, there was an outpouring of sympathy for Kate and Gerry, the parents who decided to leave no stone unturned to find their missing daughter. Locals joined the police in combing every inch of the immediate countryside, and British police went to assist their Portuguese counterparts. Massive publicity brought news of sightings from different countries, which turned out to be false leads, and the parents engaged a firm of private detectives to join in the search. But still Madeline was nowhere to be found.

Then the mood changed. Critical comments began appearing in the media, asking what kind of parents would leave their children unsupervised while having a "good time" with friends. The Express Newspapers joined in the attack with damning allegations of their own. Worst of all, the Portuguese Police formally placed the parents on "arguido" status—making them formal suspects in the disappearance of their daughter.

The Express subsequently recanted and agreed to pay the McCanns £550,000 in an out of court settlement for libel, which was credited to the "Find Madeleine Fund." And Alipio Robeiro, National Director of the Portuguese Judicial Police admitted in a radio interview that the Police had been unduly hasty in declaring the McCanns "arguidos."

It is not a happy lot to have your child missing, and the parents of Jesus knew all about that. The circumstances were altogether different, but the emotions and reactions are the same.

As practising Jews doing their utmost to bring up their son in the way of God, Joseph and Mary evidently had a habit of going with Him to Jerusalem annually to celebrate the feast of the Passover. The one and only story we know of His growing years was their taking Him with them on this journey as a precocious twelve-year-old. All went well, and it was time to return. We can visualise numerous parties of happy pilgrims on their way back to their rural homes after the excitement of the boisterous festive city, the men in the company of fellow men and the women and the children with other women and children. It is not unusual in any culture for boys of a certain age to opt for the company of their peers instead of travelling with their mothers. Another year and Jesus would graduate into adulthood at his Bar Mitzvah. Mary and Joseph were most certainly not being careless for not knowing how and when Junior quietly chose a different route in order to pursue His own agenda. Was it perhaps when He failed to show up for the evening meal they first became aware that something was amiss? They checked with family and friends. They hadn't seen him either. Help! Whatever has happened to Jesus?

And so Joseph and Mary knew all the anguish of being parents to a missing child. What must have been passing through their minds as they made their way back to Jerusalem? What sympathetic and not so sympathetic comments did they receive from friends, neighbours, and relations?

It was not until the third day before they found Him in the temple, and He was disappointed in them! Did they not know that there was only one obvious place for Him to be?

"And he said to them, 'Why were you looking for me? Did you not know that I must be in my Father's house?' And they did not understand the saying that he spoke to them" (Luke 2:49-50).

It is only natural that all our sympathy should be with the parents. But perhaps we too should not be surprised that the One who was later to commend Mary the sister of Martha and Lazarus for choosing the better option of listening to God's Word would prefer to spend more time discussing it with the teachers in Jerusalem when the festivals were over.

Joseph and Mary took their son to the Temple without fail. May the Lord enable us too to follow their good example. Their son chose to linger in the house of the Lord. May God grant us children whose hearts are similarly inclined to Him!

Sadly, we live in a world where children are increasingly unsafe. The ease of international travel and the explosion in global communications mean that paedophile gangs operate with greater facility than ever before. Parents therefore need to be extra vigilant and governments more supportive if we are to overcome the enemy's designs on our vulnerable children.

Question for Reflection

Have you ever had reason to give thought to the plight of a missing child? Is there anything we can do about the problem as God's people?

Mother, Behold Your Son!

There are some things that are not too clear to us about the human family of the Lord. One of them is the exact status of His mother, Mary, later in her life. At what stage did she become a widow, for example? It does look very much like if she was a single mother. The last reference we have to her husband, Joseph, was in that incident when He was twelve years old.

"When his parents saw him, they were astonished. And his mother said to him, 'Son, why have you treated us so? Behold, your father and I have been searching for you in great distress'" (Luke 2:48).

He was invited to the wedding in Cana in Galilee at the beginning of His public ministry, and His mother was also there, but there was no mention of Joseph. We know He had brothers who shared His mother's concern for Him:

> And his mother and his brothers came, and standing outside they sent to him and called him. And a crowd was sitting around him, and they said to him, "Your mother and your brothers are outside, seeking you." (Mark 3:31-32).

We can only speculate as to why they were looking for Him, but His reply was not what we would have expected of a dutiful son and older brother. If His father was already deceased at this time, presumably He would have some responsibility for His mother and younger siblings unless they were already able to look after themselves. Evidently, there was no crisis in the family—at least not one He adjudged to be of sufficient import to require

FLAWED SAINTS

Him to abandon the "mother and brothers" who were listening to His teaching on this occasion.

The crunch came when He was dying on the cross. He knew He had to take a definite step to assure the welfare of the mother He was leaving behind. What He did was to confide her to the care of John.

> When Jesus saw his mother and the disciple whom he loved standing nearby, he said to his mother, "Woman, behold, your son!" Then he said to the disciple, "Behold, your mother!" And from that hour the disciple took her to his own home.
>
> John 19:26-27

Mary would probably be close to fifty at the time of the crucifixion. Judging by average life expectancy of those times, she was already an old woman. If her husband was still alive, of course, her place was by his side, but evidently this was not the case. It was the responsibility of Jesus Christ as her first born son to look after her in her old age. If He died, then the honour would devolve on the next oldest son—for it was considered an honour and not a burden. We know that at least two brothers, James and Jude who wrote the two Letters that bear their names in the Bible, outlived Him. But the dying Jesus made a surprising decision. He conferred the honour and confided the responsibility on John, the Beloved Disciple. From that time, John took her into his own home.

"The old bush rat suckles from its offspring." Traditional societies have age-old customs of honouring their senior citizens and caring for them in their twilight years. It is part of the genius of the extended family system that there is always a relative on whom the responsibility devolves, even if the old man or woman is childless.

One of the tragedies of the market economy in post-communist Russia is the number of old ladies with begging bowls in Moscow immediately following the fall of Marxism—old ladies

JOSEPH AND MARY:
BEYOND HUMAN UNDERSTANDING

whose pension under the old regime was enough to keep body and soul together. Sadly, in the selfish philosophy of capitalist economies, it is not those who really need help but old people with substance that usually receive attention from doting relatives. The reason is simple—to be remembered in their wills!

Wilfred Lamb's only daughter did not particularly care for her aged father, but his neighbours in Kidderminster in England, Jim and Susan Loveridge, did—so much so that they offered him their own home so that he would not have to go into an old peoples' home. It was to their eleven-year-old daughter he left his estate, valued at £250,000! Not surprisingly, his daughter contested the will ...and lost.[142]

Jesus Christ showed us the way. In mortal agony on the cross, He did not forget to care for His mother. "Honour your father and your mother" is the one Commandment with a promise attached to it, and caring for them in their old age is a cardinal part of such honour. As individuals and as a society, when we fail in this, we herald the end of our civilization.

Mollie Ziegler's reminder is timely:

> There's a reason the psalmist cries, "Do not cast me away when I am old; do not forsake me when my strength is gone." Old age is almost always a time of physical and mental deterioration, of pain and loss, of fear and loneliness. Watching parents become chronically ill or senile is unbearably painful for their adult children.[143]

She readily admits that it can be very hard work indeed:

> [People caring] for dying parents are facing something their ancestors never did. They're part of smaller and less-stable extended families. They're less likely to live near their parents—sometimes they are thousands of miles away. And the amount of time spent caring for elderly family members can extend from a few tough years to many difficult decades. Even the strongest families will be

stretched to the limit when attempting to fulfil the commandment to honour one's parents.[144]

What we need to bear in mind is the teaching of the apostle James in his general epistle. "Whoever knows the right thing to do and fails to do it, for him it is sin" (James 4:17).

Our responsibility is to do it with godly devotion and to the best of our ability, trusting the good Lord to provide us with the wherewithal. It is an essential part of our Christian testimony. Writing to his young protégé, Apostle Paul did not mince words: "But if anyone does not provide for his relatives, and especially for members of his household, he has denied the faith and is worse than an unbeliever" (1 Timothy 5:8).

In providing for His mother, not only did Jesus Christ set the example for us at the point of His death, but He did it in a new way. There was the day when His mother came to request His attention in the middle of a teaching session—together with His brothers and sisters. He claimed then that those who do the will of His Father were His next of kin, thereby giving new direction to the traditional concept of the extended family.

> While he was still speaking to the people, behold, his mother and his brothers stood outside, asking to speak to him. But he replied to the man who told him, "Who is my mother, and who are my brothers?" And stretching out his hand toward his disciples, he said, "Here are my mother and my brothers! For whoever does the will of my Father in heaven is my brother and sister and mother."
>
> Matthew 12:46-50

For Him it was not mere theory. By this act at the point of death, He elevated it to the status of a legacy in His will. John was His brother into whose care He could confidently confide His mother—such was the new familial bond He was now establishing among His followers! When we speak about our brothers and sisters in Christ, therefore, this is the quality of the relationship He has bequeathed on us.

There is a concept of love that binds blood relations together, and "Blood," they say, "is thicker than water." Of all blood relationships, how inexpressibly more binding is that which makes us one because it is the blood of the Son of the Living God!

Question for Reflection

Why do you think it was John that Jesus Christ chose to look after His mother?

The Tragedy of Alienation

One of the most memorable among the parables Jesus told is about two sons alienated from their father. Although the prodigal generosity of the father deserves the greater emphasis, it is popularly known as the "Parable of the Prodigal Son."

> And he said, "There was a man who had two sons. And the younger of them said to his father, 'Father, give me the share of property that is coming to me.' And he divided his property between them. Not many days later, the younger son gathered all he had and took a journey into a far country, and there he squandered his property in reckless living. And when he had spent everything, a severe famine arose in that country, and he began to be in need. So he went and hired himself out to one of the citizens of that country, who sent him into his fields to feed pigs. And he was longing to be fed with the pods that the pigs ate, and no one gave him anything. But when he came to himself, he said, 'How many of my father's hired servants have more than enough bread, but I perish here with hunger! I will arise and go to my father, and I will say to him, "Father, I have sinned against heaven and before you. I am no longer worthy to be called your son. Treat me as one of your hired servants."' And he arose and came to his

father. But while he was still a long way off, his father saw him and felt compassion, and ran and embraced him and kissed him. And the son said to him, 'Father, I have sinned against heaven and before you. I am no longer worthy to be called your son.' But the father said to his servants, 'Bring quickly the best robe, and put it on him, and put a ring on his hand, and shoes on his feet. And bring the fattened calf and kill it, and let us eat and celebrate. For this my son was dead, and is alive again; he was lost, and is found.' And they began to celebrate."

Luke 15:11-24

In May 2006, the state of Maine in the United States officially acknowledged parental alienation syndrome as a serious issue. Governor John E. Baldacci signed a proclamation recognising April 25 as "Parental Alienation Awareness Day."

There is a whole variety of factors that can bring about alienation between parent and child, including insidious manipulation of the child by one parent against the other, especially in cases of divorce. This is what led to the tragedy of Rick James Lohstroh, who was fatally shot by his ten-year-old son in the summer of 2004. At first convicted of the crime, the boy was discharged and acquitted on appeal on the grounds that he genuinely believed himself in imminent danger from the father.[145]

Some children, however, are alienated from the parent without the intervention of any scheming third party. Such are the two sons in the parable of Jesus. Neither the younger nor the elder brother loved their father as father, but each one was primarily concerned about what he expected to get from him.

The younger brother demonstrates this by being very bad. The older brother wanted the money too, but his style was the opposite—to be very "good" to the extent that father would notice and reward him accordingly. Even though he remained at home and was both loyal and dutiful, it was all because of what he expected to get out of it in the end.

Now his older son was in the field, and as he came and drew near to the house, he heard music and dancing. And he called one of the servants and asked what these things meant. And he said to him, "Your brother has come, and your father has killed the fattened calf because he has received him back safe and sound." But he was angry and refused to go in. His father came out and entreated him, but he answered his father, "Look, these many years I have served you, and I never disobeyed your command, yet you never gave me a young goat, that I might celebrate with my friends. But when this son of yours came, who has devoured your property with prostitutes, you killed the fattened calf for him!" And he said to him, "Son, you are always with me, and all that is mine is yours. It was fitting to celebrate and be glad, for this your brother was dead, and is alive; he was lost, and is found."

Luke 15:25-32

The father was extremely patient with both of them. The younger one—was he perhaps an impetuous teenage rebel contemptuous of his "foolish old man"? The type abounds among us, but fortunately they do not always remain in that state. It was Mark Twain who observed, "When I was a boy of fourteen, my father was so ignorant I could hardly stand to have the old man around. But when I got to be twenty-one, I was astonished at how much he had learned in seven years."[146]

But perhaps this particular younger son was not so very young—only he was dissolutely impatient. Although he did not go to the extent of killing his father, he made it clear that he would rather have him dead. He wanted his portion of the inheritance and requested that it be handed over right away.

Denying his younger son his request would only keep the disgruntled youth at home against his will. By granting it, this man demonstrated a love that is able to let go of his own personal interests by liberating the young man to be himself. This love was perennially on the look-out for the son's change of heart after he had learned his lesson—however painfully.

As for the older brother, the father taught him the lesson he needed with regard to forgiveness. And, patiently, he also gave him a sense of self-worth as he explained to him that the privileges of being a son do not accrue only after father's death but can and should also be enjoyed today.

All of these lessons are relevant to us.

In our own different ways, we too are alienated from our Father—God. This is how the prophet Isaiah describes our plight: "All we like sheep have gone astray; we have turned every one to his own way; and the Lord has laid on him the iniquity of us all" (Isaiah 53:6).

Our heavenly Father does not cling to us at any cost. He gives us the freedom to go wrong if we choose, and this is precisely what we do. But He longs for our repentance and return to the life of abundance, which is available only in Him. This life is for us to enjoy to the full, whatever our wayward "brothers" may be doing all around us in this present world. And in the afterlife, we have eternal pleasures awaiting us that human tongue cannot describe.

What makes it all possible is the fact that the Son of God was once alienated from the Father, and we were the reason for it. It happened on that momentous day when He hung upon the cross.

"And at the ninth hour Jesus cried with a loud voice, '*Eloi, Eloi, lema sabachthani?*' which means, 'My God, my God, why have you forsaken me?'" (Mark 15:34).

Why, indeed?

He is the God described by the prophet Habakkuk: "You who are of purer eyes than to see evil and cannot look at wrong" (Habakkuk 1:13).

From eternity, He has always looked at the Son with divine approval. His baptism was one of several instances where He said so for the entire world to hear: "This is my beloved Son, with whom I am well pleased" (Matthew 3:17).

The day came, however, when Jesus Christ took our sins upon Himself on the cross, and those sins alienated Him from the

Father. "For our sake he made him to be sin who knew no sin, so that in him we might become the righteousness of God" (2 Corinthians 5:21).

Consider what it would feel like if you were to fall into a cesspit and be covered in muck from head to toe. The experience Jesus Christ had was much worse. He was immersed in human sin to the extent that the Apostle's description is that "He became sin." He did it for a purpose, "that we might die to sin and live to righteousness. By his wounds you have been healed" (1 Peter 2:24).

This is how John Stott explains it:

> Jesus had been condemned in a Jewish court for blasphemy by duly authorized legal procedures. He was then sentenced and executed for sedition by the Romans. Worse, he had been "hanged on a tree" and therefore (according to Deuteronomy 21:22-23) had died under the curse of God … And in raising him, God reversed the verdict which had been passed on him... Condemned for blasphemy, he was now designated Son of God by the resurrection. Executed for sedition, for claiming to be a king, God made him "both Lord and Christ". Hanged on a tree under the curse of God, he was vindicated as the Saviour of sinners, the curse he bore being due to us and not to him.[147]

As the hymn writer Stuart Townsend puts it,

> How great the pain of searing loss
> The Father turns His face away
> As wounds which mar the Chosen One
> Bring many sons to glory.[148]

It is this glory He invites us to share with Him as sons and daughters in the Family of Faith. Death could not hold on to Him, and the grave could not contain Him. He accomplished His purpose of reversing our alienation to the Father.

Therefore remember that at one time you Gentiles in the flesh, called "the uncircumcision" by what is called the circumcision, which is made in the flesh by hands—remember that you were at that time separated from Christ, alienated from the commonwealth of Israel and strangers to the covenants of promise, having no hope and without God in the world. But now in Christ Jesus you who once were far off have been brought near by the blood of Christ. For he himself is our peace, who has made us both one and has broken down in his flesh the dividing wall of hostility by abolishing the law of commandments expressed in ordinances, that he might create in himself one new man in place of the two, so making peace, and might reconcile us both to God in one body through the cross, thereby killing the hostility. And he came and preached peace to you who were far off and peace to those who were near. For through him we both have access in one Spirit to the Father..

Ephesians 2:11-18

Consider the privilege that is ours—we who were once alienated from God but are saved through faith in the finished work of Christ. Adopted into the family of God, we now have direct access to our loving Father any time of day or night. It is true that this does not shield us from the problems of our human existence in a fallen world, and family problems can be truly horrendous. We are invited, however, to cast all our cares on Him, because He cares for us and is able to do much more than we can ask or even imagine. In Him and through Him can be found the solution to all the family problems we ever encounter. What better response than to seek to live our lives according to His Word and in utter dependence on Him while we joyfully extol the praise of His glory?

"To the King of ages, immortal, invisible, the only God, be honor and glory forever and ever. Amen" (1 Timothy 1:17).

Taking It Further

1. "Safe sex" is the official answer to the epidemic of teenage pregnancy. What is the church's answer, and how best can it be delivered?

2. Natural and man-made disasters bring about floods of refugees. What answer is there for this plague, and what is our role in it? How should this play out with regards to members of the Family of Faith?

3. The most vulnerable in our societies, notably children and the aged, are increasingly unsafe. Would you agree that the response of our governments often cause as many problems as they solve? What should we be doing about it as Christians, both individually and corporately?

4. Does the modern lifestyle of two working parents increase the danger of alienation from children? How can the church help?

5. What would someone in the position of Mary, Joseph, or Mary's parents find most difficult if they were in your church today?

6. What are the differences between our Christian family and our natural family?

FLAWED SAINTS, FAMILY PROBLEMS, AND LESSONS OF GRACE

Flawed Saints and Their Family Problems

The people whose family problems we have studied from the Bible were each called and chosen by God and set apart for their particular role in His divine economy. That is the meaning of being a saint.

It is not because they were good or great or wise or wonderful, but because God simply decided to bestow His special grace on them. In fact, they were in every way as imperfect as we are. We do not know how many years it lasted, but only the first two chapters of the Bible describe a world where God looked at everything and said that it was good. After that, as a result of the Fall, flawed human beings lived in flawed families in a flawed world. Imperfect husbands married imperfect wives and raised imperfect sons and daughters in blemished homes. That was their story, and it is our story too.

Like them, we too are highly favoured men and women of God. We are included among the people Paul described when he wrote, "To the church of God that is in Corinth, to those sanctified in Christ Jesus, *called to be saints* together with all those who in every place call upon the name of our Lord Jesus Christ, both their Lord and ours" (1 Corinthians 1:2, italics added).

The nature and degree of our human flaws vary widely, and so does the severity of the pains we have to bear. "Before you complain about the weight of your burden, open your eyes and you will see that your neighbour has an even bigger one!" I expect these pages have demonstrated beyond doubt that whatever problem we may be facing in our own families, there were many other people who have had it even worse among the saints of whom we read in Scripture.

Sometimes it was entirely their own fault. Lot, David, and Solomon, for example, have no one else to blame but themselves. Some of the problems we face in our families today are like that. They result directly from some flaw in our character, like Abraham's desire for self-preservation at all costs; or some bad habit for which we have no excuse, like Samson's or Solomon's unbridled sexual appetite; or some momentary lapse in judgement, like Jephthah's oath; or some deliberate, wilful sin, like David committing adultery, trying to cover it up, and eventually ending up with murder.

Other times it was the fault of others. Adam and Eve suffered bereavement because their son killed his brother. Joseph went into slavery because his brothers sold him, and he went to prison because his master's wife lied against him. Hosea suffered untold anguish because his wife went into prostitution. Joseph and Mary became refugees because Herod was going to kill their son. In a similar way, the problems confronting us in our families may be caused by others. These may be people who for their own devious reasons wish us ill. But they could also be people whose unplanned actions harm us—like the drunken driver who causes an accident that kills or maims.

For others however, the causes were a lot more complex. Who exactly was to blame when "the fire of God fell from heaven" to burn up Job's sheep and servants or when "a great wind came across the wilderness and struck the four corners of the house" where his children were having a feast? Elimelech took practical steps to look after his family by emigrating with them to avoid the famine in his home country, but the end result was his death and the death of his two sons, leaving three desperate widows behind. Joseph and Mary suffered three days of anguish looking for a missing child who had simply gone about His Father's business. Some of our family problems are like these.

However the problems arise, they have the potential to destabilise or perhaps even derail our entire family life. Thankfully, we have something great going for us.

Lessons of Grace

Enormous as their problems were, these Bible saints were not ultimately sunk under the weight of the burdens they had to bear. The lessons we need to learn have to do with what enabled them to triumph. From the stories analysed and illustrated in these pages, we have been able to see many factors that are relevant to our needs, all of them tied to the grace of God.

- There is no alternative to trusting God.

    We saw many examples of people trying out alternatives to an implicit trust in God. Abraham had a baby with his slave girl. Lot went to hide with his daughters in a cave. Rebecca plotted against her first-born son. David killed Uriah to protect his image. They lived to regret it in every case. If indeed we are sons and daughters of God, we can rest assured that our heavenly Father looks after our best interests. Even when we do not see the way clearly—perhaps I should say, *especially* when we do not see the way ahead clearly—it is best to heed the advice of the Wise Man, "Trust in the Lord with all your heart, and do not lean on your own understanding. In all your ways acknowledge him, and he will make straight your paths" (Proverbs 3:5-6).

    When we rest our hope entirely in Him we cannot ultimately end up disappointed.

- The problem is not intractable.

    Our God is always able to turn things around. He put an end to the barrenness of Sarah and of Hannah. He rehabilitated Jacob and King David and Solomon. He made a new family for Ruth. He won a spectacular victory through Samson after he was made blind by his enemies. He restored Hosea's wife. And out of unpromising material such as you and me, He created a new Israel as the Bride for His Son. As He said through the prophet Jeremiah, "I am the LORD, the God of all flesh. Is anything too hard for me?" (Jeremiah 32:27). Whatever the complexity or the severity of the problems we face in our families, therefore, we can rest in this God who can always work things out to the praise of His glory.

- There is never a need to despair.

    Sometimes we know in our heart of hearts that God is able to solve our problems, but because we do not see the answer to our prayers we feel we have arrived at the end of our tether. We have waited on God all we know how, but it does not seem to make any difference. That was the experience of Abraham and of Job, and of Naomi. When the situation we face is entirely hopeless in our human way of seeing things, then we should remember that that is exactly what it is: our human way of seeing things *for now*. We belong to Someone who can see round the bend on the road, Someone who knows the end from the beginning. He has already won the victory on our behalf, even with regard to that battle we think is lost. He has not only won the battle, He has won the war! What we need to do is to hold on to Him with both hands.

- God's grace wins out.

    Our final resort is to the grace of God. We have noted how God's grace operated in the calling of men and women in Bible times to fulfil His purposes. Their Creator God was mindful of all the flaws in their lives and in the circumstances that surrounded them. He did amazing things to overrule blatant errors such as Abraham's and David's in order to work out the purposes of His grace. Thus the Son of Promise was born to Abraham, and the Messiah was born of David's line through the wife of Uriah. It is by that same grace that we too have been called and chosen in the first place. St Paul reminds us, "For by grace you have been saved through faith. And this is not your own doing; it is the gift of God, not a result of works, so that no one may boast" (Ephesians 2:8-9). This grace is at work in our lives and in our families in ways too wonderful for us to fathom. It is by no means a licence to sin; but we know that God's grace is enough to overcome all the flaws in our fallen world. We can confidently entrust our families to the grace of God and the God of grace!

- It does not end here.

  The God in whom we trust operates not only in this time/space dimension but on the scale of eternity. In His dealings with us and our families, we are works in progress. The last chapter of the story is yet to be written. There are prodigal sons out there on their way home unknown to us, and also wives like Hosea's. Even at the end of our lives in this world, it is not yet finished. We do not know what happened to Cain in the end, or what happened to Samuel's sons. It is enough for now to see with the eyes of faith. The day is coming when that faith will be turned into sight. This is how CS Lewis puts it: "We discern the freshness and purity of the morning, but they do not make us fresh and pure. We cannot mingle with the pleasures we see. But all the pages of the New Testament rustle with the rumour that it will not always be so. Some day, God willing, we shall get in."[149] It is only then that we shall get the full picture. We shall see with our own eyes how the grace of God wins out in the end!

ENDNOTES

1   The sad story of the "Safari Boy" was widely reported in the British Press in early 1996. The facts outlined here derive from Polly Toynbee's article in *The Independent*, 19 February 1996

2   Mark Twain: *Pudd'nhead Wilson's Calendar*, 1894

3   Jonathan Aitken was converted in prison and subsequently wrote two autobiographical works to describe his experience: *"Pride and Perjury"* (Harper Collins and Continuum, 2000) and *Porridge and Passion*, (Continuum, 2005)."

4   Christopher J.H. Wright: "The Mission of God's People, A Biblical Theology of the church's Mission." Jonathan Lunde, General Editor, Biblical Theology for Life. Zondervan 2010, p.40

5   BBC News October 29, 1999. 5 June 2011 <http://news.bbc.co.uk/1/hi/uk/492853.stm>

6   Paul Solotaroff : Rolling Stone, 4 June 2004. Quoted in The Methodist Church *Forgiving the Murderer* 8 June 2011 *<http://www.willsworld.com/~mvfhr/walt's.htm>*

7   Y.W.A.M. News release, February 1997

8   Margaret Mizen. BBC Radio Five interview. 12 May 2008

9   Hassan M. Fatah: "German Suspects From Opposite Sides of a Lebanese Town" *New York Times*, 29 August 2006. 8 June 2011 <http://www.nytimes.com/2006/08/29/world/europe/29lebanon.html?ex=1314504000&en=b6476a7988f5e716&ei=5088&partner=rssnyt&emc=rss>

10 ABC. "Colorado Gunman wrote suicide note before Siege." *Good Morning America*. 29 September 2006. *8* June 2011 < *http://abc-news.go.com/GMA/story?id=2506517&page=1>*

11   Channel3000.com. "Principal killed in School shooting." 29 September 2006. 10 June 2011 <http://www.channel3000.com/news/9963173/detail.html>

12   Kim Ngan Nguyen, Wayne Harrison and Kristy Armstrong, Staff Writers: "Gunman's Motives Remain Unclear As New Clues Surface." *Denver News*, 29 September 29, 2006. 8 June 2011<http://www.thedenverchannel.com/news/9958178/detail.html>

13   Jeff Jacoby: "Undeserved Forgiveness" 8 October 2006. 17 May 2011 <http://www.jeffjacoby.com/5858/undeserved-forgiveness 8 October 2006 accessed>

14   This chapter highlights the wife's role as exemplified by Sarah. It needs to be understood along with chapter 11, which majors on the complementary responsibility of the husband.

15   JewishEncyclopaedia.com. *Benedictions* 9 June 2011 <http://jewishencyclopedia.com/view.jsp?artid=697&letter=B&search=>

16   Pseudo-Demosthenes, *Speeches: Against Neaera*, 59:122. 9 June 2011 <http://www.perseus.tufts.edu/hopper/text?doc=Dem.+59+122&redirect=true>

17   There are many different ways of spelling the holy book of Islam. Other than where it occurs as part of a quotation which uses a different form, "Qur'an" is the version adopted throughout this book. "Surah" stands for "verse."

18   The Qur'an. Authorised English Translation by Dr. Rashad Khalifa: *Women (Al-Nesaa')* Surah 4:176

19   J W Stott. *The Message of Ephesians.* The Bible Speaks Today series: Leicester: IVP, 1979, p. 221.

20   J W Stott. *Issues Facing Christians Today,* London: Collins/Marshall Pickering, 1990, p. 269.

21   C S Lewis: "Essay on Prayer." *The World's Last Night, and Other Essays"* Harvest Book, September 1984

22   Jon Livesey. *Burnley and Pendle Citizen._2* July 2010. 19 May 2011 <http://www.burnleycitizen.co.uk/news/8252970. Pendle_man_is_oldest_new_dad_at_78/>

23   Washington State University. *The Code of Hammurabi.* Code 170, June 2011 <http://www.wsu.edu/~dee/MESO/CODE.HTM>

24   Women's Aid. "Domestic Violence Statistics." Domestic Abuse Directory 19 May2011 <http://www.womensaid.org.uk>

25   Patricia Tjaden and Nancy Thoennes: *Extent, Nature, and Consequences of Intimate Partner Violence.* Findings From the National Violence Against Women Survey, July 2000 NCJ 181867.

26   Women's Aid. Op.cit.

27   Whitney Kuniholm, *Essential 100* Scripture Union, E100 Edition, 2010, p. 23

28   Editions Magnificat. *St. Teresa of Avila, Virgin, Reformer of the Carmelite Order, (1515-1582).* 9 June 2011 <http://www.magnifi-cat.ca/cal/engl/10-15.htm>

29   Charles Tindley, *"When the Morning Comes."* All the verses available in many hymnals.

30   C S Lewis. *A Grief Observed,"* written after the death of his wife from cancer. It was first published under the pseudonym of N W Clerk in 1961 as Lewis did not wish to be identified as its author. It was not until after his death that it was published under his own name.

31   Nick Vujicic: "No Arms, No Legs, No Worries." YouTube positron66, 18 March 2008. 18 June 2011 <http://www.youtube.com/watch?v=u3LFBqvvW-M&feature=related>

32   Associated Press. "Report Says Stella Walsh Had Male Organs" *New York Times,* 23 January1981. 19 May 2011 <http://www.nytimes.com/1981/01/23/sports/report-says-stella-walsh-had-male-sex-organs.html> The competitor who beat Stella Walsh was investigated on the allegation of being a man. Ironically, 44 years

later, when Stella Walsh was killed by a stray bullet in a parking lot in Cleveland, Ohio, her autopsy revealed a surprise: it was she who was really a man, possessing male genitals and both male and female chromosomes!

33   The Rev. Canon David C. Anderson President, American Anglican Council and Secretary of the Anglican Communion Network. *Church of England Newspaper*, 2 August 2007

34   The Episcopal Church 76th General Council *General Convention 2009 Legislation, Resolution: D025*. 19 May 2011 <http://gc2009. org/ViewLegislation/view_leg_detail.aspx?id=986&type=Final>

35   Rowan Williams: "Communion, Covenant and our Anglican Future" Reflections on the Episcopal Church's 2009 General Convention. *Transfigurations*. 27 July 2009. 19 May 2011 <http:// transfigurations.blogspot.com/2009/07/rowan-williams-reflec-tions-on-episcopal.html>

36   Dr. J I Parker: "Why I Walked" *Christianity Today*, January 2003.

37   David L. Edwards and John Stott. *Essentials*. London: Hodder and Stoughton, 1988, p. 272.

38   JW Stott. *Issues Facing Christians Today* London: Collins/Marshall Pickering, 1990. p. 336

39   GayChristianNetwork. Justin Lee. "Gay Christian Anwers#6" *YouTube*. 19 May 2011 <http://www.youtube.com/ view_play_list?p=DA1EBE6901CF9CE4>

40   Ibid. Justin Lee *The Great Debate*. 20 May 2011 <www.gaychris-tian.net/greatdebate.php>

41   Ibid. Dr. Caompolo: "Building Bridges of Understanding: Tony and Peggy Campolo on Homosexuality" 20 May 2011 <www.gay-christian.net/campolos.php>

42   Ibid. Ron Beglau: "Love that Does Not Count the Cost" 2003. 20 May 2011 <www.gaychristian.net/rons_view.php>

43   Ibid

44   Ibid

45   Ibid

46   The only exceptions exist where strict Islamic Sharia law is fol-
      lowed. Syed Shahabuddin cites the case of the Nigerian woman
      who was sentenced to be stoned to death by a Sharia court in
      northern Nigeria until she got a reprieve from the Islamic Appeal
      Court and notes that only a handful of countries have this law on
      their books: Afghanistan, Iran, Nigeria and Saudi Arabia. (See
      Syed Shahabuddin: "Should the Islamic punishment of Adultery be
      reconsidered?" 11 June 2011 <http://www.guidedones.com/meta-
      page/gems/adultery.htm>

47   Fishcantfly.com.ATJ   Murray.   http://www.fishcantfly.com/
      ShawnPage.html 20 May 2011

48   Mario Bergner. *Setting Love in Order : Hope and Healing for the
      Homosexual* Baker, 1995.

49   Frank Worthen. *Ex-Gay: Fact, Fraud or Fantasy?* 10 June 2011
      <www.newhope123.org/xgay_fact.htm>

50   Stanton, L. Jones; Mark A. Yarhouse September 2007 *Ex-Gays?:
      A Longitudinal Study of Religiously Mediated Change In Sexual
      Orientation.* Sexual Orientation and Faith Tradition Symposium;
      American Psychiatric Association Convention, 2009.

51   Peter Tatchell. *British Journalism Review*, Volume 9, Number 2,
      June 1998

52   Rob Marshall. *Hope the Archbishop,* Continuum 2004

53   *The Book of Common Prayers* of the Anglican Church was first
      published in its complete form in 1662. It is still in use in various
      updated forms in churches of the Anglican Communion today.

54   Karl Vick. "Trial By Fury: Scandal Sentenced Ted Haggard to a
      New Life." *Washington Post.* 5 January 2009. 2 June 2011 <http://

www.washingtonpost.com/wp-dyn/content/article/2009/01/23/
AR2009012300879_2.html?sid=ST2009012900164>

55   Gordon Macdonald: *Rebuilding Your Broken World.* Thomas Nelson,
      1988

56   Hanna Rosin: "Ministers to Give Clintons 'Pastoral Care.'"
      Washington Post 16 September 1998. 11 June 2011. <http://www.
      washingtonpost.com/wp-srv/politics/special/clinton/stories/min-
      isters091698.htm>

57   Whitney Kuniholm: *Essential 100*, op. cit. p.24

58   Grace E.A. Onamusi: *Child Upbringing – Rearing Godly Children."*
      Amazing Grace Publications, Kano, 1998

59   John Milton: *Paradise Lost*, Book 3, 116-121

60   Op. cit. Codes 162-163

61   This story was recounted by the Rev. Dr. John Mpaayei, himself
      a Maasai Elder, at the World Vision Church Leaders Advisory
      Consultation in Nairobi, in which I participated in November 1980.

62   Kalpana Sharma. *THE HINDU* 19 March 2006

63   The case for actual infertility is not settled, but there is univer-
      sal agreement on the other deleterious effects of inbreeding. See
      for example Eugene Ochap: *Genetics 535* 3-22-04. 16 June 2011
      <http://www.as.wvu.edu/~kgarbutt/QuantGen/Gen535_2_2004/
      Inbreeding_Humans.htm>

64   UK Department of Health: "Abortion Statistics" *Statistical Bulletin,
      England and Wales:* 2007. The records indicate that 81 percent were
      for single women.

65   John Battersby: *New York Times* October 2, 1987.

66   *"Peanuts"* is a syndicated cartoon series illustrated by Charles
      M. Schulz which ran from 1950 to the day after his death in
      February 2000.

67   Adam Fresco and Steve Bird. *The Times,* London July 20, 2007

68   Diana Lammi. Joane: "Suicide for honour" *International Campaign Against Honour Killings.* 13 November 2007. <http://www.stophonourkillings.com/?q=node/2170> 21 May 2011

69   Sigmund Freud, *Die Traumdeutung.* 1899.

70   Chlamydia is called the silent disease because, even though it can cause serious havoc with reproductive health, it often does not have any symptoms. 80 percent of women and 50 percent of men who have it do not have any sign of infection!

71   Daniel Martin, *The Daily Mail,* July 8 2009.

72   UK National Health Service, Sheffield. *"Pleasure"* Produced by Sheffield NHS Primary Health Care Unit and distributed to pupils, parents and teachers in July 2009.

73   John Ortberg: *"If you want to walk on water you've got to get out of the Boat"* The Christian Book Club, Devon 2001

74   Whitney Kuniholm: *Essential 100. Op. cit.* p 31.

75   Philip Yancey *What's so Amazing About Grace?* Zondervan 1997 p.45

76   C.S. Lewis. "Mere Christianity" Book 4, Chapter 10.

77   The Qur'an, Surah 5:89

78   Ibid Surah 2:225

79   Afif A. Tabbarah, *The Spirit of Islam* p. 247. Tabbarah is a Muslim scholar writing an apologetic for his religion.

80   Article 18 of both the Universal Declaration of Human Rights and the International Covenant on Civil and Political Rights states that everyone has the fundamental human right to freedom of thought, conscience and belief. This is where Forum 18 takes its name.

81   Forum 18, Oslo, Norway. *Freedom of Religion. Attachment 2, Egypt* <http://www.forum18.org/PDF/freedomofreligion.pdf> 1 June 2011.

82   George Duffield, Jr., 1818-1888 *Stand Up, Stand Up for Jesus*

83   Although the advertisement has been widely attributed to Shackleton, its existence in *The Times* or other contemporary London sources has never been confirmed.

84   Dietrich Bonhoeffer, *The Cost of Discipleship*. SCM Press 1959, translated by RH Fuller from the German *Nachfolge* first published 1937

85   There was a possible exception. Egyptian tomb art work dating from about 2300BC indicates the practice of circumcision, but it is believed to be limited to priests.

86   BBC News.. "Police Chief's suicide law worry." 29 August 2009 <http://news.bbc.co.uk/1/hi/wales/8228171.stm> 13 June 2011.

87   Baroness Ilora Finlay of Llandaff. *TIMESONLINE* April 1 2009.

88   Quoted by his biographer, Timothy Dudley-Smith at his Memorial Service held at St Paul's Cathedral, London, on January 13, 2012.

89   Jerry Bridges. *The Discipline of Grace* (NavPress, 1994, 2006) p. 34-5 on Eph 4:29.

90   These are the more popular words. The original concludes: "But in the hardness, God gives to you, Chances of proving that you are true."

91   Philip Yancey. *Disappointment with God*. Grand Rapids: Zondervan, 1988. p. 213.

92   Harold Kushner: *When Bad Things Happen to Good People* Anchor Books, 1981

93   C S Lewis *A Grief Observed* (Faber Paperbacks, 1961)

94   Don W. King. *Bulletin of the New York C. S. Lewis Society* 32, March 2001. 1-7.

95   C S Lewis. *The Problem of Pain.* 1940

96   Alistair McGrath. *Evangelicalism and the Future of Christianity.* Hodder 1988

97   Esther Kerr Rusthoi. *When We See Christ.* Words and Music (c) Renewal 1969 Singspiration, Inc.

98   Gingerbread – Single Parents, Equal Families *Gingerbread Factfile* <http://www.gingerbread.org.uk/content.aspx?CategoryID=365& ArticleID=267> 2 June 2011

99   www.parliament.uk. Parliamentary business. "Memorandum submitted by One Parent families (CP 29)." 3 October 2003. *Publications and Records.* <http://www.publications.parliament.uk/ pa/cm200304/cmselect/cmworpen/85/85we47.htm> 2 June 2011

100   Miriam Neff: The Widow's Might. *Christianity Today,* January 2008

101   North American Mission Board of the Southern Baptist Convention. "Widowhood: Guidance for Coping" 2 June 2011 <http://www.namb. net/nambpbsharing.aspx?pageid=8589980133&ekfxmen_noscript =1&ekfxmensel=e9edebdff_8589934591_8589935195>

102   Ojwang, J.W and J.N.K. Mugambi (editors), *The S.M. Otieno Case, Death and Burial in Modern Kenya,* Nairobi University Press, Nairobi, 1989.

103   Mark Schoofs: "The Complete HIV/AIDS Resource." *THE BODY,* December 1999.

104   "Burkina Faso" is the African country which used to be called Upper Volta. "Burkinabé " in the local language literally means "people of integrity" and "Burkina Faso" "the land of people of integrity."

105   Quote from the 1984 film Amadeus, directed by Miloš Forman

106   John W. Kennedy: "Help for the Sexually Desperate." *Christianity Today*, March 7, 2008.

107   Psalms 19:4-5

108   Robert Hendrickson: "Facts on File" *Encyclopedia of Word and Phrase Origins*, New York, 1997.

109   Revd G.D. Watson, (1845-1924): *Others May, but You Cannot.*

110   Scott Solary & Luci Westphal, (Producers), Good Hardworking People. *All God's Children*, 2008

111   Brandon Fibbs. *Christianity Today.* August 2009

112   ibid

113   Does this perhaps have something to do with the fact, which has now been statistically demonstrated and documented, that girls are more intelligent than boys? See for example the University of Cambridge research paper, Dr. Molly Warrington & Mr. Mike Younger "The Gender Gap in Education".(British Educational Research Journal 26.3, 393-407. <www.geog.cam.ac.uk/research/projects/educationgendergap> 2 June 2011.

114   Charles-Daniel et Évelyne Maire : « *Famille, points de repère* », Editions LLB, Valence 2001 pp 22 & 23. (This author's translation)

115   Leslie Leyland Fields: The Myth of the Perfect Parent, *Christianity Today*, January 2010

116   Ibid

117   Duncan Bannatyne: "*Anyone Can Do It.*" Bannatyne Media Ltd. 2006, p. 231. The fact that a certain Sister Martha promised, two pages further on, to pray for him every day for the rest of her life makes it even more likely that, in His own good time, God will one day re-engage Duncan Bannatyne in that conversation.

118   Colin Chettle, Sermon at St. Paul's Church, Oadby, Leicester, 17 October 2009

119 For full transcript of his broadcast, see CNN website <http://edition.cnn.com/ALLPOLITICS/1998/08/17/speech/transcript.html> 2 June 2011

120 These are Rachel, Abigail, Esther, Tamar, her niece, (Absalom's daughter), also called Tamar, and the unnamed girl in the Song of Songs.

121 Jonathan Lamb: *"INTEGRITY – Leading with God watching"* IVP, 2006, p.44.

122 This concept is very helpfully developed by Bill Perkins in his book, *When Good Men Are Tempted* Zondervan, 1997. See especially, Chapter 2, *Why Other Women Look Better,* and chapter 11, *The Lost Art of Buddyship.*

123 William Shakespeare, Sonnet 129

124 The Oprah Winfrey Show: "Support Rape Victims" 22 September 2009. <www.oprah.com/oprahshow/How-to-Help-Rape-Victims-Around-the-World> 3 June 2011

125 Carol Martin: Angelfire *RAPE, THE VICTIM AND GETTING HELP* <http://www.angelfire.com/nj2/carolslittleangels/untitled.html> 3 June 2011

126 Victim Support. "Rape and Sexual Assault: Information for men." 16 June 2011 <http://www.victimsupport.org.uk/Help percent20for percent20victims/Different percent20types percent20of percent20crime/Rape percent20sexual percent20assault percent20men>

127 Listed in 2 Samuel 3: 2-6 as Amnon, Chileab, Absalom, Adonijah, Shephatiah, and Ithream.

128 Reader's Digest, *Does money really buy happiness?* March 2006

129 NIV Study Bible (Zondervan, 1995). See Commentary on Ephesians 5:21

130 Don Durham. *Happily Ever After (and Other Myths About Divorce).* Victor Books, 1992, p.44.

131   David Instone-Brewer *Divorce and Remarriage in the Church* (IVP 2007)

132   David Instone-Brewer: "What God Has Joined" *Christianity Today,* 5 October 2007

133   Francis Thompson: "The Hound of Heaven" first published in *The Oxford book of English Verse*, 1917.

134   JRR Tolkien quoted in The Neuman Press book of *Verse*, 1988

135   Alister McGrath: *Evangelicalism and the future of Christianity* Hodder, 1988

136   See, for example, < http://pewforum.org/Religion-News/ Evangelicals-Shift-Toward-Acceptance-on-Divorce.aspx>   The article contains this sad statement: "A study this year by The Barna Group, a California research firm, showed that 27 percent of "born-again" Christians have been divorced, compared to 25 percent of non-born-again Americans."

137   Tony Jordan. *The Nativity:* a four part drama for BBC1 Television at Christmas, 2010. Jordan confessed how this led to his "Damascus Road experience" in an interview with *The Telegraph* on 18 December 2010: "I don't think I'm anybody's fool. I was expelled from school at 14. I've been in trouble. I know that people from my sort of background have always discounted the story of the nativity and I certainly didn't believe it when I started on it three years ago. But now I do."

138   J W Stott: *"The Authentic Jesus"* (London: Marshalls; Downers Grove: IVP, 1985), p. 66).

139   Tour Egypt. *The Holy Family in Egypt* <*www.touregypt.net/holy-family2.htm*> and www.holyfamilyegypt.com/map/> 4 June 2011

140   Politics.co.uk 27 March 2008. www.politics.co.uk/news/com-munities-and-local-government/asylum-system-not-fit-for-pur-pose—$1215698.htm> 4 June 2011

141 Lawyers' Committee for Human Rights: "Testing the Faithful: A Briefing Paper Prepared for the Roundtable on Religion-based Persecution Claims" November 2002

142 BBC Home. "Judge approves girl's inheritance" 31 January 2005. 16 June 2011 <http://news.bbc.co.uk/1/hi/england/hereford/worcs/4222867.stm>

143 Mollie Ziegler: "'Honour Thy Father' for Grownups" *Christianity Today*, 17 July, 2009

144 Ibid

145 Karen Stephenson: "Parental Alienation Syndrome." September 18 2008. 4 June 2011 <http://abuse.suite101.com/article.cfm/pas_parental_alienation_syndrome>

146 Mark Twain: "Old Times on the Mississippi" *Atlantic Monthly*, 1874

147 JW Stott: *The Authentic Jesus* IVP, 1985. p. 45.

148 Worship Together. "How deep the Father's love for us" Stuart Townsend, 1995. *Thank You Music.* 16 June 2011 <http://www.worshiptogether.com/songs/songdetail.aspx?iid=577430>

149 CS Lewis: *Transposition and other Addresses* (Geoffrey Bles, London 1949)